Eugene O'Neill (1888–1953) was born in New York City. His first big success was *Beyond the Horizon* (1920), which won the Pulitzer Prize. Other plays from his early period include *The Emperor Jones* (1920), the Pulitzer Prize–winning *Anna Christie* (1921), and *Desire Under the Elms* (1924). His third Pulitzer Prize–winning play, *Strange Interlude* (1928), was followed by the trilogy *Mourning Becomes Electra* (1932), and the uncharacteristically comic *Ah, Wilderness!* (1933). A hiatus from the theater followed, during which O'Neill was awarded the Nobel Prize in 1936, the only American playwright to be so honored. He ended his twelve-year absence from Broadway with *The Iceman Cometh* in 1946. His masterpiece, *Long Day's Journey Into Night*, was written in 1941, but published and produced posthumously in 1956, when it won O'Neill's fourth Pulitzer Prize.

A. R. Gurney, winner of the 1987 Award of Merit from the American Academy and Institute of Arts and Letters, is the author of numerous plays, including *The Dining Room*, *The Cocktail Hour*, *Love Letters*, and *Later Life*. He taught literature at MIT for twenty-five years and in 2006 was elected a member of the American Academy of Arts and Letters.

Arthur Gelb and **Barbara Gelb** are authors of the 1962 seminal bestselling biography *O'Neill*. The first volume of their revised O'Neill biography was published in 2000, and they are at work on the final volume. Mr. Gelb is former managing editor of *The New York Times* and has had a long career as an author outside the paper, most recently with his memoir, *City Room*. Ms. Gelb is the author of *My Gene*, a play based on O'Neill's widow starring Collen Dewhurst. She is the author of, among other books, *So Short a Time*, a biography of John Reed and Louise Bryant, early colleagues of O'Neill. In 2006 the Gelbs collaborated with Ric Burns in writing the PBS documentary *O'Neill*.

4
PLAYS
by
Eugene O'Neill

Beyond the Horizon
The Emperor Jones
Anna Christie
The Hairy Ape

With an Introduction by
A. R. Gurney

and a New Afterword by
Arthur and Barbara Gelb

𝒪
SIGNET CLASSICS

SIGNET CLASSICS
Published by New American Library, a division of
Penguin Group (USA) Inc., 375 Hudson Street,
New York, New York 10014, USA
Penguin Group (Canada), 90 Eglinton Avenue East, Suite 700, Toronto,
Ontario M4P 2Y3, Canada (a division of Pearson Penguin Canada Inc.)
Penguin Books Ltd., 80 Strand, London WC2R 0RL, England
Penguin Ireland, 25 St. Stephen's Green, Dublin 2,
Ireland (a division of Penguin Books Ltd.)
Penguin Group (Australia), 250 Camberwell Road, Camberwell, Victoria 3124,
Australia (a division of Pearson Australia Group Pty. Ltd.)
Penguin Books India Pvt. Ltd., 11 Community Centre, Panchsheel Park,
New Delhi - 110 017, India
Penguin Group (NZ), 67 Apollo Drive, Rosedale, North Shore 0745,
Auckland, New Zealand (a division of Pearson New Zealand Ltd.)
Penguin Books (South Africa) (Pty.) Ltd., 24 Sturdee Avenue,
Rosebank, Johannesburg 2196, South Africa

Penguin Books Ltd., Registered Offices:
80 Strand, London WC2R 0RL, England

Published by Signet Classics, an imprint of New American Library,
a division of Penguin Group (USA) Inc.

First Signet Classics Printing, February 1998
First Signet Classics Printing (Gelb Afterword), August 2007
10 9 8 7 6 5 4 3

Introduction copyright © A. R. Gurney, 1998
Afterword copyright © Stone Group, Inc., 2007
All rights reserved

 REGISTERED TRADEMARK—MARCA REGISTRADA

Printed in the United States of America

CONTENTS

INTRODUCTION
by A. R. Gurney

These early plays not only stand as valuable windows into the main body of work of America's foremost playwright, but are also formidable pieces of theater in themselves. The two longer plays, *Beyond the Horizon* and *Anna Christie*, are written in the realistic style to which O'Neill returned many times during the course of his prolific career. *The Emperor Jones* and *The Hairy Ape* are both bold examples of his recurrent attempts to experiment with style and structure, and stretch the traditional boundaries of theater.

Since so much of O'Neill's work is illuminated by his life, it might help to remind ourselves of a number of salient benchmarks in his biography. Born in New York in 1888, he was the second son of a popular Irish-American matinee idol, James O'Neill, who spent most of his artistic life touring the country in melodramas, particularly a dramatization of the Alexander Dumas novel *The Count of Monte Cristo*. The playwright's mother was a reclusive innocent who was addicted to narcotics during most of his youth. Both parents were lapsed Catholics. O'Neill spent his early years rebelling against the conventional life his parents yearned to attain. He was suspended from Princeton, toured the bars of New York with his dissolute older brother, married and fathered a child, shipped off on a tramp steamer to South Africa and South America, divorced, and in 1912 returned to live with his family in New London, Connecticut, only to discover he had contracted tuberculosis. During his convalescence at a nearby sanitorium, he immersed himself in contemporary European drama and began to write short plays of his own.

In 1914 O'Neill enrolled in George Pierce Baker's celebrated course on playwriting at Harvard, and in the summer of 1916 he moved to Provincetown, on Cape Cod, where he associated with a number of other young artists who put on plays in a small theater, built on a wharf. Their work was successful enough for the group, calling themselves the Playwrights Theatre, to stage a season of one-acts in New York. By now, encouraged by his father and by the reactions of audiences and critics, O'Neill was beginning to trust himself as a serious playwright.

The plays in this volume belong to his fledgling period. *Beyond the Horizon*, his first significant full-length work, opened in New York in 1920. The producer hedged his bets by presenting the play only for matinees so that the actors could perform more established plays at night. O'Neill's play was received well enough to settle into a conventional run, winning the Pulitzer Prize at the end of the season. *The Emperor Jones* opened the following fall, and *Anna Christie* and *The Hairy Ape* soon after. *Anna Christie* won another Pulitzer in 1922.

Within a short span of years Eugene O'Neill had become an important figure in the American theater, and he continued to write play after play that challenged audiences and critics in both form and content, and caused the works of his contemporaries to seem increasingly trivial and old-fashioned. He experimented constantly, working with masks, choruses, asides, and myths, delving into Expressionism and Surrealism, exploring Freudian, Jungian, and Nietszchean themes, and always, even in his failures, telling stories on stage in fresh and challenging ways. Several of his plays (particularly *Strange Interlude* and *Mourning Becomes Electra*) took longer to perform than most audiences had been used to, but Americans saw him as their first significant voice in the theater and bestowed on him the attention he deserved. He was equally celebrated abroad, and won the Nobel Prize for Literature in 1936 for what was by then an extraordinary body of work.

O'Neill's private life was marred by three turbulent marriages, along with disastrous relationships with his three children. Constantly changing domiciles, never finding a place he could truly call home, falling out of favor in the late thirties and forties, he nonetheless continued to write large and compelling plays. Some he refused to release, some were inadequately produced, and some he ruthlessly destroyed toward the end of his life. Racked by bad health, he died in Boston in 1953, under the impression that the world was no longer much interested in his work.

It was only after his death that O'Neill's reputation came into its full flowering. A revival of *The Iceman Cometh* in Greenwich Village in 1956, which also spearheaded the new Off-Broadway movement, was followed by major productions of *Long Day's Journey into Night, A Touch of the Poet,* and *A Moon for the*

Misbegotten. Only the last play had been previously produced, and all four were immediately celebrated as profoundly moving works. Many of O'Neill's earlier plays were soon revived both on Broadway and off, and today there is little argument that he deserves his crown as America's most inventive and distinguished playwright. His masterpiece, *Long Day's Journey into Night,* which is an autobiographical account of a day with his family in New London when he is found to have tuberculosis, can be considered one of the great domestic dramas of all time.

In any case, the playwright's complicated life informs much of his work. His father's career in nineteenth-century melodramas is reflected in the son's highly charged dramaturgy. His suspicion and mistrust of most women comes out of his tempestuous relationships with his three wives, and the erratic behavior of his addicted mother. The yearning for a sense of the absolute echoes the lapsed Catholicism which must have pervaded his early home life. And of course, the recurrent image of the sea as an arena for escape, adventure, and loneliness comes out of the restless excursions of his youth.

These themes emerge with an ingratiating simplicity in the four early plays included here. *Beyond the Horizon* explores the debilitating nature of domestic responsibilities, as opposed to the liberating and romantic possibilities of a life at sea. *Anna Christie* treats the sea in a more complicated way, since it serves both as a cleansing influence for Anna, and also as a destructive "davil" which lures men from their roots. Both *The Emperor Jones* and *The Hairy Ape* are studies of masterful, intuitive men brought low by a growing awareness of the emptiness at the core of their lives, reminding us of O'Neill's father, whose promising acting career degenerated into hollow revivals of a second-rate vehicle.

Moreover, since these fledgling works were all written and produced very close together, we notice that they also echo each other in many ways. In *Beyond the Horizon*, Robert Mayo's disgust with the obligations and corruptions which come with family and land is repeated in Anna Christie's experiences on her cousin's farm in Minnesota and her need to be cleansed by the sea. The compulsion to escape is constantly juxtaposed with the desperate longing for a place to "belong," which we see in Andrew Mayo, Anna, Brutus Jones, and Yank, the "hairy ape." None of these actions, searching or staying, brings happiness in the end. Yank and Brutus Jones, aware of their precarious roles in the world, are destroyed by their struggles to better themselves, and even Matt Burke in *Anna Christie*, who has some of their dynamic, instinctive power, avoids a self-destructive life only by arriving at a tentative understanding with Anna. As O'Neill suggests in the moving last line of *Long Day's Journey*, the major choices we make in life—to marry, to leave home, to seek a new existence—may make us happy "for a time," but we can be sure that sooner or later fate will catch up with us and bring us down, in one way or another.

A valid sense of fate is a tough thing to dramatize on stage, particularly in the twentieth century. Sophocles could call on unimpeachable oracles; Shakespeare could rely on soothsayers, witches, and a built-in sense of cosmic order; but O'Neill had to forge other means to create a palpable sense of inevitability. For example, in *Anna Christie,* Chris Christopherson's repetitive allusions to "dat ole davil sea," which laps away at the hull of the barge in which most of the play takes place, endows the sea with a portentous influence that makes the choices of the characters resonate with importance. The offstage tom-tom beat in *The Emperor Jones,* which, according to O'Neill's stage directions, "starts at a rate exactly corresponding to a normal pulse beat . . . and continues at a gradually accelerating rate . . . to the end of the play," is not only an ingenious attempt to establish a physiological synchronicity between actor and audience, but also becomes an image for the inescapable pull of Jones's African roots as he wades deeper and deeper into his psychological and historical beginnings.

The Hairy Ape finds its sense of doom partly in its choral effects, which are intended to suggest Greek tragedy, but more often in the repetitive use of its very title. Yank is dubbed a "hairy ape" by the rich passenger Mildred Douglas, who visits the engine room on a slumming trip from First Class. She is almost a vindictive goddess endowing him with an irrevocable curse. From then on, the action of the play is, at one level, Yank's attempt to expiate this curse by proving it false, until finally, in a grotesque parody of the classical tradition, he is crushed by his own fate in the form of an actual gorilla he has released from the zoo. *Beyond the Horizon,* on the other hand, calls primarily on its scenery to impose its tragic overtones. O'Neill was criticized for breaking the dramatic momentum of the last act by shifting to the out-of-doors, but he wanted to have the open set contrast with the cramped interiors which have diminished the spirit of his dying protagonist.

O'Neill's compulsion to endow his plays with a more general and cosmic import is one quality which sets him apart from most twentieth-century playwrights. While it might be argued that his strivings are occasionally repetitious and crude in the four plays considered here, he would become a master of this sort of effect in his later plays. For example, the recurrent foghorn in *Long Day's Journey* takes the tomtom motif from *The Emperor Jones* and transmutes it into something pervasive and profound. In *Desire Under the Elms*, the overarching elms, brooding over the house "like exhausted women," give the play a continual scenic pressure which can only be inadequately hinted at in *Beyond the Horizon*, while the subtle reflection of Leonardo's *Last Supper* in the composition and staging of the banquet scene of *The Iceman Cometh* shows how he came to master the subliminal effects of stage pictures. What is admirable in his earlier plays, however, is not that O'Neill does everything well, but that he does it at all, exhibiting even at the start of his career an intense desire to say something big and significant about the human condition.

If these four plays have value as adumbrations of O'Neill's more sophisticated and subtle works to come later, they are also well worth considering on their own. *Beyond the Horizon*, for example, may now seem somewhat primitive in construction and obvious in theme, but it would be too easy to explain its initial popularity simply by comparing it to the hokey melodramas showing on Broadway when it first appeared.

The play is about the American conviction that every individual must be free to follow the promptings of one's soul, and to go against this grain is to destroy oneself. Moreover, this theme is presented less schematically than one would first think. Robert's wasting away in domestic drudgery may seem inevitable, but it is counterbalanced by the energy of his love for his young daughter. Similarly Andrew's ostensible success at sea is modified by a sense of loneliness and deracination. If the play is about making the wrong choice, Ruth stands as a contrast to both men, changing with the wind, never really choosing at all. Her mother becomes a visual image of the debilitating effects of farm life, while her mother-in-law stands an example of the quiet endurance this life demands. Only James Mayo, the father, seems disappointing as a character, being a thin imitation of the sturdier father figures O'Neill would present in later plays.

Even today the play displays a good portion of raw emotional power. The urgency of Robert Mayo's yearnings to escape is conveyed in strong enough terms that we feel a real shudder of dismay when he decides to stay on the farm. Similarly, Andrew's decision to leave feels equally wrong. Without using any heavy metaphysical machinery to warn us, O'Neill manages to dramatize the moral terms of the play simply through the intensity and seriousness of the two brothers' feelings. Furthermore, this is still a play that makes us eager to find out, on the most basic level, what happens next. This sense of suspense comes from the authentic pain and anguish imbedded in the feelings of its main characters. If drama is finally about two boards and a passion, the passion is undoubtedly palpable here.

Anna Christie, too, is validated by its bursts of authentic emotion. At one level, its plot of boy-meets-girl, boy-loses-girl is fairly old hat, and the fact that the girl happens to be a "woman with a past" isn't particularly original, either. Yet what remains exciting about the play is how its characters, including the subordinate ones, are forced by circumstances to express their feelings, if not articulately, with an intense honesty. The sea becomes a kind of elemental sounding board for their attempts to reach others, and if Chris Christopherson apostrophizes it once too often, it still dramatizes the tidal push and pull of fate as well as a cleansing element from the corruptions of life ashore.

The plot of *Anna Christie* is compelling enough to have been filmed twice, the second time as a vehicle to present the silent screen star Greta Garbo in her first talkie. Anna's opening speech, "Gimme a whiskey—ginger ale on the side. And don't be stingy, baby," was thereby made memorable. The play has been revived professionally on stage many times, most recently on Broadway in 1995 (starring Natasha Richardson and Liam Neeson), where it proved to be extremely successful. Anna herself, as a lost innocent attempting to redeem her life, is the mother of Tennessee Williams's Blanche DuBois and a number of other American dramatic heroines, and Matt, as the inarticulate, lovable lug, has many offspring, too. The play sounds a number of common American chords and reaches us still.

The Emperor Jones is distinguished for a number of reasons, not the least of which is that it was the first

American play to employ an African-American actor, Charles Gilpin, in a leading role. The movie version became a vehicle for Paul Robeson. O'Neill would go on to explore racial issues in *All God's Chillun Got Wings,* but *The Emperor Jones* is most fruitfully viewed today as a play about a chase. It is simultaneously a journey in space and in time, as Jones tries to escape into the jungle of his diminishing domain and into the expanding world of his own past, as well as into the past of his race. Much of its dialogue, or at least Jones's monologues, seems nowadays to be badly stereotyped, and its dramaturgy occasionally seems episodic and crude. For example, how do you keep the suspense taut with so many scene changes, and how do you costume "little formless fears"? On the other hand, the character of Brutus Jones displays an admirable sense of raw pride and power, particularly when viewed in contrast to his sleazy white sidekick, Smithers. In his fall from a high place and in his honesty as he moves through a kind of desperate psychoanalysis, Jones seems worthy of the silver bullet which he himself has designated for his death.

O'Neill called *The Hairy Ape* "a comedy of ancient and modern life." Borrowing from the devices of German Expressionism, he strives for a grotesque and sardonic tone, but the play, like *The Emperor Jones,* is still basically another chase. Here Yank chases himself, stumbling through the urban jungle of contemporary capitalistic America, to find what he thinks is true brotherhood only with a gorilla in a cage. As in *The Emperor Jones,* the violent death of the protagonist is primarily of his own making.

The Hairy Ape sometimes seems top-heavy in its

repetitive choral chants, and its best scenes are those when O'Neill is writing more simply and immediately out of his own bones. Yank's confrontation with Mildred, which takes place fairly early in the play, is a powerful moment, and the scene when he tries to join the Industrial Workers of the World builds up a good head of steam. There is also a powerful passage when an old seaman recalls the days of sailing ships, which gave men a more authentic connection with the sea. The ending, as with much of O'Neill, catches one unawares, and is surprisingly moving. Finally, for all the labored artificiality of *The Hairy Ape,* and its repetitive insistence on the theme of belonging, the basic story seems to hold. The play became a fairly successful movie, and was revived to some acclaim on Broadway in 1997.

In summing up, one must acknowledge that O'Neill is not without his faults as a playwright. In his struggle to move beyond the prosaic, his language at times becomes labored and inept. Possibly because he doesn't trust his words, he overloads his scripts with excessively novelistic stage directions which, if actors followed them, would allow little room for the collaborative creativity which is so much a part of good theater. These early plays, too, reflect a number of crudities in stagecraft. The machinery of getting characters on- and offstage seems sometimes bald and predictable, and there is often some awkward dead air when people are left alone on stage. Even in such a realistic play as *Anna Christie,* O'Neill occasionally falls back on old-fashioned "asides" to reveal a character's thoughts, and the gun in Act II seems dragged in as a melodramatic gimmick. O'Neill had the luxury of being able to call on elaborate scenery and large casts, but the problems of staging the journey in *The Emperor Jones* or the ending of *The Hairy Ape* remain daunting for any director.

Yet for all these difficulties, and after all these years, these early plays manage to seize us, hold us, and move us in ways that so many other plays don't. Eugene O'Neill was enough the son of his father to know the value of giving an audience a strong narrative, a passionate hero, a wealth of events, and theatrically stagy effects. He was also enough of his own man to try to stretch and expand, in every way he could, the worn-out theatrical forms he grew up with, and to instill in everything he wrote a constant and passionate thrust for a significance beyond itself.

BEYOND THE HORIZON

CHARACTERS

JAMES MAYO, *a farmer*
KATE MAYO, *his wife*
CAPTAIN DICK SCOTT, *of the bark "Sunda,"*
her brother
ANDREW MAYO } *sons of* JAMES MAYO
ROBERT MAYO
RUTH ATKINS
MRS. ATKINS, *her widowed mother*
MARY
BEN, *a farm hand*
DOCTOR FAWCETT

SCENES

ACT ONE

SCENE 1: The Road. Sunset of a day in Spring.
SCENE 2: The Farm House. The same night.

ACT TWO

(*Three years later*)
SCENE 1: The Farm House. Noon of a Summer day.
SCENE 2: The top of a hill on the farm overlooking the sea. The following day.

ACT THREE

(*Five years later*)
SCENE 1: The Farm House. Dawn of a day in late Fall.
SCENE 2: The Road. Sunrise.

ACT ONE
Scene 1

*A section of country highway. The road runs diago-
nally from the left, forward, to the right, rear, and can
be seen in the distance winding toward the horizon like
a pale ribbon between the low, rolling hills with their
freshly plowed fields clearly divided from each other,
checkerboard fashion, by the lines of stone walls and
rough snake-fences.*

*The forward triangle cut off by the road is a section
of a field from the dark earth of which myriad bright-
green blades of fall-sown rye are sprouting. A strag-
gling line of piled rocks, too low to be called a wall,
separates this field from the road.*

*To the rear of the road is a ditch with a sloping,
grassy bank on the far side. From the center of this an
old, gnarled apple tree, just budding into leaf, strains
its twisted branches heavenwards, black against the pal-
lor of distance. A snake-fence sidles from left to right
along the top of the bank, passing beneath the apple
tree.*

*The hushed twilight of a day in May is just begin-
ning. The horizon hills are still rimmed by a faint line
of flame, and the sky above them glows with the crimson flush of the sunset. This fades gradually as the action of the scene progresses.*

*At the rise of the curtain, ROBERT MAYO is discov-
ered sitting on the fence. He is a tall, slender young
man of twenty-three. There is a touch of the poet about*

5

him expressed in his high forehead and wide, dark eyes. His features are delicate and refined, leaning to weakness in the mouth and chin. He is dressed in gray corduroy trousers pushed into high laced boots, and a blue flannel shirt with a bright colored tie. He is reading a book by the fading sunset light. He shuts this, keeping a finger in to mark the place, and turns his head toward the horizon, gazing out over the fields and hills. His lips move as if he were reciting something to himself.

His brother ANDREW *comes along the road from the right, returning from his work in the fields. He is twenty-seven years old, an opposite type to* ROBERT— *husky, sun-bronzed, handsome in a large-featured, manly fashion—a son of the soil, intelligent in a shrewd way, but with nothing of the intellectual about him. He wears overalls, leather boots, a gray flannel shirt open at the neck, and a soft, mud-stained hat pushed back on his head. He stops to talk to* ROBERT, *leaning on the hoe he carries.*

ANDREW (*seeing* ROBERT *has not noticed his presence—in a loud shout*): Hey there! (ROBERT *turns with a start. Seeing who it is, he smiles*) Gosh, you do take the prize for day-dreaming! And I see you've toted one of the old books along with you. (*He crosses the ditch and sits on the fence near his brother*) What is it this time—poetry, I'll bet. (*He reaches for the book*) Let me see.

ROBERT (*handing it to him rather reluctantly*): Look out you don't get it full of dirt.

ANDREW (*glancing at his hands*): That isn't dirt—it's good clean earth. (*He turns over the pages. His eyes read something and he gives an exclamation of disgust*) Humph! (*With a provoking grin at his brother he reads aloud in a doleful, sing-song voice*) "I have loved wind and light and the bright sea. But Holy and most sacred night, not as I love and have loved thee." (*He hands the book back*) Here! Take it and bury it. I suppose it's that year in college gave you a liking for that kind of stuff. I'm darn glad I stopped at high school, or maybe I'd been crazy too. (*He grins and slaps* ROBERT *on the back affectionately*) Imagine me reading poetry and plowing at the same time. The team'd run away, I'll bet.

ROBERT (*laughing*): Or picture me plowing.

ANDREW: You should have gone back to college last fall, like I know you wanted to. You're fitted for that sort of thing—just as I ain't.

ROBERT: You know why I didn't go back, Andy. Pa didn't like the idea, even if he didn't say so; and I know he wanted the money to use improving the farm. And besides, I'm not keen on being a student, just because you see me reading books all the time. What I want to do now is keep on moving so that I won't take root in any one place.

ANDREW: Well, the trip you're leaving on tomorrow will keep you moving all right. (*At this mention of the trip they both fall silent. There is a pause. Finally* ANDREW *goes on, awkwardly, attempting to speak casually*) Uncle says you'll be gone three years.

ROBERT: About that, he figures.

ANDREW (*moodily*): That's a long time.

ROBERT: Not so long when you come to consider it. You know the "Sunda" sails around the Horn for Yokohama first, and that's a long voyage on a sailing ship; and if we go to any of the other places Uncle Dick mentions—India, or Australia, or South Africa, or South America—they'll be long voyages, too.

ANDREW: You can have all those foreign parts for all of me. (*After a pause*) Ma's going to miss you a lot, Rob.

ROBERT: Yes—and I'll miss her.

ANDREW: And Pa ain't feeling none too happy to have you go—though he's been trying not to show it.

ROBERT: I can see how he feels.

ANDREW: And you can bet that I'm not giving any cheers about it. (*He puts one hand on the fence near* ROBERT)

ROBERT (*putting one hand on top of* ANDREW'S *with a gesture almost of shyness*): I know that, too, Andy.

ANDREW: I'll miss you as much as anybody, I guess. You see, you and I ain't like most brothers—always fighting and separated a lot of the time, while we've always been together—just the two of us. It's different with us. That's why it hits so hard, I guess.

ROBERT (*with feeling*): It's just as hard for me, Andy—believe that! I hate to leave you and the old folks—but—I feel I've got to. There's something calling me— (*He points to the horizon*) Oh, I can't just explain it to you, Andy.

ANDREW: No need to, Rob. (*Angry at himself*) Hell! You want to go—that's all there is to it; and I wouldn't have you miss this chance for the world.

ROBERT: It's fine of you to feel that way, Andy.

ANDREW: Huh! I'd be a nice son-of-a-gun if I didn't, wouldn't I? When I know how you need this sea trip to make a new man of you—in the body, I mean—and give you your full health back.

ROBERT (*a trifle impatiently*): All of you seem to keep harping on my health. You were so used to seeing me lying around the house in the old days that you never will get over the notion that I'm a chronic invalid. You don't realize how I've bucked up in the past few years. If I had no other excuse for going on Uncle Dick's ship but just my health, I'd stay right here and start in plowing.

ANDREW: Can't be done. Farming ain't your nature.

There's all the difference shown in just the way us two feel about the farm. You—well, you like the home part of it, I expect; but as a place to work and grow things, you hate it. Ain't that right?

ROBERT: Yes, I suppose it is. For you it's different. You're a Mayo through and through. You're wedded to the soil. You're as much a product of it as an ear of corn is, or a tree. Father is the same. This farm is his life-work, and he's happy in knowing that another Mayo, inspired by the same love, will take up the work where he leaves off. I can understand your attitude, and Pa's; and I think it's wonderful and sincere. But I—well, I'm not made that way.

ANDREW: No, you ain't; but when it comes to understanding, I guess I realize that you've got your own angle of looking at things.

ROBERT (*musingly*): I wonder if you do, really.

ANDREW (*confidently*): Sure I do. You've seen a bit of the world, enough to make the farm seem small, and you've got the itch to see it all.

ROBERT: It's more than that, Andy.

ANDREW: Oh, of course. I know you're going to learn navigation, and all about a ship, so's you can be an officer. That's natural, too. There's fair pay in it, I expect, when you consider that you've always got a home and grub thrown in; and if you're set on traveling, you can go anywhere you're a mind to without paying fare.

ROBERT (*with a smile that is half sad*): It's more than that, Andy.

ANDREW: Sure it is. There's always a chance of a good thing coming your way in some of those foreign ports or other. I've heard there are great opportunities for a young fellow with his eyes open in some of those new countries that are just being opened up. (*Jovially*) I'll bet that's what you've been turning over in your mind under all your quietness! (*He slaps his brother on the back with a laugh*) Well, if you get to be a millionaire all of a sudden, call 'round once in a while and I'll pass the plate to you. We could use a lot of money right here on the farm without hurting it any.

ROBERT (*forced to laugh*): I've never considered that practical side of it for a minute, Andy.

ANDREW: Well, you ought to.

ROBERT: No, I oughtn't. (*Pointing to the horizon—dreamily*) Supposing I was to tell you that it's just Beauty that's calling me, the beauty of the far off and unknown, the mystery and spell of the East which lures me in the books I've read, the need of the freedom of great wide spaces, the joy of wandering on and on—in quest of the secret which is hidden over there, beyond the horizon? Suppose I told you that was the one and only reason for my going?

ANDREW: I should say you were nutty.

ROBERT (*frowning*): Don't, Andy, I'm serious.

ANDREW: Then you might as well stay here, because we've got all you're looking for right on this farm. There's wide space enough, Lord knows; and you can have all the sea you want by walking a mile down to the beach; and there's plenty of horizon to look at, and beauty enough for anyone except in the winter. (*He grins*) As for the mystery and spell, I haven't met 'em yet, but they're probably lying around somewheres. I'll have you understand this is a first class farm with all the fixings. (*He laughs.*)

ROBERT (*joining in the laughter in spite of himself*): It's no use talking to you, you chump!

ANDREW: You'd better not say anything to Uncle Dick about spells and things when you're on the ship. He'll likely chuck you overboard for a Jonah.

(*He jumps down from fence*) I'd better run along. I've got to wash up some as long as Ruth's Ma is coming over for supper.

ROBERT (*pointedly—almost bitterly*): And Ruth.

ANDREW (*confused—looking everywhere except at* ROBERT—*trying to appear unconcerned*): Yes, Ruth'll be staying too. Well, I better hustle, I guess, and— (*He steps over the ditch to the road while he is talking.*)

ROBERT (*who appears to be fighting some strong inward emotion—impulsively*): Wait a minute, Andy! (*He jumps down from the fence*) There is something I want to—(*He stops abruptly, biting his lips, his face coloring.*)

ANDREW (*facing him; half-defiantly*): Yes?

ROBERT (*confusedly*): No—never mind—it doesn't matter, it was nothing.

ANDREW (*after a pause, during which he stares fixedly at* ROBERT'S *averted face*): Maybe I can guess what—you were going to say—but I guess you're right not to talk about it. (*He pulls* ROBERT'S *hand from his side and grips it tensely; the two brothers stand looking into each other's eyes for a minute*) We can't help those things, Rob. (*He turns away, suddenly releasing* ROBERT'S *hand*) You'll be coming along shortly, won't you?

ROBERT (*dully*): Yes.

ANDREW: See you later, then. (*He walks off down the road to the left.* ROBERT *stares after him for a moment; then climbs to the fence rail again, and looks out over the hills, an expression of deep grief on his face. After a moment or so,* RUTH *enters hurriedly from the left. She is a healthy, blonde, out-of-door girl of twenty, with a graceful, slender figure. Her face, though inclined to roundness, is undeniably pretty, its large eyes of a deep blue set off strikingly by the sun-bronzed complexion. Her small, regular features are marked by a certain strength—an underlying, stubborn fixity of purpose hidden in the frankly appealing charm of her fresh youthfulness. She wears a simple white dress but no hat.*)

RUTH (*seeing him*): Hello, Rob!

ROBERT (*startled*): Hello, Ruth!

RUTH (*jumps the ditch and perches on the fence beside him*): I was looking for you.

ROBERT (*pointedly*): Andy just left here.

RUTH: I know. I met him on the road a second ago. He told me you were here. (*Tenderly playful*) I wasn't looking for Andy, Smarty, if that's what you mean. I was looking for *you*.

ROBERT: Because I'm going away tomorrow?

RUTH: Because your mother was anxious to have you come home and asked me to look for you. I just wheeled Ma over to your house.

ROBERT (*perfunctorily*): How is your mother?

RUTH (*a shadow coming over her face*): She's about the same. She never seems to get any better or any worse. Oh, Rob, I do wish she'd try to make the best of things that can't be helped.

ROBERT: Has she been nagging at you again?

RUTH (*nods her head, and then breaks forth rebelliously*): She never stops nagging. No matter what I do for her she finds fault. If only Pa was still living— (*She stops as if ashamed of her outburst*) I suppose I shouldn't complain this way. (*She sighs*) Poor Ma, Lord knows it's hard enough for her. I suppose it's natural to be cross when you're not able ever to walk a step. Oh, I'd like to be going away some place—like you!

ROBERT: It's hard to stay—and equally hard to go, sometimes.

RUTH: There! If I'm not the stupid body! I swore I

wasn't going to speak about your trip—until after you'd gone; and there I go, first thing!

ROBERT: Why didn't you want to speak of it?

RUTH: Because I didn't want to spoil this last night you're here. Oh, Rob, I'm going to—we're all going to miss you so awfully. Your mother is going around looking as if she'd burst out crying any minute. You ought to know how I feel. Andy and you and I— why it seems as if we'd always been together.

ROBERT (*with a wry attempt at a smile*): You and Andy will still have each other. It'll be harder for me without anyone.

RUTH: But you'll have new sights and new people to take your mind off; while we'll be here with the old, familiar place to remind us every minute of the day. It's a shame you're going—just at this time, in spring, when everything is getting so nice. (*With a sigh*) I oughtn't to talk that way when I know going's the best thing for you. You're bound to find all sorts of opportunities to get on, your father says.

ROBERT (*heatedly*): I don't give a damn about that! I wouldn't take a voyage across the road for the best opportunity in the world of the kind Pa thinks of. (*He smiles at his own irritation*) Excuse me, Ruth, for getting worked up over it; but Andy gave me an overdose of the practical considerations.

RUTH (*slowly, puzzled*): Well, then, if it isn't— (*With sudden intensity*) Oh, Rob, why *do* you want to go?

ROBERT (*turning to her quickly, in surprise—slowly*): Why do you ask that, Ruth?

RUTH (*dropping her eyes before his searching glance*): Because— (*Lamely*) It seems such a shame.

ROBERT (*insistently*): Why?

RUTH: Oh, because—everything.

ROBERT: I could hardly back out now, even if I wanted to. And I'll be forgotten before you know it.

RUTH (*indignantly*): You won't! I'll never forget— (*She stops and turns away to hide her confusion.*)

ROBERT (*softly*): Will you promise me that?

RUTH (*evasively*): Of course. It's mean of you to think that any of us would forget so easily.

ROBERT (*disappointedly*): Oh!

RUTH (*with an attempt at lightness*): But you haven't told me your reason for leaving yet.

ROBERT (*moodily*): I doubt if you'll understand. It's difficult to explain, even to myself. Either you feel it, or you don't. I can remember being conscious of it first when I was only a kid—you haven't forgotten what a sickly specimen I was then, in those days, have you?

RUTH (*with a shudder*): Let's not think about them.

ROBERT: You'll have to, to understand. Well, in those days, when Ma was fixing meals, she used to get me out of the way by pushing my chair to the west window and telling me to look out and be quiet. That wasn't hard. I guess I was always quiet.

RUTH (*compassionately*): Yes, you always were—and you suffering so much, too!

ROBERT (*musingly*): So I used to stare out over the fields to the hills, out there— (*He points to the horizon*) and somehow after a time I'd forget any pain I was in, and start dreaming. I knew the sea was over beyond those hills—the folks had told me— and I used to wonder what the sea was like, and try to form a picture of it in my mind. (*With a smile*) There was all the mystery in the world to me then about that—far-off sea—and there still is! It called to me then just as it does now. (*After a slight pause*) And other times my eyes would follow this road, winding off into the distance, toward the hills, as if it, too, was searching for the sea. And I'd promise myself that when I grew up and was strong, I'd follow that road, and it and I would find the sea together. (*With a smile*) You see, my making this trip is only keeping that promise of long ago.

RUTH (*charmed by his low, musical voice telling the dreams of his childhood*): Yes, I see.

ROBERT: Those were the only happy moments of my life then, dreaming there at the window. I liked to be all alone—those times, I got to know all the different kinds of sunsets by heart. And all those sunsets took place over there— (*He points*) beyond the horizon. So gradually I came to believe that all the wonders of the world happened on the other side of those hills. There was the home of the good fairies who performed beautiful miracles. I believed in fairies then. (*With a smile*) Perhaps I still do believe in them. Anyway, in those days they were real enough, and sometimes I could actually hear them calling to me to come out and play with them, dance with them down the road in the dusk in a game of hide-and-seek to find out where the sun was hiding himself. They sang their little songs to me, songs that told of all the wonderful things they had in their home on the other side of the hills; and they promised to show me all of them, if I'd only come, come! But I couldn't come then, and I used to cry sometimes and Ma would think I was in pain. (*He breaks off suddenly with a laugh*) That's why I'm going now, I suppose. For I can still hear them calling. But the horizon is as far away and as luring as ever. (*He turns to her—softly*) Do you understand now, Ruth?

RUTH (*spellbound, in a whisper*): Yes.

ROBERT: You feel it then?

RUTH: Yes, yes, I do! (*Unconsciously she snuggles close against his side. His arm steals about her as if he were not aware of the action*) Oh, Rob, how could I help feeling it? You tell things so beautifully!

ROBERT (*suddenly realizing that his arm is around her, and that her head is resting on his shoulder, gently takes his arm away. RUTH, brought back to herself, is overcome with confusion*): So now you know why I'm going. It's for that reason—that and one other.

RUTH: You've another? Then you must tell me that, too.

ROBERT (*looking at her searchingly. She drops her eyes before his gaze*): I wonder if I ought to! You'll promise not to be angry—whatever it is?

RUTH (*softly, her face still averted*): Yes, I promise.

ROBERT (*simply*): I love you. That's the other reason.

RUTH (*hiding her face in her hands*): Oh, Rob!

ROBERT: I wasn't going to tell you, but I feel I have to. It can't matter now that I'm going so far away, and for so long—perhaps forever. I've loved you all these years, but the realization never came 'til I agreed to go away with Uncle Dick. Then I thought of leaving you, and the pain of that thought revealed to me in a flash—that I loved you, had loved you as long as I could remember. (*He gently pulls one of RUTH's hands away from her face*) You mustn't mind my telling you this, Ruth. I realize how impossible it all is—and I understand; for the revelation of my own love seemed to open my eyes to the love of others. I saw Andy's love for you—and I knew that you must love him.

RUTH (*breaking out stormily*): I don't! I don't love Andy! I don't! (*ROBERT stares at her in stupid astonishment. RUTH weeps hysterically*) Whatever—put such a fool notion into—into your head? (*She suddenly throws her arms about his neck and hides her head on his shoulder*) Oh, Rob! Don't go away!

Please! You mustn't, now! You can't! I won't let you! It'd break my—my heart!

ROBERT (*the expression of stupid bewilderment giving way to one of overwhelming joy. He presses her close to him—slowly and tenderly*): Do you mean that—that you love me?

RUTH (*sobbing*): Yes, yes—of course I do—what d'you s'pose? (*She lifts up her head and looks into his eyes with a tremulous smile*) You stupid thing! (*He kisses her*) I've loved you right along.

ROBERT (*mystified*): But you and Andy were always together!

RUTH: Because you never seemed to want to go any place with me. You were always reading an old book, and not paying attention to me. I was too proud to let you see I cared because I thought the year you had away to college had made you stuck-up, and you thought yourself too educated to waste any time on me.

ROBERT (*kissing her*): And I was thinking— (*with a laugh*) What fools we've both been!

RUTH (*overcome by a sudden fear*): You won't go away on the trip, will you, Rob? You'll tell them you can't go on account of me, won't you? You can't go now! You can't!

ROBERT (*bewildered*): Perhaps—you can come too.

RUTH: Oh, Rob, don't be so foolish. You know I can't. Who'd take care of Ma? Don't you see I couldn't go—on her account? (*She clings to him imploringly*) Please don't go—not now. Tell them you've decided not to. They won't mind. I know your mother and father'll be glad. They'll all be. They don't want you go to so far away from them. Please, Rob! We'll be so happy here together where it's natural and we know things. Please tell me you won't go!

ROBERT (*face to face with a definite, final decision,*

betrays the conflict going on within him): But—
Ruth—I—Uncle Dick—

RUTH: He won't mind when he knows it's for your
happiness to stay. How could he? (*As* ROBERT *remains silent she bursts into sobs again*) Oh, Rob!
And you said—you loved me!

ROBERT (*conquered by this appeal—an irrevocable decision in his voice*): I won't go, Ruth. I promise you.
There! Don't cry! (*He presses her to him, stroking
her hair tenderly. After a pause he speaks with happy
hopefulness*) Perhaps after all Andy was right—
righter than he knew—when he said I could find all
the things I was seeking for here, at home on the
farm. I think love must have been the secret—the
secret that called to me from over the world's rim—
the secret beyond every horizon; and when I did
not come, it came to me. (*He clasps* RUTH *to him
fiercely*) Oh, Ruth, our love is sweeter than any distant dream! (*He kisses her passionately and steps to
the ground, lifting* RUTH *in his arms and carrying
her to the road where he puts her down.*)

RUTH (*with a happy laugh*): My, but you're strong!

ROBERT: Come! We'll go and tell them at once.

RUTH (*dismayed*): Oh, no, don't, Rob, not 'til after
I've gone. There'd be bound to be such a scene with
them all together.

ROBERT (*kissing her—gayly*): As you like—little Miss
Common Sense!

RUTH: Let's go, then. (*She takes his hand, and they
start to go off left.* ROBERT *suddenly stops and turns
as though for a last look at the hills and the dying
sunset flush.*)

ROBERT (*looking upward and pointing*): See! The first
star. (*He bends down and kisses her tenderly*) Our
star!

RUTH (*in a soft murmur*): Yes. Our very own star.

(*They stand for a moment looking up at it, their arms around each other. Then* RUTH *takes his hand again and starts to lead him away*) Come, Rob, let's go. (*His eyes are fixed again on the horizon as he half turns to follow her.* RUTH *urges*) We'll be late for supper, Rob.

ROBERT (*shakes his head impatiently, as though he were throwing off some disturbing thought—with a laugh*): All right. We'll run then. Come on! (*They run off laughing as the curtain falls.*)

ACT ONE
Scene 2

The small sitting room of the Mayo farmhouse about nine o'clock same night. On the left, two windows looking out on the fields. Against the wall between the windows, an old-fashioned walnut desk. In the left corner, rear, a sideboard with a mirror. In the rear wall to the right of the sideboard, a window looking out on the road. Next to the window a door leading out into the yard. Farther right, a black horsehair sofa, and another door opening on a bedroom. In the corner, a straight-backed chair. In the right wall, near the middle, an open doorway leading to the kitchen. Farther forward a double-heater stove with coal scuttle, etc. In the center of the newly-carpeted floor, an oak dining-room table with a red cover. In the center of the table, a large oil reading lamp. Four chairs, three rockers with crocheted tidies on their backs, and one straight-backed, are placed about the table. The walls are papered a dark red with a scrolly-figured pattern.

Everything in the room is clean, well-kept, and in its exact place, yet there is no suggestion of primness about the whole. Rather the atmosphere is one of the orderly comfort of a simple, hard-earned prosperity, enjoyed and maintained by the family as a unit.

JAMES MAYO, *his wife, her brother,* CAPTAIN DICK SCOTT, *and* ANDREW *are discovered.* MAYO *is his son* ANDREW *over again in body and face—an* ANDREW *sixty-five years old with a short, square, white beard.*

MRS. MAYO *is a slight, round-faced, rather prim-look-ing woman of fifty-five who had once been a school teacher. The labors of a farmer's wife have bent but not broken her, and she retains a certain refinement of movement and expression foreign to the* MAYO *part of the family. Whatever of resemblance* ROBERT *has to his parents may be traced to her. Her brother, the* CAP-TAIN, *is short and stocky, with a weather-beaten, jovial face and a white mustache—a typical old salt, loud of voice and given to gesture. He is fifty-eight years old.*

JAMES MAYO *sits in front of the table. He wears spectacles, and a farm journal which he has been read-ing lies in his lap. The* CAPTAIN *leans forward from a chair in the rear, his hands on the table in front of him.* ANDREW *is tilted back on the straight-backed chair to the left, his chin sunk forward on his chest, staring at the carpet, preoccupied and frowning.*

As the curtain rises the CAPTAIN *is just finishing the relation of some sea episode. The others are pretending an interest which is belied by the absent-minded expres-sions on their faces.*

THE CAPTAIN (*chuckling*): And that mission woman, she hails me on the dock as I was acomin' ashore, and she says—with her silly face all screwed up seri-ous as judgment—"Captain," she says, "would you be so kind as to tell me where the sea-gulls sleeps at nights?" Blow me if them warn't her exact words! (*He slaps the table with the palms of his hands and laughs loudly. The others force smiles*) Ain't that just like a fool woman's question? And I looks at her serious as I could. "Ma'm," says I, "I couldn't rightly answer that question. I ain't never seed a sea-gull in his bunk yet. The next time I hears one snorin'," I says, "I'll make a note of where he's turned in, and write out a letter 'bout it." And then

she calls me a fool real spiteful and tacks away from
me quick. (*He laughs again uproariously*) So I got
rid of her that way. (*The others smile but immediately relapse into expressions of gloom again.*)

MRS. MAYO (*absent-mindedly—feeling that she has to
say something*): But when it comes to that, where
do sea-gulls sleep, Dick?

SCOTT (*slapping the table*): Ho! Ho! Listen to her,
James. 'Nother one! Well, if that don't beat all
hell—'scuse me for cussin', Kate.

MAYO (*with a twinkle in his eyes*): They unhitch their
wings, Katey, and spreads 'em out on a wave for
a bed.

SCOTT: And then they tells the fish to whistle to 'em
when it's time to turn out. Ho! Ho!

MRS. MAYO (*with a forced smile*): You men folks are
too smart to live, aren't you? (*She resumes her knitting.* MAYO *pretends to read his paper;* ANDREW
stares at the floor.)

SCOTT (*looks from one to the other of them with a
puzzled air. Finally he is unable to bear the thick
silence a minute longer, and blurts out*): You folks
look as if you was settin' up with a corpse. (*With
exaggerated concern*) God A'mighty, there ain't anyone dead, be there?

MAYO (*sharply*): Don't play the dunce, Dick! You
know as well as we do there ain't no great cause to
be feelin' chipper.

SCOTT (*argumentatively*): And there ain't no cause to
be wearin' mourning, either, I can make out.

MRS. MAYO (*indignantly*): How can you talk that way,
Dick Scott, when you're taking our Robbie away
from us, in the middle of the night, you might say,
just to get on that old boat of yours on time! I
think you might wait until morning when he's had
his breakfast.

SCOTT (*appealing to the others hopelessly*): Ain't that a woman's way o' seein' things for you? God A'mighty, Kate, I can't give orders to the tide that it's got to be high just when it suits me to have it. I ain't gettin' no fun out o' missing sleep and leavin' here at six bells myself. (*Protestingly*) And the "Sunda" ain't an old ship—leastways, not very old—and she's good's she ever was.

MRS. MAYO (*her lips trembling*): I wish Robbie weren't going.

MAYO (*looking at her over his glasses—consolingly*): There, Katey!

MRS. MAYO (*rebelliously*): Well, I *do* wish he wasn't!

SCOTT: You shouldn't be taking it so hard, 's far as I kin see. This vige'll make a man of him. I'll see to it he learns how to navigate, 'n' study for a mate's c'tificate right off—and it'll give him a trade for the rest of his life, if he wants to travel.

MRS. MAYO: But I don't want him to travel all his life. You've got to see he comes home when this trip is over. Then he'll be all well, and he'll want to—to marry—(ANDREW *sits forward in his chair with an abrupt movement*)—and settle down right here. (*She stares down at the knitting in her lap—after a pause*) I never realized how hard it was going to be for me to have Robbie go—or I wouldn't have considered it a minute.

SCOTT: It ain't no good goin' on that way, Kate, now it's all settled.

MRS. MAYO (*on the verge of tears*): It's all right for *you* to talk. You've never had any children. You don't know what it means to be parted from them—and Robbie my youngest, too. (ANDREW *frowns and fidgets in his chair.*)

ANDREW (*suddenly turning to them*): There's one thing none of you seem to take into consideration—that

Rob wants to go. He's dead set on it. He's been dreaming over this trip ever since it was first talked about. It wouldn't be fair to him not to have him go. (*A sudden uneasiness seems to strike him*) At least, not if he still feels the same way about it he did when he was talking to me this evening.

MAYO (*with an air of decision*): Andy's right, Katey. That ends all argyment, you can see that. (*Looking at his big silver watch*) Wonder what's happened to Robert? He's been gone long enough to wheel the widder to home, certain. He can't be out dreamin' at the stars his last night.

MRS. MAYO (*a bit reproachfully*): Why didn't you wheel Mrs. Atkins back tonight, Andy? You usually do when she and Ruth come over.

ANDREW (*avoiding her eyes*): I thought maybe Robert wanted to tonight. He offered to go right away when they were leaving.

MRS. MAYO: He only wanted to be polite.

ANDREW (*gets to his feet*): Well, he'll be right back, I guess. (*He turns to his father*) Guess I'll go take a look at the black cow, Pa—see if she's ailing any.

MAYO: Yes—better had, son. (ANDREW *goes into the kitchen on the right.*)

SCOTT (*as he goes out—in a low tone*): There's the boy that would make a good, strong sea-farin' man—if he'd a mind to.

MAYO (*sharply*): Don't you put no such fool notions in Andy's head, Dick—or you'n' me's goin' to fall out. (*Then he smiles*) You couldn't tempt him, no ways. Andy's a Mayo bred in the bone, and he's a born farmer and a damn good one, too. He'll live and die right here on this farm, like I expect to. (*With proud confidence*) And he'll make this one of the slickest, best-payin' farms in the state, too, afore he gits through!

SCOTT: Seems to me it's a pretty slick place right now.

MAYO (*shaking his head*): It's too small. We need more land to make it amount to much, and we ain't got the capital to buy it. (ANDREW *enters from the kitchen. His hat is on, and he carries a lighted lantern in his hand. He goes to the door in the rear leading out.*)

ANDREW (*opens the door and pauses*): Anything else you can think of to be done, Pa?

MAYO: No, nothin' I know of. (ANDREW *goes out, shutting the door.*)

MRS. MAYO (*after a pause*): What's come over Andy tonight, I wonder? He acts so strange.

MAYO: He does seem sort o' glum and out of sorts. It's 'count o' Robert leavin', I s'pose. (*To* SCOTT) Dick, you wouldn't believe how them boys o' mine sticks together. They ain't like most brothers. They've been thick as thieves all their lives, with nary a quarrel I kin remember.

SCOTT: No need to tell me that. I can see how they take to each other.

MRS. MAYO (*pursuing her train of thought*): Did you notice, James, how queer everyone was at supper? Robert seemed stirred up about something; and Ruth was so flustered and giggly; and Andy sat there dumb, looking as if he'd lost his best friend; and all of them only nibbled at their food.

MAYO: Guess they was all thinkin' about tomorrow, same as us.

MRS. MAYO (*shaking her head*): No. I'm afraid somethin's happened—somethin' else.

MAYO: You mean—'bout Ruth?

MRS. MAYO: Yes.

MAYO (*after a pause—frowning*): I hope her and Andy ain't had a serious fallin'-out. I always sorter hoped

they'd hitch up together sooner or later. What d'you
say, Dick? Don't you think them two'd pair up well?

SCOTT (*nodding his head approvingly*): A sweet,
wholesome couple they'd make.

MAYO: It'd be a good thing for Andy in more ways
than one. I ain't what you'd call calculatin' gener-
ally, and I b'lieve in lettin' young folks run their
affairs to suit themselves; but there's advantages for
both o' them in this match you can't overlook in
reason. The Atkins farm is right next to ourn. Jined
together they'd make a jim-dandy of a place, with
plenty o' room to work in. And bein' a widder with
only a daughter, and laid up all the time to boot,
Mrs. Atkins can't do nothin' with the place as it
ought to be done. She needs a man, a first-class
farmer to take hold o' things; and Andy's just the
one.

MRS. MAYO (*abruptly*): I don't think Ruth loves Andy.

MAYO: You don't? Well, maybe a woman's eyes is
sharper in such things—but they're always together.
And if she don't love him now, she'll likely come
around to it in time. (*As* MRS. MAYO *shakes her
head*) You seem mighty fixed in your opinion,
Katey. How d'you know?

MRS. MAYO: It's just—what I feel.

MAYO (*a light breaking over him*): You don't mean to
say— (MRS. MAYO *nods.* MAYO *chuckles scornfully*)
Shucks! I'm losin' my respect for your eyesight,
Katey. Why, Robert ain't got no time for Ruth,
'cept as a friend!

MRS. MAYO (*warningly*): Sss-h-h! (*The door from the
yard opens, and* ROBERT *enters. He is smiling happily, and humming a song to himself, but as he
comes into the room an undercurrent of nervous uneasiness manifests itself in his bearing.*)

MAYO: So here you be at last! (ROBERT *comes for-*

ward and sits on ANDY'S *chair.* MAYO *smiles slyly at his wife*) What have you been doin' all this time—countin' the stars to see if they all come out right and proper?

ROBERT: There's only one I'll ever look for any more, Pa.

MAYO (*reproachfully*): You might've even not wasted time lookin' for that one—your last night.

MRS. MAYO (*as if she were speaking to a child*): You ought to have worn your coat a sharp night like this, Robbie.

SCOTT (*disgustedly*): God A'mighty, Kate, you treat Robert as if he was one year old!

MRS. MAYO (*notices* ROBERT'S *nervous uneasiness*): You look all worked up over something, Robbie. What is it?

ROBERT (*swallowing hard, looks quickly from one to the other of them—then begins determinedly*): Yes, there *is* something—something I must tell you—all of you. (*As he begins to talk* ANDREW *enters quietly from the rear, closing the door behind him, and setting the lighted lantern on the floor. He remains standing by the door, his arms folded, listening to* ROBERT *with a repressed expression of pain on his face.* ROBERT *is so much taken up with what he is going to say that he does not notice* ANDREW'S *presence*) Something I discovered only this evening—very beautiful and wonderful—something I did not take into consideration previously because I hadn't dared to hope that such happiness could ever come to me. (*Appealingly*) You must all remember that fact, won't you?

MAYO (*frowning*): Let's get to the point, son.

ROBERT (*with a trace of defiance*): Well, the point is this, Pa: I'm not going—I mean—I can't go tomorrow with Uncle Dick—or at any future time, either.

MRS. MAYO (*with a sharp sigh of joyful relief*): Oh, Robbie, I'm so glad!

MAYO (*astounded*): You ain't serious, be you, Robert? (*Severely*) Seems to me it's a pretty late hour in the day for you to be upsettin' all your plans so sudden!

ROBERT: I asked you to remember that until this evening I didn't know myself. I had never dared to dream—

MAYO (*irritably*): What is this foolishness you're talkin' of?

ROBERT (*flushing*): Ruth told me this evening that—she loved me. It was after I'd confessed I loved her. I told her I hadn't been conscious of my love until after the trip had been arranged, and I realized it would mean—leaving her. That was the truth. I *didn't* know until then. (*As if justifying himself to the others*) I hadn't intended telling her anything but—suddenly—I felt I must. I didn't think it would matter, because I was going away. And I thought she loved—someone else. (*Slowly—his eyes shining*) And then she cried and said it was I she'd loved all the time, but I hadn't seen it.

MRS. MAYO (*rushes over and throws her arms about him*): I knew it! I was just telling your father when you came in—and, oh, Robbie, I'm so happy you're not going!

ROBERT (*kissing her*): I knew you'd be glad, Ma.

MAYO (*bewilderedly*): Well, I'll be damned! You do beat all for gettin' folks' minds all tangled up, Robert. And Ruth too! Whatever got into her of a sudden? Why, I was thinkin'—

MRS. MAYO (*hurriedly—in a tone of warning*): Never mind what you were thinking, James. It wouldn't be any use telling us that now. (*Meaningly*) And what you were hoping for turns out just the same almost, doesn't it?

MAYO (*thoughtfully—beginning to see this side of the argument*): Yes, I suppose you're right, Katey. (*Scratching his head in puzzlement*) But how it ever come about! It do beat anything ever I heard. (*Finally he gets up with a sheepish grin and walks over to* ROBERT) We're glad you ain't goin', your Ma and I, for we'd have missed you terrible, that's certain and sure; and we're glad you've found happiness. Ruth's a fine girl and'll make a good wife to you.

ROBERT (*much moved*): Thank you, Pa. (*He grips his father's hand in his.*)

ANDREW (*his face tense and drawn comes forward and holds out his hand, forcing a smile*): I guess it's my turn to offer congratulations, isn't it?

ROBERT (*with a startled cry when his brother appears before him so suddenly*): Andy! (*Confused*) Why— I—I didn't see you. Were you here when—

ANDREW: I heard everything you said; and here's wishing you every happiness, you and Ruth. You both deserve the best there is.

ROBERT (*taking his hand*): Thanks, Andy, it's fine of you to— (*His voice dies away as he sees the pain in* ANDREW's *eyes.*)

ANDREW (*giving his brother's hand a final grip*): Good luck to you both! (*He turns away and goes back to the rear where he bends over the lantern, fumbling with it to hide his emotions from the others.*)

MRS. MAYO (*to the* CAPTAIN, *who has been too flabbergasted by* ROBERT's *decision to say a word*): What's the matter, Dick? Aren't you going to congratulate Robbie?

SCOTT (*embarrassed*): Of course I be! (*He gets to his feet and shakes* ROBERT's *hand, muttering a vague*) Luck to you, boy. (*He stands beside* ROBERT *as if*

*he wanted to say something more but doesn't know
how to go about it.*)

ROBERT: Thanks, Uncle Dick.

SCOTT: So you're not acomin' on the "Sunda" with
me? (*His voice indicates disbelief.*)

ROBERT: I can't, Uncle—not now. I wouldn't miss it
for anything in the world under any other circumstances. (*He sighs unconsciously*) But you see I've
found—a bigger dream. (*Then with joyous high spir-
its*) I want you all to understand one thing—I'm not
going to be a loafer on your hands any longer. This
means the beginning of a new life for me in every·
way. I'm going to settle right down and take a real
interest in the farm, and do my share. I'll prove to
you, Pa, that I'm as good a Mayo as you are—or
Andy, when I want to be.

MAYO (*kindly but skeptically*): That's the right spirit,
Robert. Ain't none of us doubts your willin'ness,
but you ain't never learned—

ROBERT: Then I'm going to start learning right away,
and you'll teach me, won't you?

MAYO (*mollifyingly*): Of course I will boy, and be glad
to, only you'd best go easy at first.

SCOTT (*who has listened to this conversation in mingled
consternation and amazement*): You don't mean to
tell me you're going to let him stay, do you, James?

MAYO: Why, things bein' as they be, Robert's free to
do as he's a mind to.

MRS. MAYO: *Let him!* The very idea!

SCOTT (*more and more ruffled*): Then all I got to say
is, you're a soft, weak-willed critter to be permittin'
a boy—and women, too—to be layin' your course
for you wherever they damn pleases.

MAYO (*slyly amused*): It's just the same with me as
'twas with you, Dick. You can't order the tides on

the seas to suit you, and I ain't pretendin' I can reg'late love for young folks.

SCOTT (*scornfully*): Love! They ain't old enough to know love when they sight it! Love! I'm ashamed of you, Robert, to go lettin' a little huggin' and kissin' in the dark spile your chances to make a man out o' yourself. It ain't common sense—no siree, it ain't—not by a hell of a sight! (*He pounds the table with his fists in exasperation*).

MRS. MAYO (*laughing provokingly at her brother*): A fine one you are to be talking about love, Dick— an old cranky bachelor like you. Goodness sakes!

SCOTT (*exasperated by their joking*): I've never been a damn fool like most, if that's what you're steerin' at.

MRS. MAYO (*tauntingly*): Sour grapes, aren't they, Dick? (*She laughs.* ROBERT *and his father chuckle.* SCOTT *sputters with annoyance*) Good gracious, Dick, you do act silly, flying into a temper over nothing.

SCOTT (*indignantly*): Nothin'! You talk as if I wasn't concerned nohow in this here business. Seems to me I've got a right to have my say. Ain't I made all arrangements with the owners and stocked up with some special grub all on Robert's account?

ROBERT: You've been fine, Uncle Dick; and I appreciate it. Truly.

MAYO: 'Course; we all does, Dick.

SCOTT (*unplacated*): I've been countin' sure on havin' Robert for company on this vige—to sorta talk to and show things to, and teach, kinda, and I got my mind so set on havin' him I'm goin' to be double lonesome this vige. (*He pounds on the table, attempting to cover up this confession of weakness*) Darn all this silly lovin' business, anyway. (*Irritably*) But all this talk ain't tellin' me what I'm to do with that sta'b'd cabin I fixed up. It's all painted white, an' a bran new mattress on the bunk, 'n' new sheets 'n' blankets 'n' things. And Chips built in a book-case so's Robert could take his books along—with a slidin' bar fixed across't it, mind, so's they couldn't fall out no matter how she rolled. (*With excited consternation*) What d'you suppose my officers is goin' to think when there's no one comes aboard to oc-cupy that sta'b'd cabin? And the men what did the work on it—what'll *they* think? (*He shakes his finger indignantly*) They're liable as not to suspicion it was a *woman* I'd planned to ship along, and that she gave me the go-by at the last moment! (*He wipes his perspiring brow in anguish at this thought*) Gawd A'mighty! They're only lookin' to have the laugh on me for something like that. They're liable to b'lieve anything, those fellers is!

MAYO (*with a wink*): Then there's nothing to it but for you to get right out and hunt up a wife some-wheres for that spick 'n' span cabin. She'll have to be a pretty one, too, to match it. (*He looks at his watch with exaggerated concern*) You ain't got much time to find her, Dick.

SCOTT (*as the others smile—sulkily*): You kin go to thunder, Jim Mayo!

ANDREW (*comes forward from where he has been standing by the door, rear, brooding. His face is set in a look of grim determination*): You needn't worry about that spare cabin, Uncle Dick, if you've a mind to take me in Robert's place.

ROBERT (*turning to him quickly*): Andy! (*He sees at once the fixed resolve in his brother's eyes, and real-izes immediately the reason for it—in consternation*) Andy, you mustn't!

ANDREW: You've made your decision, Rob, and now I've made mine. You're out of this, remember.

ROBERT (*hurt by his brother's tone*): But Andy—

ANDREW: Don't interfere, Rob—that's all I ask. (*Turning to his uncle*) You haven't answered my question, Uncle Dick.

SCOTT (*clearing his throat, with an uneasy side glance at* JAMES MAYO *who is staring at his elder son as if he thought he had suddenly gone mad*): O' course, I'd be glad to have you, Andy.

ANDREW: It's settled then. I can pack the little I want to take in a few minutes.

MRS. MAYO: Don't be a fool, Dick. Andy's only joking you.

SCOTT (*disgustedly*): It's hard to tell who's jokin' and who's not in this house.

ANDREW (*firmly*): I'm not joking, Uncle Dick. (*As* SCOTT *looks at him uncertainly*) You needn't be afraid I'll go back on my word.

ROBERT (*hurt by the insinuation he feels in* ANDREW's *tone*): Andy! That isn't fair!

MAYO (*frowning*): Seems to me this ain't no subject to joke over—not for Andy.

ANDREW (*facing his father*): I agree with you, Pa, and I tell you again, once and for all, that I've made up my mind to go.

MAYO (*dumbfounded—unable to doubt the determination in* ANDREW's *voice—helplessly*): But why, son? Why?

ANDREW (*evasively*): I've always wanted to go.

ROBERT: Andy!

ANDREW (*half angrily*): You shut up, Rob! (*Turning to his father again*) I didn't ever mention it because as long as Rob was going I knew it was no use; but now Rob's staying on here, there isn't any reason for me not to go.

MAYO (*breathing hard*): No reason? Can you stand there and say that to me, Andrew?

MRS. MAYO (*hastily—seeing the gathering storm*): He doesn't mean a word of it, James.

MAYO (*making a gesture to her to keep silence*): Let me talk, Katey. (*In a more kindly tone*) What's come over you so sudden, Andy? You know's well as I do that it wouldn't be fair o' you to run off at a moment's notice right now when we're up to our necks in hard work.

ANDREW (*avoiding his eyes*): Rob'll hold his end up as soon as he learns.

MAYO: Robert was never cut out for a farmer, and you was.

ANDREW: You can easily get a man to do my work.

MAYO (*restraining his anger with an effort*): It sounds strange to hear you, Andy, that I always thought had good sense, talkin' crazy like that. (*Scornfully*) Get a man to take your place! You ain't been workin' here for no hire, Andy, that you kin give me your notice to quit like you've done. The farm is your'n as well as mine. You've always worked on it with that understanding; and what you're sayin' you intend doin' is just skulkin' out o' your rightful responsibility.

ANDREW (*looking at the floor—simply*): I'm sorry, Pa. (*After a slight pause*) It's no use talking any more about it.

MRS. MAYO (*in relief*): There! I knew Andy'd come to his senses!

ANDREW: Don't get the wrong idea, Ma. I'm not backing out.

MAYO: You mean you're goin' in spite of—everythin'?

ANDREW: Yes I'm going. I've got to. (*He looks at his father defiantly*) I feel I oughtn't to miss this chance to get out into the world and see things, and—I want to go.

MAYO (*with bitter scorn*): So—you want to go out into

the world and see thin's? (*His voice raised and quivering with anger*) I never thought I'd live to see the day when a son o' mine'd look me in the face and tell a bare-faced lie! (*Bursting out*) You're a liar, Andy Mayo, and a mean one to boot!

MRS. MAYO: James!

ROBERT: Pa!

SCOTT: Steady there, Jim!

MAYO (*waving their protests aside*): He is and he knows it.

ANDREW (*his face flushed*): I won't argue with you, Pa. You can think as badly of me as you like.

MAYO (*shaking his finger at* ANDY, *in a cold rage*): You know I'm speakin' truth—that's why you're afraid to argy! You lie when you say you want to go 'way—and see thin's! You ain't got no likin' in the world to go. I've watched you grow up, and I know your ways, and they're my ways. You're runnin' against your own nature, and you're goin' to be a'mighty sorry for it if you do. 'S if I didn't know your real reason for runnin' away! And runnin' away's the only words to fit it. You're runnin' away 'cause you're put out and riled 'cause your own brother's got Ruth 'stead o' you, and—

ANDREW (*his face crimson—tensely*): Stop, Pa! I won't stand hearing that—not even from you!

MRS. MAYO (*rushing to* ANDY *and putting her arms about him protectingly*): Don't mind him, Andy dear. He don't mean a word he's saying! (ROBERT *stands rigidly, his hands clenched, his face contracted by pain.* SCOTT *sits dumbfounded and open-mouthed.* ANDREW *soothes his mother who is on the verge of tears.*)

MAYO (*in angry triumph*): It's the truth, Andy Mayo! And you ought to be bowed in shame to think of it!

ROBERT (*protestingly*): Pa!

MRS. MAYO (*coming from* ANDREW *to his father; puts her hands on his shoulders as though to try to push him back in the chair from which he has risen*): Won't you be still, James? Please won't you?

MAYO (*looking at* ANDREW *over his wife's shoulder—stubbornly*): The truth—God's truth!

MRS. MAYO: Sh-h-h! (*She tries to put a finger across his lips, but he twists his head away.*)

ANDREW (*who has regained control over himself*): You're wrong, Pa, it isn't truth. (*With defiant assertiveness*) I don't love Ruth. I never loved her, and the thought of such a thing never entered my head.

MAYO (*with an angry snort of disbelief*): Hump! You're pilin' lie on lie.

ANDREW (*losing his temper—bitterly*): I suppose it'd be hard for you to explain anyone's wanting to leave this blessed farm except for some outside reason like that. But I'm sick and tired of it—whether you want to believe me or not—and that's why I'm glad to get a chance to move on.

ROBERT: Andy! Don't! You're only making it worse.

ANDREW (*sulkily*): I don't care. I've done my share of work here. I've earned my right to quit when I want to. (*Suddenly overcome with anger and grief; with rising intensity*) I'm sick and tired of the whole damn business. I hate the farm and every inch of ground in it. I'm sick of digging in the dirt and sweating in the sun like a slave without getting a word of thanks for it. (*Tears of rage starting to his eyes—hoarsely*) I'm through, through for good and all; and if Uncle Dick won't take me on his ship, I'll find another. I'll get away somewhere, somehow.

MRS. MAYO (*in a frightened voice*): Don't you answer him, James. He doesn't know what he's saying. Don't say a word to him 'til he's in his right senses again. Please James, don't—

MAYO (*pushes her away from him; his face is drawn and pale with the violence of his passion. He glares at* ANDREW *as if he hated him*): You dare to—you dare to speak like that to me? You talk like that 'bout this farm—the Mayo farm—where you was born—you—you— (*He clenches his fist above his head and advances threateningly on* ANDREW) You damned whelp!

MRS. MAYO (*with a shriek*): James! (*She covers her face with her hands and sinks weakly into* MAYO'S *chair.* ANDREW *remains standing motionless, his face pale and set.*)

SCOTT (*starting to his feet and stretching his arms across the table toward* MAYO): Easy there, Jim!

ROBERT (*throwing himself between father and brother*): Stop! Are you mad?

MAYO (*grabs* ROBERT'S *arm and pushes him aside— then stands for a moment gasping for breath before* ANDREW. *He points to the door with a shaking finger*): Yes—go—go! You're no son o' mine—no son o' mine! You can go to hell if you want to! Don't let me find you here—in the mornin'—or—or—I'll *throw* you out!

ROBERT: Pa! For God's sake! (MRS. MAYO *bursts into noisy sobbing*).

MAYO (*he gulps convulsively and glares at* ANDREW): You go—tomorrow mornin'—and by God—don't come back—don't dare come back—by God, not while I'm livin'—or I'll—I'll (*He shakes over his muttered threat and strides toward the door rear, right.*)

MRS. MAYO (*rising and throwing her arms around him—hysterically*): James! James! Where are you going?

MAYO (*incoherently*): I'm goin'—to bed, Katey. It's late, Katey—it's late. (*He goes out.*)

MRS. MAYO (*following him, pleading hysterically*): James! Take back what you've said to Andy, James! (*She follows him out.* ROBERT *and the* CAPTAIN *stare after them with horrified eyes.* ANDREW *stands rigidly looking straight in front of him, his fists clenched at his sides.*)

SCOTT (*the first to find his voice—with an explosive sigh*): Well, if he ain't the devil himself when he's roused! You oughtn't to have talked to him that way, Andy, 'bout the damn farm, knowin' how touchy he is about it. (*With another sigh*) Well, you won't mind what he's said in anger. He'll be sorry for it when he's calmed down a bit.

ANDREW (*in a dead voice*): You don't know him. (*Defiantly*) What's said is said and can't be unsaid; and I've chosen.

ROBERT (*with violent protest*): Andy! You can't go! This is all so stupid—and terrible!

ANDREW (*coldly*): I'll talk to you in a minute, Rob. (*Crushed by his brother's attitude* ROBERT *sinks down into a chair, holding his head in his hands.*)

SCOTT (*comes and slaps* ANDREW *on the back*): I'm damned glad you're shippin' on, Andy. I like your spirit, and the way you spoke up to him. (*Lowering his voice to a cautious whisper*) The sea's the place for a young feller like you that isn't half dead 'n' alive. (*He gives* ANDY *a final approving slap*) You 'n' me'll get along like twins, see if we don't. I'm goin' aloft to turn in. Don't forget to pack your dunnage. And git some sleep, if you kin. We'll want to sneak out extra early b'fore they're up. It'll do away with more argyments. Robert can drive us down to the town, and bring back the team. (*He goes to the door in the rear, left*) Well, good night.

ANDREW: Good night. (SCOTT *goes out. The two brothers remain silent for a moment. Then* ANDREW *comes over to his brother and puts a hand on his back. He speaks in a low voice, full of feeling*) Buck up, Rob. It ain't any use crying over spilt milk; and it'll all turn out for the best—let's hope. It couldn't be helped—what's happened.

ROBERT (*wildly*): But it's a lie, Andy, a lie!

ANDREW: Of course it's a lie. You know it and I know it, —but that's all ought to know it.

ROBERT: Pa'll never forgive you. Oh, the whole affair is so senseless—and tragic. Why did you think you must go away?

ANDREW: You know better than to ask that. You know why. (*Fiercely*) I can wish you and Ruth all the good luck in the world, and I do, and I mean it; but you can't expect me to stay around here and watch you two together, day after day—and me alone. I couldn't stand it—not after all the plans I'd made to happen on this place thinking— (*His voice breaks*) thinking she cared for me.

ROBERT (*putting a hand on his brother's arm*): God! It's horrible! I feel so guilty—to think that I should be the cause of your suffering, after we've been such pals all our lives. If I could have foreseen what'd happen, I swear to you I'd have never said a word to Ruth. I swear I wouldn't have, Andy!

ANDREW: I know you wouldn't; and that would've been worse, for Ruth would've suffered then. (*He pats his brother's shoulder*) It's best as it is. It had to be, and I've got to stand the gaff, that's all. Pa'll see how I felt—after a time. (*As* ROBERT *shakes his head*)—and if he don't—well, it can't be helped.

ROBERT: But think of Ma! God, Andy, you can't go! You can't!

ANDREW (*fiercely*): I've got to go—to get away! I've got to, I tell you. I'd go crazy here, bein' reminded every second of the day what a fool I'd made of

myself. I've got to get away and try and forget, if I
can. And I'd hate the farm if I stayed, hate it for
bringin' things back. I couldn't take interest in the
work any more, work with no purpose in sight.
Can't you see what a hell it'd be? You love her
too, Rob. Put yourself in my place, and remember
I haven't stopped loving her, and couldn't if I was
to stay. Would that be fair to you or to her? Put
yourself in my place. (*He shakes his brother fiercely
by the shoulder*) What'd you do then? Tell me the
truth! You love her. What'd you do?

ROBERT (*chokingly*): I'd—I'd go, Andy! (*He buries his
face in his hands with a shuddering sob*) God!

ANDREW (*seeming to relax suddenly all over his
body—in a low, steady voice*): Then you know why
I got to go; and there's nothing more to be said.

ROBERT (*in a frenzy of rebellion*): Why did this have
to happen to us? It's damnable! (*He looks about
him wildly, as if his vengeance were seeking the responsible fate.*)

ANDREW (*soothingly—again putting his hands on his
brother's shoulder*): It's no use fussing any more,
Rob. It's done. (*Forcing a smile*) I guess Ruth's got
a right to have who she likes. She made a good
choice—and God bless her for it!

ROBERT: Andy! Oh, I wish I could tell you half I feel
of how fine you are!

ANDREW (*interrupting him quickly*): Shut up! Let's go
to bed. I've got to be up long before sun-up. You,
too, if you're going to drive us down.

ROBERT: Yes. Yes.

ANDREW (*turning down the lamp*): And I've got to
pack yet. (*He yawns with utter weariness*) I'm as
tired as if I'd been plowing twenty-four hours at a
stretch. (*Dully*) I feel—dead. (ROBERT *covers his
face again with his hands.* ANDREW *shakes his head*

as if to get rid of his thoughts, and continues with a poor attempt at cheery briskness) I'm going to douse the light. Come on. (*He slaps his brother on the back.* ROBERT *does not move.* ANDREW *bends over and blows out the lamp. His voice comes from the darkness*) Don't sit there mourning, Rob. It'll all come out in the wash. Come and get some sleep. Everything'll turn out all right in the end. (ROBERT *can be heard stumbling to his feet, and the dark figures of the two brothers can be seen groping their way toward the doorway in the rear as the curtain falls.*)

ACT TWO
Scene 1

*Same as Act One, Scene 2. Sitting room of the farm-
house about half past twelve in the afternoon of a hot,
sun-baked day in mid-summer, three years later. All
the windows are open, but no breeze stirs the soiled
white curtains. A patched screen door is in the rear.
Through it the yard can be seen, its small stretch of
lawn divided by the dirt path leading to the door from
the gate in the white picket fence which borders the
road.*

*The room has changed, not so much in its outward
appearance as in its general atmosphere. Little significant details give evidence of carelessness, of inefficiency,
of an industry gone to seed. The chairs appear shabby
from lack of paint; the table cover is spotted and askew;
holes show in the curtains: a child's doll, with one arm
gone, lies under the table; a hoe stands in a corner; a
man's coat is flung on the couch in the rear; the desk
is cluttered with odds and ends; a number of books are
piled carelessly on the sideboard. The noon enervation
of the sultry, scorching day seems to have penetrated
indoors, causing even inanimate objects to wear an as-
pect of despondent exhaustion.*

*A place is set at the end of the table, left, for some-
one's dinner. Through the open door to the kitchen
comes the clatter of dishes being washed, interrupted at
intervals by a woman's irritated voice and the peevish
whining of a child.*

42

At the rise of the curtain MRS. MAYO *and* MRS. AT-
KINS *are discovered sitting facing each other,* MRS.
MAYO *to the rear,* MRS. ATKINS *to the right of the table.*
MRS. MAYO'S *face has lost all character, disintegrated,
become a weak mask wearing a helpless, doleful expression of being constantly on the verge of comfortless
tears. She speaks in an uncertain voice, without assertiveness, as if all power of willing had deserted her.*
MRS. ATKINS *is in her wheel chair. She is a thin, pale-
faced, unintelligent-looking woman of about forty-eight,
with hard, bright eyes. A victim of partial paralysis for
many years, condemned to be pushed from day to day
of her life in a wheel chair, she has developed the
selfish, irritable nature of the chronic invalid. Both
women are dressed in black.* MRS. ATKINS *knits nervously as she talks. A ball of unused yarn, with needles
stuck through it, lies on the table before* MRS. MAYO.

MRS. ATKINS (*with a disapproving glance at the place
set on the table*): Robert's late for his dinner again, as
usual. I don't see why Ruth puts up with it, and I've
told her so. Many's the time I've said to her, "It's
about time you put a stop to his nonsense. Does he
suppose you're running a hotel—with no one to help
with things?" But she don't pay no attention. She's as
bad as he is, a'most—thinks she knows better than an
old, sick body like me.

MRS. MAYO (*dully*): Robbie's always late for things.
He can't help it, Sarah.

MRS. ATKINS (*with a snort*): Can't help it! How you
do go on, Kate, findin' excuses for him! Anybody
can help anything they've a mind to—as long as
they've got health, and ain't rendered helpless like
me—(*She adds as a pious afterthought*)—through
the will of God.

MRS. MAYO: Robbie can't.

MRS. ATKINS: Can't! It do make me mad, Kate Mayo, to see folks that God gave all the use of their limbs to potterin' round and wastin' time doin' everything the wrong way—and me powerless to help and at their mercy, you might say. And it ain't that I haven't pointed the right way to 'em. I've talked to Robert thousands of times and told him how things ought to be done. You know that, Kate Mayo. But d'you s'pose he takes any notice of what I say? Or Ruth, either—my own daughter? No, they think I'm a crazy, cranky old woman, half dead a'ready, and the sooner I'm in the grave and out o' their way the better it'd suit them.

MRS. MAYO: You mustn't talk that way, Sarah. They're not as wicked as that. And you've got years and years before you.

MRS. ATKINS: You're like the rest, Kate. You don't know how near the end I am. Well, at least I can go to my eternal rest with a clear conscience. I've done all a body could do to avert ruin from this house. On their heads be it!

MRS. MAYO (*with hopeless indifference*): Things might be worse. Robert never had any experience in farming. You can't expect him to learn in a day.

MRS. ATKINS (*snappily*): He's had three years to learn, and he's gettin' worse 'stead of better. Not on'y your place but mine too is driftin' to rack and ruin, and I can't do nothin' to prevent.

MRS. MAYO (*with a spark of assertiveness*): You can't say but Robbie works hard, Sarah.

MRS. ATKINS: What good's workin' hard if it don't accomplish anythin', I'd like to know?

MRS. MAYO: Robbie's had bad luck against him.

MRS. ATKINS: Say what you've a mind to, Kate, the proof of the puddin's in the eatin'; and you can't

deny that things have been goin' from bad to worse
ever since your husband died two years back.

MRS. MAYO (*wiping tears from her eyes with her handkerchief*): It was God's will that he should be taken.

MRS. ATKINS (*triumphantly*): It was God's punishment
on James Mayo for the blasphemin' and denyin' of
God he done all his sinful life! (MRS. MAYO *begins
to weep softly*) There, Kate, I shouldn't be remindin'
you, I know. He's at peace, poor man, and forgiven,
let's pray.

MRS. MAYO (*wiping her eyes—simply*): James was a
good man.

MRS. ATKINS (*ignoring this remark*): What I was sayin'
was that since Robert's been in charge things've
been goin' down hill steady. You don't know *how*
bad they are. Robert don't let on to you what's
happenin'; and you'd never see it yourself if 'twas
under your nose. But, thank the Lord, Ruth still
comes to me once in a while for advice when she's
worried near out of her senses by his goin's-on. Do
you know what she told me last night? But I forgot,
she said not to tell you—still I think you've got a
right to know, and it's my duty not to let such things
go on behind your back.

MRS. MAYO (*wearily*): You can tell me if you want to.

MRS. ATKINS (*bending over toward her—in a low
voice*): Ruth was almost crazy about it. Robert told
her he'd have to mortgage the farm—said he didn't
know how he'd pull through 'til harvest without it,
and he can't get money any other way. (*She straightens up—indignantly*) Now what do you think of
your Robert?

MRS. MAYO (*resignedly*): If it has to be—

MRS. ATKINS: You don't mean to say you're goin' to
sign away your farm, Kate Mayo—after me war-
nin' you?

MRS. MAYO: I'll do what Robbie says is needful.

MRS. ATKINS (*holding up her hands*): Well, of all the foolishness!—well, it's your farm, not mine, and I've nothin' more to say.

MRS. MAYO: Maybe Robbie'll manage till Andy gets back and sees to things. It can't be long now.

MRS. ATKINS (*with keen interest*): Ruth says Andy ought to turn up any day. When does Robert figger he'll get here?

MRS. MAYO: He says he can't calculate exactly on account o' the "Sunda" being a sail boat. Last letter he got was from England, the day they were sailing for home. That was over a month ago, and Robbie thinks they're overdue now.

MRS. ATKINS: We can praise to God then that he'll be back in the nick o' time. He ought to be tired of travelin' and anxious to get home and settle down to work again.

MRS. MAYO: Andy *has* been working. He's head officer on Dick's boat, he wrote Robbie. You know that.

MRS. ATKINS: That foolin' on ships is all right for a spell, but he must be right sick of it by this.

MRS. MAYO (*musingly*): I wonder if he's changed much. He used to be so fine-looking and strong. (*With a sigh*) Three years! It seems more like three hundred. (*Her eyes filling—piteously*) Oh, if James could only have lived 'til he came back—and forgiven him!

MRS. ATKINS: He never would have—not James Mayo! Didn't he keep his heart hardened against him till the last in spite of all you and Robert did to soften him?

MRS. MAYO (*with a feeble flash of anger*): Don't you dare say that! (*Brokenly*) Oh, I know deep down in his heart he forgave Andy, though he was too stubborn ever to own up to it. It was that brought on his death—breaking his heart just on account of his stubborn pride. (*She wipes her eyes with her handkerchief and sobs.*)

MRS. ATKINS (*piously*): It was the will of God. (*The whining crying of the child sounds from the kitchen. MRS. ATKINS frowns irritably*) Drat that young one! Seems as if she cries all the time on purpose to set a body's nerves on edge.

MRS. MAYO (*wiping her eyes*): It's the heat upsets her. Mary doesn't feel any too well these days, poor little child!

MRS. ATKINS: She gets it right from her Pa—being sickly all the time. You can't deny Robert was always ailin' as a child. (*She sighs heavily*) It was a crazy mistake for them two to get married. I argyed against it at the time, but Ruth was so spelled with Robert's wild poetry notions she wouldn't listen to sense. Andy was the one would have been the match for her.

MRS. MAYO: I've often thought since it might have been better the other way. But Ruth and Robbie seem happy enough together.

MRS. ATKINS: At any rate it was God's work—and His will be done. (*The two women sit in silence for a moment. RUTH enters from the kitchen, carrying in her arms her two-year-old daughter, MARY, a pretty but sickly and anemic-looking child with a tear-stained face. RUTH has aged appreciably. Her face has lost its youth and freshness. There is a trace in her expression of something hard and spiteful. She sits in the rocker in front of the table and sighs wearily. She wears a gingham dress with a soiled apron tied around her waist.*)

RUTH: Land sakes, if this isn't a scorcher! That kitchen's like a furnace. Phew! (*She pushes the damp hair back from her forehead.*)

MRS. MAYO: Why didn't you call me to help with the dishes?

RUTH (*shortly*): No. The heat in there'd kill you.

MARY (*sees the doll under the table and struggles on her mother's lap*): Dolly, Mama! Dolly!

RUTH (*pulling her back*): It's time for your nap. You can't play with Dolly now.

MARY (*commencing to cry whiningly*): Dolly!

MRS. ATKINS (*irritably*): Can't you keep that child still? Her racket's enough to split a body's ears. Put her down and let her play with the doll if it'll quiet her.

RUTH (*lifting MARY to the floor*): There! I hope you'll be satisfied and keep still. (MARY *sits down on the floor before the table and plays with the doll in silence.* RUTH *glances at the place set on the table*) It's a wonder Rob wouldn't try to get to meals on time once in a while.

MRS. MAYO (*dully*): Something must have gone wrong again.

RUTH (*wearily*): I s'pose so. Something always going wrong these days, it looks like.

MRS. ATKINS (*snappily*): It wouldn't if you possessed a bit of spunk. The idea of you permittin' him to come in to meals at all hours—and you doin' the work! I never heard of such a thin'. You're too easy goin', that's the trouble.

RUTH: Do stop your nagging at me, Ma! I'm sick of hearing you. I'll do as I please about it; and thank you for not interfering. (*She wipes her moist forehead—wearily*) Phew! It's too hot to argue. Let's talk of something pleasant. (*Curiously*) Didn't I hear you speaking about Andy a while ago?

MRS. MAYO: We were wondering when he'd get home.

RUTH (*brightening*): Rob says any day now he's liable to drop in and surprise us—him and the Captain. It'll certainly look natural to see him around the farm again.

MRS. ATKINS: Let's hope the farm'll look more natural, too, when he's had a hand at it. The way thing's are now!

RUTH (*irritably*): Will you stop harping on that, Ma? We all know things aren't as they might be. What's the good of your complaining all the time?

MRS. ATKINS: There, Kate Mayo! Ain't that just what I told you? I can't say a word of advice to my own daughter even, she's that stubborn and self-willed.

RUTH (*putting her hands over her ears—in exasperation*): For goodness sakes, Ma!

MRS. MAYO (*dully*): Never mind. Andy'll fix everything when he comes.

RUTH (*hopefully*): Oh, yes, I know he will. He always did know just the right thing ought to be done. (*With weary vexation*) It's a shame for him to come home and have to start in with things in such a topsy-turvy.

MRS. MAYO: Andy'll manage.

RUTH (*sighing*): I s'pose it isn't Rob's fault things go wrong with him.

MRS. ATKINS (*scornfully*): Hump! (*She fans herself nervously*) Land o' Goshen, but it's bakin' in here! Let's go out in under the trees where there's a breath of fresh air. Come, Kate (MRS. MAYO *gets up obediently and starts to wheel the invalid's chair toward the screen door*) You better come too, Ruth. It'll do you good. Learn him a lesson and let him get his own dinner. Don't be such a fool.

RUTH (*going and holding the screen door open for them—listlessly*): He wouldn't mind. He doesn't eat

much. But I can't go anyway. I've got to put baby
to bed.

MRS. ATKINS: Let's go, Kate. I'm boilin' in here. (MRS.
MAYO *wheels her out and off left.* RUTH *comes back
and sits down in her chair.*)

RUTH (*mechanically*): Come and let me take off your
shoes and stockings, Mary, that's a good girl. You've
got to take your nap now. (*The child continues to
play as if she hadn't heard, absorbed in her doll. An
eager expression comes over* RUTH'S *tired face. She
glances toward the door furtively—then gets up and
goes to the desk. Her movements indicate a guilty
fear of discovery. She takes a letter from a pigeon-
hole and retreats swiftly to her chair with it. She
opens the envelope and reads the letter with great
interest, a flush of excitement coming to her cheeks.*
ROBERT *walks up the path and opens the screen door
quietly and comes into the room. He, too, has aged.
His shoulders are stooped as if under too great a
burden. His eyes are dull and lifeless, his face burned
by the sun and unshaven for days. Streaks of sweat
have smudged the layer of dust on his cheeks. His
lips drawn down at the corners give him a hopeless,
resigned expression. The three years have accentuated
the weakness of his mouth and chin. He is dressed
in overalls, laced boots, and a flannel shirt open at
the neck.*)

ROBERT (*throwing his hat over on the sofa—with a
great sigh of exhaustion*): Phew! The sun's hot
today! (RUTH *is startled. At first she makes an instinctive motion as if to hide the letter in her bosom.
She immediately thinks better of this and sits with
the letter in her hands looking at him with defiant
eyes. He bends down and kisses her.*)

RUTH (*feeling of her cheek—irritably*): Why don't you
shave? You look awful.

ROBERT (*indifferently*): I forgot—and it's too much trouble this weather.

MARY (*throwing aside her doll, runs to him with a happy cry*): Dada! Dada!

ROBERT (*swinging her up above his head—lovingly*): And how's this little girl of mine this hot day, eh?

MARY (*screeching happily*): Dada! Dada!

RUTH (*in annoyance*): Don't do that to her! You know it's time for her nap and you'll get her all waked up; then I'll be the one that'll have to sit beside her till she falls asleep.

ROBERT (*sitting down in the chair on the left of table and cuddling* MARY *on his lap*): You needn't bother. I'll put her to bed.

RUTH (*shortly*): You've got to get back to your work, I s'pose.

ROBERT (with a sigh): Yes, I was forgetting. (*He glances at the open letter on* RUTH'S *lap*) Reading Andy's letter again? I should think you'd know it by heart by this time.

RUTH (*coloring as if she'd been accused of something— defiantly*): I've got a right to read it, haven't I? He says it's meant for all of us.

ROBERT (*with a trace of irritation*): Right? Don't be so silly. There's no question of right. I was only saying that you must know all that's in it after so many readings.

RUTH: Well, I don't. (*She puts the letter on the table and gets wearily to her feet*) I s'pose you'll be wanting your dinner now.

ROBERT (*listlessly*): I don't care. I'm not hungry.

RUTH: And here I been keeping it hot for you!

ROBERT (*irritably*): Oh, all right then. Bring it in and I'll try to eat.

RUTH: I've got to get her to bed first. (*She goes to lift*

MARY *off his lap*) Come, dear. It's after time and you can hardly keep your eyes open now.

MARY (*crying*): No, no! (*Appealing to her father*) Dada! No!

RUTH (*accusingly to* ROBERT): There! Now see what you've done! I told you not to—

ROBERT (*shortly*): Let her alone, then. She's all right where she is. She'll fall asleep on my lap in a minute if you'll stop bothering her.

RUTH (*hotly*): She'll not do any such thing! She's got to learn to mind me! (*shaking her finger at* MARY) You naughty child! Will you come with Mama when she tells you for your own good?

MARY (*clinging to her father*): No, Dada!

RUTH (*losing her temper*): A good spanking's what you need, my young lady—and you'll get one from me if you don't mind better, d'you hear? (MARY *starts to whimper frightenedly.*)

ROBERT (*with sudden anger*): Leave her alone! How often have I told you not to threaten her with whipping? I won't have it. (*Soothing the wailing* MARY) There! There, little girl! Baby mustn't cry. Dada won't like you if you do. Dada'll hold you and you must promise to go to sleep like a good little girl. Will you when Dada asks you?

MARY (*cuddling up to him*): Yes, Dada.

RUTH (*looking at them, her pale face set and drawn*): A fine one you are to be telling folks how to do things! (*She bites her lips. Husband and wife look into each other's eyes with something akin to hatred in their expressions; then* RUTH *turns away with a shrug of affected indifference*) All right, take care of her then, if you think it's so easy. (*She walks away into the kitchen.*)

ROBERT (*smoothing* MARY'S *hair—tenderly*): We'll show Mama you're a good little girl, won't we?

MARY (*crooning drowsily*): Dada, Dada.

ROBERT: Let's see: Does your mother take off your shoes and stockings before your nap?

MARY (*nodding with half-shut eyes*): Yes, Dada.

ROBERT (*taking off her shoes and stockings*): We'll show Mama we know how to do those things, won't we? There's one old shoe off—and there's the other old shoe—and here's one old stocking—and there's the other old stocking. There we are, all nice and cool and comfy. (*He bends down and kisses her*) And now will you promise to go right to sleep if Dada takes you to bed? (MARY *nods sleepily*) That's the good little girl. (*He gathers her up in his arms carefully and carries her into the bedroom. His voice can be heard faintly as he lulls the child to sleep. RUTH comes out of the kitchen and gets the plate from the table. She hears the voice from the room and tiptoes to the door to look in. Then she starts for the kitchen but stands for a moment thinking, a look of ill-concealed jealousy on her face. At a noise from inside she hurriedly disappears into the kitchen. A moment later ROBERT re-enters. He comes forward and picks up the shoes and stockings which he shoves carelessly under the table. Then, seeing no one about, he goes to the sideboard and selects a book. Coming back to his chair, he sits down and immediately becomes absorbed in reading. RUTH returns from the kitchen bringing his plate heaped with food, and a cup of tea. She sets those before him and sits down in her former place. ROBERT continues to read, oblivious to the food on the table.*)

RUTH (*after watching him irritably for a moment*): For heaven's sakes, put down that old book! Don't you see your dinner's getting cold?

ROBERT (*closing his book*): Excuse me, Ruth, I didn't

notice. (*He picks up his knife and fork and begins to eat gingerly, without appetite.*)

RUTH: I should think you might have some feeling for me, Rob, and not always be late for meals. If you think it's fun sweltering in that oven of a kitchen to keep things warm for you, you're mistaken.

ROBERT: I'm sorry, Ruth, really I am. Something crops up every day to delay me. I mean to be here on time.

RUTH (*with a sigh*): Mean-tos don't count.

ROBERT (*with a conciliating smile*): Then punish me, Ruth. Let the food get cold and don't bother about me.

RUTH: I'd have to wait just the same to wash up after you.

ROBERT: But I can wash up.

RUTH: A nice mess there'd be then!

ROBERT (*with an attempt at lightness*); The food is lucky to be able to get cold this weather. (*As RUTH doesn't answer or smile he opens his book and resumes his reading, forcing himself to take a mouthful of food every now and then. RUTH stares at him in annoyance.*)

RUTH: And besides, you've got your own work that's got to be done.

ROBERT (*absent-mindedly, without taking his eyes from the book*): Yes, of course.

RUTH (*spitefully*): Work you'll never get done by reading books all the time.

ROBERT (*shutting the book with a snap*): Why do you persist in nagging at me for getting pleasure out of reading? Is it because— (*He checks himself abruptly.*)

RUTH (*coloring*): Because I'm too stupid to understand them, I s'pose you were going to say.

ROBERT (*shame-facedly*): No—no. (*In exasperation*)

Why do you goad me into saying things I don't mean? Haven't I got my share of troubles trying to work this cursed farm without your adding to them? You know how hard I've tried to keep things going in spite of bad luck—

RUTH (*scornfully*): Bad luck!

ROBERT: And my own very apparent unfitness for the job, I was going to add; but you can't deny there's been bad luck to it, too. Why don't you take things into consideration? Why can't we pull together? We used to. I know it's hard on you also. Then why can't we help each other instead of hindering?

RUTH (*sullenly*): I do the best I know how.

ROBERT (*gets up and puts his hand on her shoulder*): I know you do. But let's both of us try to do better. We can improve. Say a word of encouragement once in a while when things go wrong, even if it is my fault. You know the odds I've been up against since Pa died. I'm not a farmer. I've never claimed to be one. But there's nothing else I can do under the circumstances, and I've got to pull things through somehow. With your help, I can do it. With you against me— (*He shrugs his shoulders. There is a pause. Then he bends down and kisses her hair— with an attempt at cheerfulness*) So you promise that; and I'll promise to be here when the clock strikes— and anytime else you tell me to. Is it a bargain?

RUTH (*dully*): I s'pose so. (*They are interrupted by the sound of a loud knock at the kitchen door*) There's someone at the kitchen door. (*She hurries out. A moment later she reappears*) It's Ben.

ROBERT (*frowning*): What's the trouble now, I wonder? (*In a loud voice*) Come on in here, Ben. (BEN *slouches in from the kitchen. He is a hulking, awkward young fellow with a heavy, stupid face and shifty, cunning eyes. He is dressed in overalls, boots, etc., and wears a broad-brimmed hat of coarse straw pushed back on his head*) Well, Ben, what's the matter?

BEN (*drawingly*): The mowin' machine's bust.

ROBERT: Why, that can't be. The man fixed it only last week.

BEN: It's bust just the same.

ROBERT: And can't you fix it?

BEN: No. Don't know what's the matter with the goll-darned thing. 'Twon't work, anyhow.

ROBERT (*getting up and going for his hat*): Wait a minute and I'll go look it over. There can't be much the matter with it.

BEN (*impudently*): Don't make no diff'rence t' me whether there be or not. I'm quittin'.

ROBERT (*anxiously*): You don't mean you're throwing up your job here?

BEN: That's what! My month's up today and I want what's owin' t' me.

ROBERT: But why are you quitting now, Ben, when you know I've so much work on hand? I'll have a hard time getting another man at such short notice.

BEN: That's for you to figger. I'm quittin'.

ROBERT: But what's your reason? You haven't any complaint to make about the way you've been treated, have you?

BEN: No. 'Tain't that. (*Shaking his finger*) Look-a-here. I'm sick o' being made fun at, that's what; an' I got a job up to Timms' place; an' I'm quittin' here.

ROBERT: Being made fun of? I don't understand you. Who's making fun of you?

BEN: They all do. When I drive down with the milk in the mornin' they all laughs and jokes at me—that boy up to Harris' and the new feller up to Slocum's, and Bill Evans down to Mead's, and all the rest on 'em.

ROBERT: That's a queer reason for leaving me flat. Won't they laugh at you just the same when you're working for Timms?

BEN: They wouldn't dare to. Timms is the best farm hereabouts. They was laughin' at me for workin' for *you*, that's what! "How're things up to the Mayo place?" they hollers every mornin'. "What's Robert doin' now—pasturin' the cattle in the cornlot? Is he seasonin' his hay with rain this year, same as last?" they shouts. "Or is he inventin' some 'lectrical milkin' engine to fool them dry cows o' his into givin' hard cider?" (*Very much ruffled*) That's like they talks; and I ain't goin' to put up with it no longer. Everyone's always knowed me as a first-class hand hereabouts, and I ain't wantin' 'em to get no different notion. So I'm quittin' you. And I wants what's comin' to me.

ROBERT (*coldly*): Oh, if that's the case, you can go to the devil. You'll get your money tomorrow when I get back from town—not before!

BEN (*turning to doorway to kitchen*): That suits me. (*As he goes out he speaks back over his shoulder*) And see that I do get it, or there'll be trouble. (*He disappears and the slamming of the kitchen door is heard.*)

ROBERT (*as RUTH comes from where she has been standing by the doorway and sits down dejectedly in her old place*): The stupid damn fool! And now what about the haying? That's an example of what I'm up against. No one can say I'm responsible for that.

RUTH: He wouldn't dare act that way with anyone else! (*Spitefully, with a glance at ANDREW's letter on the table*) It's lucky Andy's coming back.

ROBERT (*without resentment*): Yes, Andy'll see the right thing to do in a jiffy. (*With an affectionate smile*) I wonder if the old chump's changed much?

He doesn't seem to from his letters, does he? (*Shaking his head*) But just the same I doubt if he'll want to settle down to a humdrum farm life, after all he's been through.

RUTH (*resentfully*): Andy's not like you. He likes the farm.

ROBERT (*immersed in his own thoughts—enthusiastically*): Gad, the things he's seen and experienced! Think of the places he's been! All the wonderful far places I used to dream about! God, how I envy him! What a trip! (*He springs to his feet and instinctively goes to the window and stares out at the horizon.*)

RUTH (*bitterly*): I s'pose you're sorry now you didn't go?

ROBERT (*too occupied with his own thoughts to hear her—vindictively*): Oh, those cursed hills out there that I used to think promised me so much! How I've grown to hate the sight of them! They're like the walls of a narrow prison yard shutting me in from all the freedom and wonder of life! (*He turns back to the room with a gesture of loathing*) Sometimes I think if it wasn't for you, Ruth, and—(*His voice softening*)—little Mary, I'd chuck everything up and walk down the road with just one desire in my heart——to put the whole rim of the world between me and those hills, and be able to breathe freely once more! (*He sinks down into his chair and smiles with bitter self-scorn*) There I go dreaming again—my old fool dreams.

RUTH (*in a low, repressed voice—her eyes smoldering*): You're not the only one!

ROBERT (*buried in his own thoughts—bitterly*): And Andy, who's had the chance—what has he got out of it? His letters read like the diary of a—of a farmer! "We're in Singapore now. It's a dirty hole of a place and hotter than hell. Two of the crew are down with fever and we're short-handed on the work. I'll be damn glad when we sail again, although tacking back and forth in these blistering seas is a rotten job too!' (*Scornfully*) That's about the way he summed up his impressions of the East.

RUTH (*her repressed voice trembling*): You needn't make fun of Andy.

ROBERT: When I think—but what's the use? You know I wasn't making fun of Andy personally, but his attitude toward things is—

RUTH (*her eyes flashing—bursting into uncontrollable rage*): You was too making fun of him! And I ain't going to stand for it! You ought to be ashamed of yourself! (ROBERT *stares at her in amazement. She continues furiously*) A fine one to talk about anyone else—after the way you've ruined everything with your lazy loafing!—and the stupid way you do things!

ROBERT (*angrily*): Stop that kind of talk, do you hear?

RUTH: You findin' fault—with your own brother who's ten times the man you ever was or ever will be! You're jealous, that's what! Jealous because he's made a man of himself, while you're nothing but a—but a— (*She stutters incoherently, overcome by rage.*)

ROBERT: Ruth! Ruth! You'll be sorry for talking like that.

RUTH: I won't! I won't never be sorry! I'm only saying what I've been thinking for years.

ROBERT (*aghast*): Ruth! You can't mean that!

RUTH: What do you think—living with a man like you—having to suffer all the time because you've never been man enough to work and do things like other people. But no! You never own up to that. You think you're so much better than other folks, with your college education, where you never learned a thing, and always reading your stupid books instead of working. I s'pose you think I ought to be *proud* to be your wife—a poor, ignorant thing like me! (*Fiercely*) But I'm not. I hate it! I hate the sight of you. Oh, if I'd only known! If I hadn't been such a fool to listen to your cheap, silly, poetry talk that you learned out of books! If I could have seen how you were in your true self—like you are now— I'd have killed myself before I'd have married you! I was sorry for it before we'd been together a month. I knew what you were really like—when it was too late.

ROBERT (*his voice raised loudly*): And now—I'm finding out what you're really like—what a—a creature I've been living with. (*With a harsh laugh*) God! It wasn't that I haven't guessed how mean and small you are—but I've kept on telling myself that I must be wrong—like a fool!—like a damned fool!

RUTH: You were saying you'd go out on the road if it wasn't for me. Well, you can go, and the sooner the better! I don't care! I'll be glad to get rid of you! The farm'll be better off too. There's been a curse on it ever since you took hold. So go! Go and be a tramp like you've always wanted. It's all you're good for. I can get along without you, don't you worry. (*Exulting fiercely*) Andy's coming back, don't forget that! He'll attend to things like they should be. He'll show what a man can do! I don't need you. Andy's coming!

ROBERT (*they are both standing. ROBERT grabs her by the shoulders and glares into her eyes*): What do you mean? (*He shakes her violently*) What are you thinking of? What's in your evil mind, you—you— (*His voice is a harsh shout.*)

RUTH (*in a defiant scream*): Yes, I do mean it! I'd say

it if you was to kill me! I do love Andy. I do! I do! I always loved him. (*Exultantly*) And he loves me! He loves me! I know he does. He always did! And you know he did, too! So go! Go if you want to!

ROBERT (*throwing her away from him. She staggers back against the table—thickly*): You—you slut! (*He stands glaring at her as she leans back, supporting herself by the table, gasping for breath. A loud frightened whimper sounds from the awakened child in the bedroom. It continues. The man and woman stand looking at one another in horror, the extent of their terrible quarrel suddenly brought home to them. A pause. The noise of a horse and carriage comes from the road before the house. The two, suddenly struck by the same premonition, listen to it breathlessly, as to a sound heard in a dream. It stops. They hear* ANDY'S *voice from the road shouting a long hail—* "Ahoy there!")

RUTH (*with a strangled cry of joy*): Andy! Andy! (*She rushes and grabs the knob of the screen door, about to fling it open.*)

ROBERT (*in a voice of command that forces obedience*): Stop! (*He goes to the door and gently pushes the trembling* RUTH *away from it. The child's crying rises to a louder pitch*) I'll meet Andy. You better go in to Mary, Ruth. (*She looks at him defiantly for a moment, but there is something in his eyes that makes her turn and walk slowly into the bedroom.*)

ANDY'S VOICE (*in a louder shout*): Ahoy there, Rob!

ROBERT (*in an answering shout of forced cheeriness*): Hello, Andy! (*He opens the door and walks out as the curtain falls.*)

ACT TWO
Scene 2

The top of a hill on the farm. It is about eleven o'clock the next morning. The day is hot and cloudless. In the distance the sea can be seen.

The top of the hill slopes downward slightly toward the left. A big boulder stands in the center toward the rear. Further right, a large oak tree. The faint trace of a path leading upward to it from the left foreground can be detected through the bleached, sun-scorched grass.

ROBERT *is discovered sitting on the boulder, his chin resting on his hands, staring out toward the horizon seaward. His face is pale and haggard, his expression one of utter despondency.* MARY *is sitting on the grass near him in the shade, playing with her doll, singing happily to herself. Presently she casts a curious glance at her father, and, propping her doll up against the tree, comes over and clambers to his side.*

MARY (*pulling at his hand—solicitously*): Dada sick?

ROBERT (*looking at her with a forced smile*): No, dear. Why?

MARY: Play wif Mary.

ROBERT (*gently*): No, dear, not today. Dada doesn't feel like playing today.

MARY (*protestingly*): Yes, Dada!

ROBERT: No, dear. Dada does feel sick—a little. He's got a bad headache.

62

MARY: Mary see. (*He bends his head. She pats his hair*) Bad head.

ROBERT (*kissing her—with a smile*): There! It's better now, dear, thank you. (*She cuddles up close against him. There is a pause during which each of them looks out seaward. Finally* ROBERT *turns to her tenderly*) Would you like Dada to go away?—far, far, away?

MARY (*tearfully*): No! No! No, Dada, no!

ROBERT: Don't you like Uncle Andy—the man that came yesterday—not the old man with the white mustache—the other?

MARY: Mary loves Dada.

ROBERT (*with fierce determination*): He won't go away, baby. He was only joking. He couldn't leave his little Mary. (*He presses the child in his arms.*)

MARY (*with an exclamation of pain*): Oh! Hurt!

ROBERT: I'm sorry, little girl. (*He lifts her down to the grass*) Go play with Dolly, that's a good girl; and be careful to keep in the shade. (*She reluctantly leaves him and takes up her doll again. A moment later she points down the hill to the left.*)

MARY: Mans, Dada.

ROBERT (*Looking that way*): It's your uncle Andy. (*A moment later* ANDREW *comes up from the left, whistling cheerfully. He has changed but little in appearance, except for the fact that his face has been deeply bronzed by his years in the tropics; but there is a decided change in his manner. The old easy-going good nature seems to have been partly lost in a breezy, business-like briskness of voice and gesture. There is an authoritative note in his speech as though he were accustomed to give orders and have them obeyed as a matter of course. He is dressed in the simple blue uniform and cap of a merchant ship's officer.*)

ANDREW: Here you are, eh?

ROBERT: Hello, Andy.

ANDREW (*going over to* MARY): And who's this young lady I find you all alone with, eh? Who's this pretty young lady? (*He tickles the laughing, squirming* MARY, *then lifts her up arm's length over his head*) Upsy—daisy! (*He sets her down on the ground again*) And there you are! (*He walks over and sits down on the boulder beside* ROBERT *who moves to one side to make room for him*) Ruth told me I'd probably find you up top-side here; but I'd have guessed it, anyway. (*He digs his brother in the ribs affectionately*) Still up to your old tricks, you old beggar! I can remember how you used to come up here to mope and dream in the old days.

ROBERT (*with a smile*): I come up here now because it's the coolest place on the farm. I've given up dreaming.

ANDREW (*grinning*): I don't believe it. You can't have changed that much. (*After a pause—with boyish enthusiasm*) Say, it sure brings back old times to be up here with you having a chin all by our lonesomes again. I feel great being back home.

ROBERT: It's great for us to have you back.

ANDREW (*after a pause—meaningly*): I've been looking over the old place with Ruth. Things don't seem to be—

ROBERT (*his face flushing—interrupts his brother shortly*): Never mind the damn farm! Let's talk about something interesting. This is the first chance I've had to have a word with you alone. Tell me about your trip.

ANDREW: Why, I thought I told you everything in my letters.

ROBERT (*smiling*): Your letters were—sketchy, to say the least.

ANDREW: Oh, I know I'm no author. You needn't be afraid of hurting my feelings. I'd rather go through a typhoon again than write a letter.

ROBERT (*with eager interest*): Then you were through a typhoon?

ANDREW: Yes—in the China sea. Had to run before it under bare poles for two days. I thought we were bound down for Davy Jones, sure. Never dreamed waves could get so big or the wind blow so hard. If it hadn't been for Uncle Dick being such a good skipper we'd have gone to the sharks, all of us. As it was we came out minus a main topmast and had to beat back to Hong-Kong for repairs. But I must have written you all this.

ROBERT: You never mentioned it.

ANDREW: Well, there was so much dirty work getting things ship-shape again I must have forgotten about it.

ROBERT (*looking at* ANDREW—*marveling*): Forget a typhoon? (*With a trace of scorn*) You're a strange combination, Andy. And is what you've told me all you remember about it?

ANDREW: Oh, I could give you your bellyful of details if I wanted to turn loose on you. It was all-wool-and-a-yard-wide-Hell, I'll tell you. You ought to have been there. I remember thinking about you at the worst of it, and saying to myself: "This'd cure Rob of them ideas of his about the beautiful sea, if he could see it." And it would have too, you bet! (*He nods emphatically*)

ROBERT (*dryly*): The sea doesn't seem to have impressed you very favorably.

ANDREW: I should say it didn't! I'll never set foot on a ship again if I can help it—except to carry me some place I can't get to by train.

ROBERT: But you studied to become an officer!

ANDREW: Had to do something or I'd gone mad. The days were like years. (*He laughs*) And as for the East you used to rave about—well, you ought to see it, and *smell* it! One walk down one of their filthy narrow streets with the tropic sun beating on it would sicken you for life with the "wonder and mystery" you used to dream of.

ROBERT (*shrinking from his brother with a glance of aversion*): So all you found in the East was a stench?

ANDREW: A stench! Ten thousand of them!

ROBERT: But you did like some of the places, judging from your letters—Sydney, Buenos Aires—

ANDREW: Yes, Sydney's a good town. (*Enthusiastically*) But Buenos Aires—there's the place for you. Argentine's a country where a fellow has a chance to make good. You're right I like it. And I'll tell you, Rob, that's right where I'm going just as soon as I've seen you folks a while and can get a ship. I can get a berth as second officer, and I'll jump the ship when I get there. I'll need every cent of the wages Uncle's paid me to get a start at something in B.A.

ROBERT (*staring at his brother—slowly*): So you're not going to stay on the farm?

ANDREW: Why sure not! Did you think I was? There wouldn't be any sense. One of us is enough to run this little place.

ROBERT: I suppose it does seem small to you now.

ANDREW (*not noticing the sarcasm in* ROBERT'S *tone*): You've no idea, Rob, what a splendid place Argentine is. I had a letter from a marine insurance chap that I'd made friends with in Hong-Kong to his brother, who's in the grain business in Buenos Aires. He took quite a fancy to me, and what's more important, he offered me a job if I'd come back there. I'd have taken it on the spot, only I couldn't leave Uncle Dick in the lurch, and I'd promised you folks to come home. But I'm going back there, you bet, and then you watch me get on! (*He slaps* ROBERT *on the back*) But don't you think it's a big chance, Rob?

ROBERT: It's fine—for you, Andy.

ANDREW: We call this a farm—but you ought to hear about the farms down there—ten square miles where we've got an acre. It's a new country where big things are opening up—and I want to get in on something big before I die. I'm no fool when it comes to farming, and I know something about grain. I've been reading up a lot on it, too, lately. (*He notices* ROBERT'S *absent-minded expression and laughs*) Wake up, you old poetry bookworm, you! I know my talking about business makes you want to choke me, doesn't it?

ROBERT (*with an embarrassed smile*): No, Andy, I—I just happened to think of something else. (*Frowning*) There've been lots of times lately that I wished I had some of your faculty for business.

ANDREW (*soberly*): There's something I want to talk about, Rob—the farm. You don't mind, do you?

ROBERT: No.

ANDREW: I walked over it this morning with Ruth—and she told me about things— (*Evasively*) I could see the place had run down; but you mustn't blame yourself. When luck's against anyone—

ROBERT: Don't, Andy! It *is* my fault. You know it as well as I do. The best I've ever done was to make ends meet.

ANDREW (*after a pause*): I've got over a thousand saved, and you can have that.

ROBERT (*firmly*): No. You need that for your start in Buenos Aires.

ANDREW: I don't. I can—

ROBERT (*determinedly*): No, Andy! Once and for all, no! I won't hear of it!

ANDREW (*protestingly*): You obstinate old son of a gun!

ROBERT: Oh, everything'll be on a sound footing after harvest. Don't worry about it.

ANDREW (*doubtfully*): Maybe. (*After a pause*) It's too bad Pa couldn't have lived to see things through. (*With feeling*) It cut me up a lot—hearing he was dead. He never—softened up, did he—about me, I mean?

ROBERT: He never understood, that's a kinder way of putting it. He does now.

ANDREW (*after a pause*): You've forgotten all about what—caused me to go, haven't you, Rob? (ROBERT *nods but keeps his face averted*) I was a slushier damn fool in those days than you were. But it was an act of Providence I did go. It opened my eyes to how I'd been fooling myself. Why, I'd forgotten all about—that—before I'd been at sea six months.

ROBERT (*turns and looks into* ANDREW'S *eyes searchingly*): You're speaking of—Ruth?

ANDREW (*confused*): Yes, I didn't want you to get false notions in your head, or I wouldn't say anything. (*Looking* ROBERT *squarely in the eyes*) I'm telling you the truth when I say I'd forgotten long ago. It don't sound well for me, getting over things so easy, but I guess it never really amounted to more than a kid idea I was letting rule me. I'm certain now I never was in love—I was getting fun out of thinking I was—and being a hero to myself. (*He heaves a great sigh of relief*) There! Gosh, I'm glad that's off my chest. I've been feeling sort of awkward ever since I've been home, thinking of what you two might think. (*A trace of appeal in his voice*) You've got it all straight now, haven't you, Rob?

ROBERT (*in a low voice*): Yes, Andy.

ANDREW: And I'll tell Ruth, too, if I can get up the nerve. She must feel kind of funny having me round—after what used to be—and not knowing how I feel about it.

ROBERT (*slowly*): Perhaps—for her sake—you'd better not tell her.

ANDREW: For her sake? Oh, you mean she wouldn't want to be reminded of my foolishness? Still, I think it'd be worse if—

ROBERT (*breaking out—in an agonized voice*): Do as you please, Andy; but for God's sake, let's not talk about it! (*There is a pause.* ANDREW *stares at* ROBERT *in hurt stupefaction.* ROBERT *continues after a moment in a voice which he vainly attempts to keep calm*) Excuse me, Andy. This rotten headache has my nerves shot to pieces.

ANDREW (*mumbling*): It's all right, Rob—long as you're not sore at me.

ROBERT: Where did Uncle Dick disappear to this morning?

ANDREW: He went down to the port to see to things on the "Sunda." He said he didn't know exactly when he'd be back. I'll have to go down and tend to the ship when he comes. That's why I dressed up in these togs.

MARY (*pointing down to the hill to the left*): See! Mama! Mama! (*She struggles to her feet.* RUTH *appears at left. She is dressed in white, shows she has been fixing up. She looks pretty, flushed and full of life.*)

MARY (*running to her mother*): Mama!

RUTH (*kissing her*): Hello, dear! (*She walks toward the rock and addresses* ROBERT *coldly*) Jake wants to

see you about something. He finished working
where he was. He's waiting for you at the road.

ROBERT (*getting up—wearily*): I'll go down right away.
(*As he looks at* RUTH, *noting her changed appearance, his face darkens with pain.*)

RUTH: And take Mary with you, please. (*To* MARY)
Go with Dada, that's a good girl. Grandma has your
dinner 'most ready for you.

ROBERT (*shortly*): Come, Mary!

MARY (*taking his hand and dancing happily beside
him*): Dada! Dada! (*They go down the hill to the
left.* RUTH *looks after them for a moment, frowning—then turns to* ANDY *with a smile*) I'm going to
sit down. Come on, Andy. It'll be like old times.
(*She jumps lightly to the top of the rock and sits
down*) It's so fine and cool up here after the house.

ANDREW (*half-sitting on the side of the boulder*): Yes.
It's great.

RUTH: I've taken a holiday in honor of your arrival.
(*Laughing excitedly*) I feel so free I'd like to have
wings and fly over the sea. You're a man. You can't
know how awful and stupid it is—cooking and wash-
ing dishes all the time.

ANDREW (*making a wry face*): I can guess.

RUTH: Besides, your mother just insisted on getting
your first dinner to home, she's that happy at having
you back. You'd think I was planning to poison you
the flurried way she shooed me out of the kitchen.

ANDREW: That's just like Ma, bless her!

RUTH: She's missed you terrible. We all have. And
you can't deny the farm has, after what I showed
you and told you when we was looking over the
place this morning.

ANDREW (*with a frown*): Things are run down, that's
a fact! It's too darn hard on poor old Rob.

RUTH (*scornfully*): It's his own fault. He never takes any interest in things.

ANDREW (*reprovingly*): You can't blame him. He wasn't born for it; but I know he's done his best for your sake and the old folks and the little girl.

RUTH (*indifferently*): Yes, I suppose he has. (*Gaily*) But thank the Lord, all those days are over now. The "hard luck" Rob's always blaming won't last long when you take hold, Andy. All the farm's ever needed was someone with the knack of looking ahead and preparing for what's going to happen.

ANDREW: Yes, Rob hasn't got that. He's frank to own up to that himself. I'm going to try and hire a good man for him—an experienced farmer—to work the place on a salary and percentage. That'll take it off of Rob's hands, and he needn't be worrying himself to death any more. He looks all worn out, Ruth. He ought to be careful.

RUTH (*absent-mindedly*): Yes, I s'pose. (*Her mind is filled with premonitions by the first part of his statement*) Why do you want to hire a man to oversee things? Seems as if now that you're back it wouldn't be needful.

ANDREW: Oh, of course I'll attend to everything while I'm here. I mean after I'm gone.

RUTH (*as if she couldn't believe her ears*): Gone!

ANDREW: Yes. When I leave for the Argentine again.

RUTH (*aghast*): You're going away to sea!

ANDREW: Not to sea, no; I'm through with the sea for good as a job. I'm going down to Buenos Aires to get in the grain business.

RUTH: But—that's far off—isn't it?

ANDREW (*easily*): Six thousand miles more or less. It's quite a trip. (*With enthusiasm*) I've got a peach of a chance down there, Ruth. Ask Rob if I haven't. I've just been telling him all about it.

RUTH (*a flush of anger coming over her face*): And didn't he try to stop you from going?

ANDREW (*in surprise*): No, of course not. Why?

RUTH (*slowly and vindictively*): That's just like him—not to.

ANDREW (*resentfully*): Rob's too good a chum to try and stop me when he knows I'm set on a thing. And he could see just as soon's I told him what a good chance it was.

RUTH (*dazedly*): And you're bound on going?

ANDREW: Sure thing. Oh, I don't mean right off. I'll have to wait for a ship sailing there for quite a while, likely. Anyway, I want to stay to home and visit with you folks a spell before I go.

RUTH (*dumbly*): I s'pose. (*With sudden anguish*) Oh, Andy, you can't go! You can't. Why we've all thought—we've all been hoping and praying you was coming home to stay, to settle down on the farm and see to things. You mustn't go! Think of how your Ma'll take on if you go—and how the farm'll be ruined if you leave it to Rob to look after. You can see that.

ANDREW (*frowning*): Rob hasn't done so bad. When I get a man to direct things the farm'll be safe enough.

RUTH (*insistently*): But your Ma—think of her.

ANDREW: She's used to me being away. She won't object when she knows it's best for her and all of us for me to go. You ask Rob. In a couple of years down there, I'll make my pile, see if I don't; and then I'll come back and settle down and turn this farm into the crackiest place in the whole state. In the meantime, I can help you both from down there. (*Earnestly*) I tell you, Ruth, I'm going to make good right from the minute I land, if working hard and a determination to get on can do it; and I *know* they can! (*Excitedly—in a rather boastful tone*) I tell you, I feel ripe for bigger things than settling down here. The trip did that for me, anyway. It showed me the world is a larger proposition than ever I thought it was in the old days. I couldn't be content any more stuck here like a fly in molasses. It all seems trifling, somehow. You ought to be able to understand what I feel.

RUTH (*dully*): Yes—I s'pose I ought. (*After a pause— a sudden suspicion forming in her mind*) What did Rob tell you—about me?

ANDREW: Tell? About you? Why, nothing.

RUTH (*staring at him intensely*): Are you telling me the truth, Andy Mayo? Didn't he say—I— (*She stops confusedly.*)

ANDREW (*surprised*): No, he didn't mention you, I can remember. Why? What made you think he did?

RUTH (*wringing her hands*): Oh, I wish I could tell if you're lying or not!

ANDREW (*indignantly*): What're you talking about? I didn't used to lie to you, did I? And what in the name of God is there to lie for?

RUTH (*still unconvinced*): Are you sure—will you swear—it isn't the reason— (*She lowers her eyes and half turns away from him*) The same reason that made you go last time that's driving you away again? 'Cause if it is—I was going to say—you mustn't go—on that account. (*Her voice sinks to a tremulous, tender whisper as she finishes.*)

ANDREW (*confused—forces a laugh*): Oh, is *that* what you're driving at? Well, you needn't worry about that no more— (*Soberly*) I don't blame you, Ruth, feeling embarrassed having me round again, after the way I played the dumb fool about going away last time.

RUTH (*her hope crushed—with a gasp of pain*): Oh, Andy!

ANDREW (*misunderstanding*): I know I oughtn't to talk about such foolishness to you. Still I figure it's better to get it out of my system so's we three can be together same's years ago, and not be worried thinking one of us might have the wrong notion.

RUTH: Andy! Please! Don't!

ANDREW: Let me finish now that I've started. It'll help clear things up. I don't want you to think once a fool always a fool, and be upset all the time I'm here on my fool account. I want you to believe I put all that silly nonsense back of me a long time ago—and now—it seems—well—as if you'd always been my sister, that's what, Ruth.

RUTH (*at the end of her endurance—laughing hysterically*): For God's sake, Andy—won't you please stop talking! (*She again hides her face in her hands, her bowed shoulders trembling.*)

ANDREW (*ruefully*): Seems as if I put my foot in it whenever I open my mouth today. Rob shut me up with almost the same words when I tried speaking to him about it.

RUTH (*fiercely*): You told him—what you've told me?

ANDREW (*astounded*): Why sure! Why not?

RUTH (*shuddering*): Oh, my God!

ANDREW (*alarmed*): Why? Shouldn't I have?

RUTH (*hysterically*): Oh, I don't care what you do! I don't care! Leave me alone! (*ANDREW gets up and walks down the hill to the left, embarrassed, hurt, and greatly puzzled by her behavior.*)

ANDREW (*after a pause—pointing down the hill*): Hello! Here they come back—and the Captain's with them. How'd he come to get back so soon, I wonder? That means I've got to hustle down to the port and get on board. Rob's got the baby with him.

(*He comes back to the boulder.* RUTH *keeps her face averted from him*) Gosh, I never saw a father so tied up in a kid as Rob is! He just watches every move she makes. And I don't blame him. You both got a right to feel proud of her. She's surely a little winner. (*He glances at* RUTH *to see if this very obvious attempt to get back in her good graces is having any effect*) I can see the likeness to Rob standing out all over her, can't you? But there's no denying she's your young one, either. There's something about her eyes—

RUTH (*piteously*): Oh, Andy, I've a headache! I don't want to talk! Leave me alone, won't you please?

ANDREW (*stands staring at her for a moment—then walks away saying in a hurt tone*): Everybody hereabouts seems to be on edge today. I begin to feel as if I'm not wanted around. (*He stands near the path, left, kicking at the grass with the toe of his shoe. A moment later* CAPTAIN DICK SCOTT *enters, followed by* ROBERT *carrying* MARY. *The* CAPTAIN *seems scarcely to have changed at all from the jovial, booming person he was three years before. He wears a uniform similar to* ANDREW'S. *He is puffing and breathless from his climb and mops wildly at his perspiring countenance.* ROBERT *casts a quick glance at* ANDREW, *noticing the latter's discomfited look, and then turns his eyes on* RUTH *who, at their approach, has moved so her back is toward them, her chin resting on her hands as she stares out seaward.*)

MARY: Mama! Mama! (ROBERT *puts her down and she runs to her mother.* RUTH *turns and grabs her up in her arms with a sudden fierce tenderness, quickly turning away again from the others. During the following scene she keeps* MARY *in her arms.*)

SCOTT (*wheezily*): Phew! I got great news for you, Andy. Let me get my wind first. Phew! God

A'mighty, mountin' this damned hill is worser'n goin' aloft to the skys'l yard in a blow. I got to lay to a while. (*He sits down on the grass, mopping his face.*)

ANDREW: I didn't look for you this soon, Uncle.

SCOTT: I didn't figger it, neither; but I run across a bit o' news down to the Seamen's Home made me 'bout ship and set all sail back here to find you.

ANDREW (*eagerly*): What is it, Uncle?

SCOTT: Passin' by the Home I thought I'd drop in an' let 'em know I'd be lackin' a mate next trip 'count o' your leavin'. Their man in charge o' the shippin' asked after you 'special curious. "Do you think he'd consider a berth as Second on a steamer, Captain?" he asks. I was going to say no when I thinks o' you wantin' to get back down south to the Plate agen; so I asks him: "What is she and where's she bound?" "She's the 'El Paso,' a brand new tramp," he says, "and she's bound for Buenos Aires."

ANDREW (*his eyes lighting up—excitedly*): Gosh, that is luck! When does she sail?

SCOTT: Tomorrow mornin'. I didn't know if you'd want to ship away agen so quick an' I told him so. "Tell him I'll hold the berth open for him until late this afternoon," he says. So there you be, an' you can make your own choice.

ANDREW: I'd like to take it. There may not be another ship for Buenos Aires with a vacancy in months. (*His eyes roving from* ROBERT *to* RUTH *and back again—uncertainly*) Still—damn it all—tomorrow morning *is* soon. I wish she wasn't leaving for a week or so. That'd give me a chance—it seems hard to go right away again when I've just got home. And yet it's a chance in a thousand— (*Appealing to* ROBERT) What do you think, Rob? What would you do?

ROBERT (*forcing a smile*): He who hesitates, you know. (*Frowning*) It's a piece of good luck thrown in your way—and—I think you owe it to yourself to jump at it. But don't ask me to decide for you.

RUTH (*turning to look at* ANDREW—*in a tone of fierce resentment*): Yes, go, Andy! (*She turns quickly away again. There is a moment of embarrassed silence.*)

ANDREW (*thoughtfully*): Yes, I guess I will. It'll be the best thing for all of us in the end, don't you think so, Rob? (ROBERT *nods but remains silent.*)

SCOTT (*getting to his feet*): Then, that's settled.

ANDREW (*now that he has definitely made a decision his voice rings with hopeful strength and energy*): Yes, I'll take the berth. The sooner I go the sooner I'll be back, that's a certainty; and I won't come back with empty hands next time. You bet I won't!

SCOTT: You ain't got so much time, Andy. To make sure you'd best leave here soon's you kin. I got to get right back aboard. You'd best come with me.

ANDREW: I'll go to the house and repack my bag right away.

ROBERT (*quietly*): You'll both be here for dinner, won't you?

ANDREW (*worriedly*): I don't know. Will there be time? What time is it now, I wonder?

ROBERT (*reproachfully*): Ma's been getting dinner especially for you, Andy.

ANDREW (*flushing—shamefacedly*): Hell! And I was forgetting! Of course I'll stay for dinner if I missed every damned ship in the world. (*He turns to the* CAPTAIN—*briskly*) Come on, Uncle. Walk down with me to the house and you can tell me more about this berth on the way. I've got to pack before dinner. (*He and the* CAPTAIN *start down to the left.* ANDREW *calls back over his shoulder*) You're coming soon, aren't you, Rob?

ROBERT: Yes. I'll be right down. (ANDREW *and the*
CAPTAIN *leave.* RUTH *puts* MARY *on the ground and
hides her face in her hands. Her shoulders shake as
if she were sobbing.* ROBERT *stares at her with a
grim, somber expression.* MARY *walks backward
toward* ROBERT, *her wondering eyes fixed on her
mother.*)

MARY (*her voice vaguely frightened, taking her father's
hand*): Dada, Mama's cryin', Dada.

ROBERT (*bending down and stroking her hair—in a
voice he endeavors to keep from being harsh*): No,
she isn't, little girl. The sun hurts her eyes, that's
all. Aren't you beginning to feel hungry, Mary?

MARY (*decidedly*): Yes, Dada.

ROBERT (*meaningly*): It must be your dinner time now.

RUTH (*in a muffled voice*): I'm coming, Mary. (*She
wipes her eyes quickly and, without looking at* ROB-
ERT, *comes and takes* MARY'S *hand—in a dead
voice*) Come on and I'll get your dinner for you.
(*She walks out left, her eyes fixed on the ground, the
skipping* MARY *tugging at her hand.* ROBERT *waits
a moment for them to get ahead and then slowly
follows as the curtain falls.*)

ACT THREE
Scene 1

*Same as Act Two, Scene 1—The sitting room of the
farmhouse about six o'clock in the morning of a day
toward the end of October five years later. It is not yet
dawn, but as the action progresses the darkness outside
the windows gradually fades to gray.*

*The room, seen by the light of the shadeless oil lamp
with a smoky chimney which stands on the table, pres-
ents an appearance of decay, of dissolution. The curtains at the windows are torn and dirty and one of them
is missing. The closed desk is gray with accumulated
dust as if it had not been used in years. Blotches of
dampness disfigure the wall paper. Threadbare trails,
leading to the kitchen and outer doors, show in the
faded carpet. The top of the coverless table is stained
with the imprints of hot dishes and spilt food. The rung
of one rocker has been clumsily mended with a piece
of plain board. A brown coating of rust covers the
unblacked stove. A pile of wood is stacked up carelessly
against the wall by the stove.*

*The whole atmosphere of the room, contrasted with
that of former years, is one of an habitual poverty too
hopelessly resigned to be any longer ashamed or even
conscious of itself.*

At the rise of the curtain RUTH *is discovered sitting
by the stove, with hands outstretched to the warmth as
if the air in the room were damp and cold. A heavy
shawl is wrapped about her shoulders, half-concealing*

her dress of deep mourning. She has aged horribly. Her pale, deeply-lined face has the stony lack of expression of one to whom nothing more can ever happen, whose capacity for emotion has been exhausted. When she speaks her voice is without timbre, low and monotonous. The negligent disorder of her dress, the slovenly arrangement of her hair, now streaked with gray, her muddied shoes run down at the heel, give full evidence of the apathy in which she lives.

Her mother is asleep in her wheel chair beside the stove toward the rear, wrapped up in a blanket.

There is a sound from the open bedroom door in the rear as if someone were getting out of bed. RUTH turns in that direction with a look of dull annoyance. A moment later ROBERT appears in the doorway, leaning weakly against it for support. His hair is long and unkempt, his face and body emaciated. There are bright patches of crimson over his cheek bones and his eyes are burning with fever. He is dressed in corduroy pants, a flannel shirt, and wears worn carpet slippers on his bare feet.

RUTH (*dully*): S-s-s-h! Ma's asleep.

ROBERT (*speaking with an effort*): I won't wake her. (*He walks weakly to a rocker by the side of the table and sinks down in it exhausted.*)

RUTH (*staring at the stove*): You better come near the fire where it's warm.

ROBERT: No, I'm burning up now.

RUTH: That's the fever. You know the doctor told you not to get up and move round.

ROBERT (*irritably*): That old fossil! He doesn't know anything. Go to bed and stay there—that's his only prescription.

RUTH (*indifferently*): How are you feeling now?

ROBERT (*buoyantly*): Better! Much better than I've

felt in ages. Really I'm fine now—only very weak. It's the turning point, I guess. From now on I'll pick up so quick I'll surprise you—and no thanks to that old fool of a country quack, either.

RUTH: He's always tended to us.

ROBERT: Always helped us to die, you mean! He "tended" to Pa and Ma and— (*His voice breaks*) and to—Mary.

RUTH (*dully*): He did the best he knew, I s'pose. (*After a pause*) Well, Andy's bringing a specialist with him when he comes. That ought to suit you.

ROBERT (*bitterly*): Is that why you're waiting up all night?

RUTH: Yes.

ROBERT: For Andy?

RUTH (*without a trace of feeling*): Somebody had got to. It's only right for someone to meet him after he's been gone five years.

ROBERT (*with bitter mockery*): Five years! It's a long time.

RUTH: Yes.

ROBERT (*meaningly*): To *wait*!

RUTH (*indifferently*): It's past now.

ROBERT: Yes, it's past. (*After a pause*) Have you got his two telegrams with you? (RUTH *nods*) Let me see them, will you? My head was so full of fever when they came I couldn't make head or tail to them. (*Hastily*) But I'm feeling fine now. Let me read them again. (RUTH *takes them from the bosom of her dress and hands them to him.*)

RUTH: Here. The first one's on top.

ROBERT (*opening it*): New York. "Just landed from steamer. Have important business to wind up here. Will be home as soon as deal is completed." (*He smiles bitterly*) Business first was always Andy's

motto. (*He reads*) "Hope you are all well. Andy."
(*He repeats ironically*) "Hope you are all well!"

RUTH (*dully*): He couldn't know you'd been took sick
till I answered that and told him.

ROBERT (*contritely*): Of course he couldn't. I'm a fool.
I'm touchy about nothing lately. Just what did you
say in your reply?

RUTH (*inconsequentially*): I had to send it collect.

ROBERT (*irritably*): What did you say was the matter
with me?

RUTH: I wrote you had lung trouble.

ROBERT (*flying into a petty temper*): You *are* a fool!
How often have I explained to you that it's *pleurisy*
is the matter with me. You can't seem to get it in
your head that the pleura is outside the lungs, not
in them!

RUTH (*callously*): I only wrote what Doctor Smith
told me.

ROBERT (*angrily*): He's a damned ignoramus!

RUTH (*dully*): Makes no difference. I had to tell Andy
something, didn't I?

ROBERT (*after a pause, opening the other telegram*): He
sent this last evening. Let's see. (*He reads*) "Leave
for home on midnight train. Just received your wire.
Am bringing specialist to see Rob. Will motor to
farm from Port." (*He calculates*) What time is it
now?

RUTH: Round six, must be.

ROBERT: He ought to be here soon. I'm glad he's
bringing a doctor who knows something. A specialist will tell you in a second that there's nothing the
matter with my lungs.

RUTH (*stolidly*): You've been coughing an awful lot
lately.

ROBERT (*irritably*): What nonsense! For God's sake,
haven't you ever had a bad cold yourself? (RUTH

stares at the stove in silence. ROBERT *fidgets in his chair. There is a pause. Finally* ROBERT'S *eyes are fixed on the sleeping* MRS. ATKINS) Your mother is lucky to be able to sleep so soundly.

RUTH: Ma's tired. She's been sitting up with me most of the night.

ROBERT (*mockingly*): Is she waiting for Andy, too? (*There is a pause.* ROBERT *sighs*) I couldn't get to sleep to save my soul. I counted ten million sheep if I counted one. No use! I gave up trying finally and just laid there in the dark thinking. (*He pauses, then continues in a tone of tender sympathy*) I was thinking about you, Ruth—of how hard these last years must have been for you. (*Appealingly*) I'm sorry, Ruth.

RUTH (*in a dead voice*): I don't know. They're past now. They were hard on all of us.

ROBERT: Yes, on all of us but Andy. (*With a flash of sick jealousy*) Andy's made a big success of himself—the kind he wanted. (*Mockingly*) And now he's coming home to let us admire his greatness. (*Frowning—irritably*) What am I talking about? My brain must be sick, too. (*After a pause*) Yes, these years have been terrible for both of us. (*His voice is lowered to a trembling whisper*) Especially the last eight months since Mary—died. (*He forces back a sob with a convulsive shudder—then breaks out in a passionate agony*) Our last hope of happiness! I could curse God from the bottom of my soul—if there was a God! (*He is racked by a violent fit of coughing and hurriedly puts his handkerchief to his lips.*)

RUTH (*without looking at him*): Mary's better off—being dead.

ROBERT (*gloomily*): We'd all be better off for that matter. (*With a sudden exasperation*) You tell that

mother of yours she's got to stop saying that Mary's
death was due to a weak constitution inherited from
me. (*On the verge of tears of weakness*) It's got to
stop, I tell you!

RUTH (*sharply*): S-h-h! You'll wake her; and then
she'll nag at me—not you.

ROBERT (*coughs and lies back in his chair weakly—a
pause*): It's all because your mother's down on me
for not begging Andy for help.

RUTH (*resentfully*): You might have. He's got plenty.

ROBERT: How can *you* of all people think of taking
money from *him*?

RUTH (*dully*): I don't see the harm. He's your own
brother.

ROBERT (*shrugging his shoulders*): What's the use of
talking to you? Well, I couldn't. (*Proudly*) And I've
managed to keep things going, thank God. You
can't deny that without help I've succeeded in—
(*He breaks off with a bitter laugh*) My God, what
am I boasting of? Debts to this one and that, taxes,
interest unpaid! I'm a fool! (*He lies back in his chair
closing his eyes for a moment, then speaks in a low
voice*) I'll be frank, Ruth. I've been an utter failure,
and I've dragged you with me. I couldn't blame you
in all justice—for hating me.

RUTH (*without feeling*): I don't hate you. It's been my
fault, too, I s'pose.

ROBERT: No. You couldn't help loving—Andy.

RUTH (*dully*): I don't love anyone.

ROBERT (*waving her remark aside*): You needn't deny
it. It doesn't matter. (*After a pause—with a tender
smile*) Do you know, Ruth, what I've been dreaming
back there in the dark? (*With a short laugh*) I was
planning our future when I get well. (*He looks at
her with appealing eyes as if afraid she will sneer at
him. Her expression does not change. She stares at*

the stove. His voice takes on a note of eagerness)
After all, why shouldn't we have a future? We're
young yet. If we can only shake off the curse of this
farm! It's the farm that's ruined our lives, damn it!
And now that Andy's coming back—I'm going to
sink my foolish pride, Ruth! I'll borrow the money
from him to give us a good start in the city. We'll
go there where people live instead of stagnating,
and start all over again. (*Confidently*) I won't be the
failure there that I've been here, Ruth. You won't
need to be ashamed of me there. I'll prove to you
the reading I've done can be put to some use.
(*Vaguely*) I'll write, or something of that sort. I've
always wanted to write. (*Pleadingly*) You'll want to
do that, won't you, Ruth?

RUTH (*dully*): There's Ma.

ROBERT: She can come with us.

RUTH: She wouldn't.

ROBERT (*angrily*): So that's your answer! (*He trembles
with violent passion. His voice is so strange that
RUTH turns to look at him in alarm*) You're lying,
Ruth! Your mother's just an excuse. You want to
stay here. You think that because Andy's coming
back that— (*He chokes and has an attack of
coughing.*)

RUTH (*getting up—in a frightened voice*): What's the
matter? (*She goes to him*) I'll go with you, Rob.
Stop that coughing for goodness' sake! It's awful
bad for you. (*She soothes him in dull tones*) I'll go
with you to the city—soon's you're well again. Honest I will, Rob, I promise! (ROB *lies back and closes
his eyes. She stands looking down at him anxiously*)
Do you feel better now?

ROBERT: Yes. (RUTH *goes back to her chair. After a
pause he opens his eyes and sits up in his chair. His
face is flushed and happy*) Then you *will* go, Ruth?

RUTH: Yes.

ROBERT (*excitedly*): We'll make a new start, Ruth—just you and I. Life owes us some happiness after what we've been through. (*Vehemently*) It must! Otherwise our suffering would be meaningless—and that is unthinkable.

RUTH (*worried by his excitement*): Yes, yes, of course, Rob, but you mustn't—

ROBERT: Oh, don't be afraid. I feel completely well, really I do—now that I can hope again. Oh if you knew how glorious it feels to have something to look forward to! Can't you feel the thrill of it, too—the vision of a new life opening up after all the horrible years?

RUTH: Yes, yes, but do be—

ROBERT: Nonsense! I won't be careful. I'm getting back all my strength. (*He gets lightly to his feet*) See! I feel light as a feather. (*He walks to her chair and bends down to kiss her smilingly*) One kiss—the first in years, isn't it?—to greet the dawn of a new life together.

RUTH (*submitting to his kiss—worriedly*): Sit down, Rob, for goodness' sake!

ROBERT (*with tender obstinacy—stroking her hair*): I won't sit down. You're silly to worry. (*He rests one hand on the back of her chair*) Listen. All our suffering has been a test through which we had to pass to prove ourselves worthy of a finer realization. (*Exultingly*) And we did pass through it! It hasn't broken us! And now the dream is to come true! Don't you see?

RUTH (*looking at him with frightened eyes as if she thought he had gone mad*): Yes, Rob, I see; but won't you go back to bed now and rest?

ROBERT: No, I'm going to see the sun rise. It's an augury of good fortune. (*He goes quickly to the win-*

dow in the rear left, and pushing the curtains aside, stands looking out. RUTH *springs to her feet and comes quickly to the table, left, where she remains watching* ROBERT *in a tense, expectant attitude. As he peers out his body seems gradually to sag, to grow limp and tired. His voice is mournful as he speaks)* No sun yet. It isn't time. All I can see is the black rim of the damned hills outlined against a creeping grayness. *(He turns around; letting the curtains fall back, stretching a hand out to the wall to support himself. His false strength of a moment has evaporated leaving his face drawn and hollow-eyed. He makes a pitiful attempt to smile)* That's not a very happy augury, is it? But the sun'll come—soon. *(He sways weakly.)*

RUTH *(hurrying to his side and supporting him)*: Please go to bed, won't you, Rob? You don't want to be all wore out when the specialist comes, do you?

ROBERT *(quickly)*: No. That's right. He mustn't think I'm sicker than I am. And I feel as if I could sleep now— *(Cheerfully)* a good, sound, restful sleep.

RUTH *(helping him to the bedroom door)*: That's what you need most. *(They go inside. A moment later she reappears calling back)* I'll shut this door so's you'll be quiet. *(She closes the door and goes quickly to her mother and shakes her by the shoulder)* Ma! Ma! Wake up!

MRS. ATKINS *(coming out of her sleep with a start)*: Glory be! What's the matter with you?

RUTH: It was Rob. He's just been talking to me out here. I put him back to bed. *(Now that she is sure her mother is awake her fear passes and she relapses into dull indifference. She sits down in her chair and stares at the stove—dully)* He acted—funny; and his eyes looked so—so wild like.

MRS. ATKINS *(with asperity)*: And is that all you woke

me out of a sound sleep for, and scared me near
out of my wits?

RUTH: I was afraid. He talked so crazy. I couldn't
quiet him. I don't want to be alone with him that
way. Lord knows what he might do.

MRS. ATKINS (*scornfully*): Humph! A help I'd be to
you and me not able to move a step! Why didn't
you run and get Jake?

RUTH (*dully*): Jake isn't here. He quit last night. He
hasn't been paid in three months.

MRS. ATKINS (*indignantly*): I can't blame him. What
decent person'd want to work on a place like this?
(*With sudden exasperation*) Oh, I wish you'd never
married that man!

RUTH (*wearily*): You oughtn't to talk about him now
when he's sick in his bed.

MRS. ATKINS (*working herself into a fit of rage*): You
know very well, Ruth Mayo, if it wasn't for me helpin'
you on the sly out of my savin's, you'd both
been in the poor house—and all 'count of his pig-
headed pride in not lettin' Andy know the state
thin's were in. A nice thin' for me to have to support him out of what I'd saved for my last days—
and me an invalid with no one to look to!

RUTH: Andy'll pay you back, Ma. I can tell him so's
Rob'll never know.

MRS. ATKINS (*with a snort*): What'd Rob think you
and him was livin' on, I'd like to know?

RUTH (*dully*): He didn't think about it, I s'pose. (*After
a slight pause*) He said he'd made up his mind to
ask Andy for help when he comes. (*As a clock in
the kitchen strikes six*) Six o'clock Andy ought to be
here directly.

MRS. ATKINS: D'you think this special doctor'll do
Rob any good?

RUTH (*hopelessly*): I don't know. (*The two women remain silent for a time staring dejectedly at the stove.*)

MRS. ATKINS (*shivering irritably*): For goodness' sake put some wood on that fire. I'm 'most freezin'!

RUTH (*pointing to the door in the rear*): Don't talk so loud. Let him sleep if he can. (*She gets wearily from the chair and puts a few pieces of wood in the stove*) This is the last of the wood. I don't know who'll cut more now that Jake's left. (*She sighs and walks to the window in the rear, left, pulls the curtains aside, and looks out*) It's getting gray out. (*She comes back to the stove*) Looks like it'd be a nice day (*She stretches out her hands to warm them*) Must've been a heavy frost last night. We're paying for the spell of warm weather we've been having. (*The throbbing whine of a motor sounds from the distance outside.*)

MRS. ATKINS (*sharply*): S-h-h! Listen! Ain't that an auto I hear?

RUTH (*without interest*); Yes. It's Andy, I s'pose.

MRS. ATKINS (*with nervous irritation*): Don't sit there like a silly goose. Look at the state of this room! What'll this strange doctor think of us? Look at that lamp chimney all smoke! Gracious sakes, Ruth—

RUTH (*indifferently*): I've got a lamp all cleaned up in the kitchen.

MRS. ATKINS (*peremptorily*): Wheel me in there this minute. I don't want him to see me looking a sight. I'll lay down in the room the other side. You don't need me now and I'm dead for sleep. (*RUTH wheels her mother off right. The noise of the motor grows louder and finally ceases as the car stops on the road before the farmhouse. RUTH returns from the kitchen with a lighted lamp in her hand which she sets on the table beside the other. The sound of footsteps on the path is heard—then a sharp rap on the door. RUTH goes and opens it. ANDREW enters, followed by* DOCTOR FAWCETT *carrying a small black bag.* ANDREW *has changed greatly. His face seems to have grown highstrung, hardened by the look of decisiveness which comes from being constantly under a strain where judgments on the spur of the moment are compelled to be accurate. His eyes are keener and more alert. There is even a suggestion of ruthless cunning about them. At present, however, his expression is one of tense anxiety.* DOCTOR FAWCETT *is a short, dark, middle-aged man with a Vandyke beard. He wears glasses.*)

RUTH: Hello, Andy! I've been waiting—

ANDREW (*kissing her hastily*): I got here as soon as I could. (*He throws off his cap and heavy overcoat on the table, introducing* RUTH *and the* DOCTOR *as he does so. He is dressed in an expensive business suit and appears stouter*) My sister-in-law, Mrs. Mayo— Doctor Fawcett. (*They bow to each other silently.* ANDREW *casts a quick glance about the room*) Where's Rob?

RUTH (*pointing*): In there.

ANDREW: I'll take your coat and hat, Doctor. (*As he helps the* DOCTOR *with his things*) Is he very bad, Ruth?

RUTH (*dully*): He's been getting weaker.

ANDREW: Damn! This way, Doctor. Bring the lamp, Ruth. (*He goes into the bedroom, followed by the* DOCTOR *and* RUTH *carrying the clean lamp.* RUTH *reappears almost immediately closing the door behind her, and goes slowly to the outside door, which she opens, and stands in the doorway looking out. The sound of* ANDREW'S *and* ROBERT'S *voices comes from the bedroom. A moment later* ANDREW *re-enters, closing the door softly. He comes forward and sinks down in the rocker on the right of table, leaning his head on his hand. His face is drawn in a shocked expression of great grief. He sighs heavily, staring mournfully in front of him.* RUTH *turns and stands watching him. Then she shuts the door and returns to her chair by the stove, turning it so she can face him.*)

ANDREW (*glancing up quickly—in a harsh voice*): How long has this been going on?

RUTH: You mean—how long has he been sick?

ANDREW (*shortly*): Of course! What else?

RUTH: It was last summer he had a bad spell first, but he's been ailin' ever since Mary died—eight months ago.

ANDREW (*harshly*): Why didn't you let me know—cable me? Do you want him to die, all of you? I'm damned if it doesn't look that way! (*His voice breaking*) Poor old chap! To be sick in this out-of-the-way hole without anyone to attend to him but a country quack! It's a damned shame!

RUTH (*dully*): I wanted to send you word once, but he only got mad when I told him. He was too proud to ask anything, he said.

ANDREW: Proud? To ask *me*? (*He jumps to his feet and paces nervously back and forth*) I can't understand the way you've acted. Didn't you see how sick he was getting? Couldn't you realize—why, I nearly dropped in my tracks when I saw him! He looks— (*He shudders*) terrible! (*With fierce scorn*) I suppose you're so used to the idea of his being delicate that you took his sickness as a matter of course. God, if I'd only known!

RUTH (*without emotion*): A letter takes some time to get where you were—and we couldn't afford to telegraph. We owed everyone already, and I couldn't ask Ma. She'd been giving me money out of her savings till she hadn't much left. Don't say anything to Rob about it. I never told him. He'd only be mad at me if he knew. But I had to, because—God knows how we'd have got on if I hadn't.

ANDREW: You mean to say— (*His eyes seem to take in the poverty-stricken appearance of the room for the first time*) You sent that telegram to me collect. Was it because— (RUTH *nods silently.* ANDREW *pounds on the table with his fist*) Good God! And all this time I've been—why I've had everything! (*He sits down in his chair and pulls it close to* RUTH's *impulsively*) But—I can't get it through my head. Why? Why? What had happened? How did it ever come about? Tell me!

RUTH (*dully*): There's nothing much to tell. Things kept getting worse, that's all—and Rob didn't seem to care. He never took any interest since way back when your Ma died. After that he got men to take charge, and they nearly all cheated him—he couldn't tell—and left one after another. Then after Mary died he didn't pay no heed to anything any more—just stayed indoors and took to reading books again. So I had to ask Ma if she wouldn't help us some.

ANDREW (*surprised and horrified*): Why, damn it, this is frightful! Rob must be mad not to have let me know. Too proud to ask help of *me*! What's the matter with him in God's name? (*A sudden, horrible suspicion entering his mind*) Ruth! Tell me the truth. His mind hasn't gone back on him, has it?

RUTH (*dully*): I don't know. Mary's dying broke him up terrible—but he's used to her being gone by this time, I s'pose.

ANDREW (*looking at her queerly*): Do you mean to say *you're* used to it?

RUTH (*in a dead tone*): There's a time comes—when you don't mind any more—anything.

ANDREW (*looks at her fixedly for a moment—with*

great pity): I'm sorry, Ruth—if I seemed to blame you. I didn't realize— The sight of Rob lying in bed there, so gone to pieces—it made me furious at everyone. Forgive me, Ruth.

RUTH: There's nothing to forgive. It doesn't matter.

ANDREW (*springing to his feet again and pacing up and down*): Thank God I came back before it was too late. This doctor will know exactly what to do. That's the first thing to think of. When Rob's on his feet again we can get the farm working on a sound basis once more. I'll see to that—before I leave.

RUTH: You're going away again?

ANDREW: I've got to.

RUTH: You wrote Rob you was coming back to stay this time.

ANDREW: I expected to—until I got to New York. Then I learned certain facts that make it necessary (*With a short laugh*) To be candid, Ruth, I'm not the rich man you've probably been led to believe by my letters—not now. I was when I wrote them. I made money hand over fist as long as I stuck to legitimate trading; but I wasn't content with that. I wanted it to come easier, so like all the rest of the idiots, I tried speculation. Oh, I won all right! Several times I've been almost a millionaire—on paper—and then come down to earth again with a bump. Finally the strain was too much. I got disgusted with myself and made up my mind to get out and come home and forget it and really live again. (*He gives a harsh laugh*) And now comes the funny part. The day before the steamer sailed I saw what I thought was a chance to become a millionaire again. (*He snaps his fingers*) That easy! I plunged. Then, before things broke, I left—I was so confident I couldn't be wrong. But when I landed in New York—I wired you I had business to wind up, didn't I? Well, it was the business that wound me up! (*He smiles grimly, pacing up and down, his hands in his pockets.*)

RUTH (*dully*): You found—you'd lost everything?

ANDREW (*sitting down again*): Practically. (*He takes a cigar from his pocket, bites the end off, and lights it*) Oh, I don't mean I'm dead broke. I've saved ten thousand from the wreckage, maybe twenty. But that's a poor showing for five years' hard work. That's why I'll have to go back. (*Confidently*) I can make it up in a year or so down there—and I don't need but a shoestring to start with. (*A weary expression comes over his face and he sighs heavily*) I wish I didn't have to. I'm sick of it all.

RUTH: It's too bad—things seem to go wrong so.

ANDREW (*shaking off his depression—briskly*): They might be much worse. There's enough left to fix the farm. O.K. before I go. I won't leave 'til Rob's on his feet again. In the meantime I'll make things fly around here. (*With satisfaction*) I need a rest, and the kind of rest I need is hard work in the open— just like I used to do in the old days. (*Stopping abruptly and lowering his voice cautiously*) Not a word to Rob about my losing money! Remember that, Ruth! You can see why. If he's grown so touchy he'd never accept a cent if he thought I was hard up; see?

RUTH: Yes, Andy. (*After a pause, during which AN-DREW puffs at his cigar abstractedly, his mind evidently busy with plans for the future, the bedroom door is opened and DR. FAWCETT enters, carrying a bag. He closes the door quietly behind him and comes forward, a grave expression on his face. AN-DREW springs out of his chair.*)

ANDREW: Ah, Doctor! (*He pushes a chair between his own and* RUTH'S) Won't you have a chair?

FAWCETT (*glancing at his watch*): I must catch the nine o'clock back to the city. It's imperative. I have only a moment. (*Sitting down and clearing his throat—in a perfunctory, impersonal voice*) The case of your brother, Mr. Mayo, is— (*He stops and glances at* RUTH *and says meaningly to* ANDREW) Perhaps it would be better if you and I—

RUTH (*with dogged resentment*): I know what you mean, Doctor. (*Dully*) Don't be afraid I can't stand it. I'm used to bearing trouble by this time; and I can guess what you've found out. (*She hesitates for a moment—then continues in a monotonous voice*) Rob's going to die.

ANDREW (*angrily*): Ruth!

FAWCETT (*raising his hand as if to command silence*): I am afraid my diagnosis of your brother's condition forces me to the same conclusion as Mrs. Mayo's.

ANDREW (*groaning*): But, Doctor, surely—

FAWCETT (*calmly*): Your brother hasn't long to live— perhaps a few days, perhaps only a few hours. It's a marvel that he's alive at this moment. My examination revealed that both of his lungs are terribly affected.

ANDREW (*brokenly*): Good God! (RUTH *keeps her eyes fixed on her lap in a trance-like stare.*)

FAWCETT: I am sorry I have to tell you this. If there was anything that could be done—

ANDREW: There isn't anything?

FAWCETT (*shaking his head*): It's too late. Six months ago there might have—

ANDREW (*in anguish*): But if we were to take him to the mountains—go to Arizona—or—

FAWCETT: That might have prolonged his life six

months ago. (ANDREW *groans*) But now— (*He shrugs his shoulders significantly.*)

ANDREW (*appalled by a sudden thought*): Good heavens, you haven't told him this, have you, Doctor?

FAWCETT: No. I lied to him. I said a change of climate— (*He looks at his watch again nervously*) I must leave you. (*He gets up.*)

ANDREW (*getting to his feet—insistently*): But there must still be some chance—

FAWCETT (*as if he were reassuring a child*): There is always that last chance—the miracle. (*He puts on his hat and coat—bowing to* RUTH) Good-by, Mrs. Mayo.

RUTH (*without raising her eyes—dully*): Good-by.

ANDREW (*mechanically*): I'll walk to the car with you, Doctor. (*They go out of the door.* RUTH *sits motionlessly. The motor is heard starting and the noise gradually recedes into the distance.* ANDREW *re-enters and sits down in his chair, holding his head in his hands*) Ruth! (*She lifts her eyes to his*) Hadn't we better go in and see him? God! I'm afraid to! I know he'll read it in my face. (*The bedroom door is noiselessly opened and* ROBERT *appears in the doorway. His cheeks are flushed with fever, and his eyes appear unusually large and brilliant.* ANDREW *continues with a groan*) It can't be, Ruth. It can't be as hopeless as he said. There's always a fighting chance. We'll take Rob to Arizona. He's got to get well. There *must* be a chance!

ROBERT (*in a gentle tone*): Why must there, Andy? (RUTH *turns and stares at him with terrified eyes.*)

ANDREW (*whirling around*): Rob! (*Scoldingly*) What are you doing out of bed? (*He gets up and goes to him*) Get right back now and obey the Doc, or you're going to get a licking from me!

ROBERT (*ignoring these remarks*): Help me over the chair, please, Andy.

ANDREW: Like hell I will! You're going right back to bed, that's where you're going, and stay there! (*He takes hold of* ROBERT's *arm.*)

ROBERT (*mockingly*): Stay there 'til I die, eh, Andy? (*Coldly*) Don't behave like a child. I'm sick of lying down. I'll be more rested sitting up. (*As* ANDREW *hesitates—violently*) I swear I'll get out of bed every time you put me there. You'll have to sit on my chest, and that wouldn't help my health any. Come on, Andy. Don't play the fool. I want to talk to you, and I'm going to. (*With a grim smile*) A dying man has some rights, hasn't he?

ANDREW (*with a shudder*): Don't talk that way, for God's sake! I'll only let you sit down if you'll promise that. Remember. (*He helps* ROBERT *to the chair between his own and* RUTH's) Easy now! There you are! Wait, and I'll get a pillow for you. (*He goes into the bedroom.* ROBERT *looks at* RUTH *who shrinks away from him in terror.* ROBERT *smiles bitterly.* ANDREW *comes back with the pillow which he places behind* ROBERT's *back*) How's that?

ROBERT (*with an affectionate smile*): Fine! Thank you! (*As* ANDREW *sits down*) Listen, Andy. You've asked me not to talk—and I won't after I've made my position clear. (*Slowly*) In the first place I know I'm dying. (RUTH *bows her head and covers her face with her hands. She remains like this all during the scene between the two brothers.*)

ANDREW: Rob! That isn't so!

ROBERT (*wearily*): It *is* so! Don't lie to me. After Ruth put me to bed before you came, I saw it clearly for the first time. (*Bitterly*) I'd been making plans for our future—Ruth's and mine—so it came hard at first—the realization. Then when the doctor examined me, I knew—although he tried to lie about it. And then to make sure I listened at the door to what he told you. So don't mock me with fairy tales about Arizona, or any such rot as that. Because I'm dying is no reason you should treat me as an imbecile or a coward. Now that I'm sure what's happening I can say Kismet to it with all my heart. It was only the silly uncertainty that hurt. (*There is a pause.* ANDREW *looks around in impotent anguish, not knowing what to say.* ROBERT *regards him with an affectionate smile.*)

ANDREW (*finally blurts out*): It isn't foolish. You *have* got a chance. If you heard all the Doctor said that ought to prove it to you.

ROBERT: Oh, you mean when he spoke of the miracle? (*Dryly*) I don't believe in miracles—in my case. Besides, I know more than any doctor on earth *could* know—because I *feel* what's coming. (*Dismissing the subject*) But we've agreed not to talk of it. Tell me about yourself, Andy. That's what I'm interested in. Your letters were too brief and far apart to be illuminating.

ANDREW: I meant to write oftener.

ROBERT (*with a faint trace of irony*): I judge from them you've accomplished all you set out to do five years ago?

ANDREW: That isn't much to boast of.

ROBERT (*surprised*): Have you really, honestly reached that conclusion?

ANDREW: Well, it doesn't seem to amount to much now.

ROBERT: But you're rich, aren't you?

ANDREW (*with a quick glance at* RUTH): Yes, I s'pose so.

ROBERT: I'm glad. You can do to the farm all I've undone. But what did you do down there? Tell me.

You went in the grain business with that friend of yours?

ANDREW: Yes. After two years I had a share in it. I sold out last year. (*He is answering* ROBERT'S *questions with great reluctance.*)

ROBERT: And then?

ANDREW: I went in on my own.

ROBERT: Still in grain?

ANDREW: Yes.

ROBERT: What's the matter? You look as if I were accusing you of something.

ANDREW: I'm proud enough of the first four years. It's after that I'm not boasting of. I took to speculating.

ROBERT: In wheat?

ANDREW: Yes.

ROBERT: And you made money—gambling?

ANDREW: Yes.

ROBERT (*thoughtfully*): I've been wondering what the great change was in you. (*After a pause*) You—a farmer—to gamble in a wheat pit with scraps of paper. There's a spiritual significance in that picture, Andy. (*He smiles bitterly*) I'm a failure, and Ruth's another—but we can both justly lay some of the blame for our stumbling on God. But you're the deepest-dyed failure of the three, Andy. You've spent eight years running away from yourself when you loved the farm. And now— (*He stops as if seeking vainly for words*) My brain is muddled. But part of what I mean is that your gambling with the thing you used to love to create proves how far astray— So you'll be punished. You'll have to suffer to win back— (*His voice grows weaker and he sighs wearily*) It's no use. I can't say it. (*He lies back and closes his eyes, breathing pantingly.*)

ANDREW (*slowly*): I think I know what you're driving at, Rob—and it's true, I guess. (ROBERT *smiles gratefully and stretches out his hand, which* ANDREW *takes in his.*)

ROBERT: I want you to promise me to do one thing, Andy, after——

ANDREW: I'll promise anything, as God is my Judge!

ROBERT: Remember, Andy, Ruth has suffered double her share. (*His voice faltering with weakness*) Only through contact with suffering, Andy, will you—— awaken. Listen. You must marry Ruth—afterwards.

RUTH (*with a cry*): Rob! (ROBERT *lies back, his eyes closed, gasping heavily for breath.*)

ANDREW (*making signs to her to humor him—gently*): You're tired out, Rob. You better lie down and rest a while, don't you think? We can talk later on.

ROBERT (*with a mocking smile*): Later on! You always were an optimist, Andy! (*He sighs with exhaustion*) Yes, I'll go and rest a while. (*As* ANDREW *comes to help him*) It must be near sunrise, isn't it?

ANDREW: It's after six.

ROBERT (*as* ANDREW *helps him into the bedroom*): Shut the door, Andy. I want to be alone. (ANDREW *reappears and shuts the door softly. He comes and sits down on his chair again, supporting his head on his hands. His face drawn with the intensity of his dry-eyed anguish.*)

RUTH (*glancing at him—fearfully*): He's out of his mind now, isn't he?

ANDREW: He may be a little delirious. The fever would do that. (*With impotent rage*) God, what a shame! And there's nothing we can do but sit and—— wait! (*He springs from his chair and walks to the stove.*)

RUTH (*dully*): He was talking—wild—like he used to—— only this time it sounded—unnatural, don't you think?

ANDREW: I don't know. The things he said to me had

truth in them—even if he did talk them way up in the air, like he always sees things. Still— (*He glances down at* RUTH *keenly*) Why do you suppose he wanted us to promise we'd— (*Confusedly*) You know what he said.

RUTH (*dully*): His mind was wandering, I s'pose.

ANDREW (*with conviction*): No—there was something back of it.

RUTH: He wanted to make sure I'd be all right—after he'd gone, I expect.

ANDREW: No, it wasn't that. He knows very well I'd naturally look after you without—anything like that.

RUTH: He might be thinking of—something happened five years back, the time you came home from the trip.

ANDREW: What happened? What do you mean?

RUTH (*dully*): We had a fight.

ANDREW: A fight? What has that to do with me?

RUTH: It was about you—in a way.

ANDREW (*amazed*): About *me*?

RUTH: Yes, mostly. You see I'd found out I'd made a mistake about Rob soon after we were married— when it was too late.

ANDREW: Mistake? (*Slowly*) You mean—you found out you didn't love Rob?

RUTH: Yes.

ANDREW: Good God!

RUTH: And then I thought that when Mary came it'd be different, and I'd love him; but it didn't happen that way. And I couldn't bear with his blundering and book-reading—and I grew to hate him, almost.

ANDREW: Ruth!

RUTH: I couldn't help it. No woman could. It had to be because I loved someone else, I'd found out. (*She sighs wearily*) It can't do no harm to tell you now—when it's all past and gone—and dead. *You* were the one I really loved—only I didn't come to the knowledge of it 'til too late.

ANDREW (*stunned*): Ruth! Do you know what you're saying?

RUTH: It was true—then. (*With sudden fierceness*) How could I help it? No woman could.

ANDREW: Then—you loved me—that time I came home?

RUTH (*doggedly*): I'd known your real reason for leaving home the first time—everybody knew it—and for three years I'd been thinking—

ANDREW: That I loved you?

RUTH: Yes. Then that day on the hill you laughed about what a fool you'd been for loving me once—and I knew it was all over.

ANDREW: Good God, but I never thought— (*He stops, shuddering at his remembrance*) And did Rob—

RUTH: That was what I'd started to tell. We'd had a fight just before you came and I got crazy mad—and I told him all I've told you.

ANDREW (*gaping at her speechlessly for a moment*): You told Rob—you loved me?

RUTH: Yes.

ANDREW (*shrinking away from her in horror*): You—you—you mad fool, you! How could you do such a thing?

RUTH: I couldn't help it. I'd got to the end of bearing things—without talking.

ANDREW: Then Rob must have known every moment I stayed here! And yet he never said or showed— God, how he must have suffered! Didn't you know how much he loved you?

RUTH (*dully*): Yes. I knew he liked me.

ANDREW: Liked you! What kind of a woman are you? Couldn't you have kept silent? Did you have to torture him? No wonder he's dying! And you've lived together for five years with this between you?

RUTH: We've lived in the same house.

ANDREW: Does he still think—

RUTH: I don't know. We've never spoke a word about it since that day. Maybe, from the way he went on, he s'poses I care for you yet.

ANDREW: But you don't. It's outrageous. It's stupid! You don't love me!

RUTH (*slowly*): I wouldn't know how to feel love, even if I tried, any more.

ANDREW (*brutally*): And I don't love you, that's sure! (*He sinks into his chair, his head between his hands*) It's damnable such a thing should be between Rob and me. Why, I love Rob better'n anybody in the world and always did. There isn't a thing on God's green earth I wouldn't have done to keep trouble away from him. And I have to be the very one— it's damnable! How am I going to face him again? What can I say to him now? (*He groans with anguished rage. After a pause*) He asked me to promise—what am I going to do?

RUTH: You can promise—so's it'll ease his mind—and not mean anything.

ANDREW: What? Lie to him now—when he's dying? (*Determinedly*) No! It's *you* who'll have to do the lying, since it must be done. You've got a chance now to undo some of all the suffering you've brought on Rob. Go in to him! Tell him you never loved me—it was all a mistake. Tell him you only said so because you were mad and didn't know what you were saying! Tell him something, anything, that'll bring him peace!

RUTH (*dully*): He wouldn't believe me.

ANDREW (*furiously*): You've got to make him believe you, do you hear? You've got to—now—hurry—

you never know when it may be too late. (*As she hesitates—imploringly*) For God's sake, Ruth! Don't you see you owe it to him? You'll never forgive yourself if you don't.

RUTH (*dully*): I'll go. (*She gets wearily to her feet and walks slowly toward the bedroom*) But it won't do any good. (ANDREW's *eyes are fixed on her anxiously. She opens the door and steps inside the room. She remains standing there for a minute. Then she calls in a frightened voice*) Rob! Where are you? (*Then she hurries back, trembling with fright*) Andy! Andy! He's gone!

ANDREW (*misunderstanding her—his face pale with dread*): He's not—

RUTH (*interrupting him—hysterically*): He's gone! The bed's empty. The window's wide open. He must have crawled out into the yard!

ANDREW (*springing to his feet. He rushes into the bedroom and returns immediately with an expression of alarmed amazement on his face*): Come! He can't have gone far! (*Grabbing his hat he takes* RUTH's *arm and shoves her toward the door*) Come on! (*Opening the door*) Let's hope to God— (*The door closes behind them, cutting off his words as the curtain falls.*)

ACT THREE
Scene 2

Same as Act One, Scene 1—A section of country high-
way. The sky to the east is already alight with bright
color and a thin, quivering line of flame is spreading
slowly along the horizon rim of the dark hills. The
roadside, however, is still steeped in the grayness of the
dawn, shadowy and vague. The field in the foreground
has a wild uncultivated appearance as if it had been
allowed to remain fallow the preceding summer. Parts
of the snake-fence in the rear have been broken down.
The apple tree is leafless and seems dead.

ROBERT *staggers weakly in from the left. He stumbles*
into the ditch and lies there for a moment; then crawls
with a great effort to the top of the bank where he
can see the sun rise, and collapses weakly. RUTH *and*
ANDREW *come hurriedly along the road from the left.*

ANDREW (*stopping and looking about him*): There he
is! I knew it! I knew we'd find him here.

ROBERT (*trying to raise himself to a sitting position as*
they hasten to his side—with a wan smile): I thought
I'd given you the slip.

ANDREW (*with kindly bullying*): Well you didn't, you
old scoundrel, and we're going to take you right
back where you belong—in bed. (*He makes a mo-*
tion to lift ROBERT.)

ROBERT: Don't, Andy. Don't, I tell you!

ANDREW: You're in pain?

ROBERT (*simply*): No. I'm dying. (*He falls back weakly.
RUTH sinks down beside him with a sob and pillows
his head on her lap. ANDREW stands looking down
at him helplessly. ROBERT moves his head restlessly
on RUTH's lap*) I couldn't stand it back there in the
room. It seemed as if all my life—I'd been cooped
in a room. So I thought I'd try to end as I might
have—if I'd had the courage—alone—in a ditch by
the open road—watching the sun rise.

ANDREW: Rob! Don't talk. You're wasting your
strength. Rest a while and then we'll carry you—

ROBERT: Still hoping, Andy? Don't. I know. (*There is
a pause during which he breathes heavily, straining
his eyes toward the horizon*) The sun comes so
slowly. (*With an ironical smile*) The doctor told me
to go to the far-off places—and I'd be cured. He
was right. That was always the cure for me. It's too
late—for this life—but— (*He has a fit of coughing
which racks his body.*)

ANDREW (*with a hoarse sob*): Rob! (*He clenches his
fists in an impotent rage against Fate*) God! God!
(*RUTH sobs brokenly and wipes ROBERT's lips with
her handkerchief.*)

ROBERT (*in a voice which is suddenly ringing with the
happiness of hope*): You mustn't feel sorry for me.
Don't you see I'm happy at last—free—free!—freed
from the farm—free to wander on and on—eter-
nally! (*He raises himself on his elbow, his face radi-
ant, and points to the horizon*) Look! Isn't it
beautiful beyond the hills? I can hear the old voices
calling me to come— (*Exultantly*) And this time I'm
going! It isn't the end. It's a free beginning—the
start of my voyage! I've won to my trip—the right
of release—beyond the horizon! Oh, you ought to
be glad—glad—for my sake! (*He collapses weakly*)

Andy! (ANDREW *bends down to him*) Remember
Ruth—

ANDREW: I'll take care of you, I swear to you, Rob!

ROBERT: Ruth has suffered—remember, Andy—only
through sacrifice—the secret beyond there— (*He
suddenly raises himself with his last remaining
strength and points to the horizon where the edge of
the sun's disc is rising from the rim of the hills*) The
sun! (*He remains with his eyes fixed on it for a moment. A rattling noise throbs from his throat. He
mumbles*) Remember! (*And falls back and is still.
RUTH gives a cry of horror and springs to her feet,
shuddering, her hands over her eyes. ANDREW bends
on one knee beside the body, placing a hand over
ROBERT's heart, then he kisses his brother reveren-
tially on the forehead and stands up.*)

ANDREW (*facing RUTH, the body between them—in a
dead voice*): He's dead. (*With a sudden burst of
fury*) God damn you, you never told him!

RUTH (*piteously*): He was so happy without my lying
to him.

ANDREW (*pointing to the body—trembling with the violence of his rage*): This is your doing, you damn
woman, you coward, you murderess!

RUTH (*sobbing*): Don't, Andy! I couldn't help it—and
he knew how I'd suffered, too. He told you—to
remember.

ANDREW (*stares at her for a moment, his rage ebbing
away, an expression of deep pity gradually coming
over his face. Then he glances down at his brother
and speaks brokenly in a compassionate voice*): Forgive me, Ruth—for his sake—and I'll remember—
(RUTH *lets her hands fall from her face and looks at
him uncomprehendingly. He lifts his eyes to hers and
forces out falteringly*) I—you—we've both made a
mess of things! We must try to help each other—

and—in time—we'll come to know what's right— (*Desperately*) And perhaps we— (*But* RUTH, *if she is aware of his words, gives no sign. She remains silent, gazing at him dully with the sad humility of exhaustion, her mind already sinking back into that spent calm beyond the further troubling of any hope.*)

Curtain

THE EMPEROR JONES

CHARACTERS

BRUTUS JONES, *Emperor*
HENRY SMITHERS, *a Cockney trader*
AN OLD NATIVE WOMAN
LEM, *a Native Chief*
SOLDIERS, *Adherents of Lem*
The Little Formless Fears; Jeff; The Negro Convicts;
The Prison Guard; The Planters; The Auctioneer; The
Slaves; The Congo Witch-Doctor; the Crocodile God

The action of the play takes place on an island in
the West Indies as yet not self-determined by White
Marines. The form of native government is, for the
time being, an Empire.

SCENES

SCENE ONE

The audience chamber in the palace of the Emperor—a spacious, high-ceilinged room with bare, white-washed walls. The floor is of white tiles. In the rear, to the left of center, a wide archway giving out on a portico with white pillars. The palace is evidently situated on high ground for beyond the portico nothing can be seen but a vista of distant hills, their summits crowned with thick groves of palm trees. In the right wall, center, a smaller arched doorway leading to the living quarters of the palace. The room is bare of furniture with the exception of one huge chair made of uncut wood which stands at center, its back to rear. This is very apparently the Emperor's throne. It is painted a dazzling, eye-smiting scarlet. There is a brilliant orange cushion on the seat and another smaller one is placed on the floor to serve as a footstool. Strips of matting, dyed scarlet, lead from the foot of the throne to the two entrances.

It is late afternoon but the sunlight still blazes yellowly beyond the portico and there is an oppressive burden of exhausting heat in the air.

As the curtain rises, a native negro woman sneaks in cautiously from the entrance on the right. She is very old, dressed in cheap calico, bare-footed, a red bandanna handkerchief covering all but a few stray wisps of white hair. A bundle bound in colored cloth is carried over her shoulder on the end of a stick. She hesitates beside the doorway, peering back as if in extreme dread of being discovered. Then she begins to glide noiselessly, a step at a time, toward the doorway in the rear. At this moment, Smithers appears beneath the portico.

Smithers is a tall, stoop-shouldered man about forty. His bald head, perched on a long neck with an enormous Adam's apple, looks like an egg. The tropics have tanned his naturally pasty face with its small, sharp features to a sickly yellow, and native rum has painted his pointed nose to a startling red. His little, washy-blue eyes are red-rimmed and dart about him like a ferret's. His expression is one of unscrupulous meanness, cowardly and dangerous. He is dressed in a worn riding suit of dirty white drill, puttees, spurs, and wears a white cork helmet. A cartridge belt with an automatic revolver is around his waist. He carries a riding whip in his hand. He sees the woman and stops to watch her suspiciously. Then, making up his mind, he steps quickly on tiptoe into the room. The woman, looking back over her shoulder continually, does not see him until it is too late. When she does Smithers springs forward and grabs her firmly by the shoulder. She struggles to get away, fiercely but silently.

SMITHERS (*tightening his grasp—roughly*): Easy! None o' that, me birdie. You can't wriggle out, now I got me 'ooks on yer.

WOMAN (*seeing the uselessness of struggling, gives way to frantic terror, and sinks to the ground, embracing his knees supplicatingly*): No tell him! No tell him, Mister!

SMITHERS (*with great curiosity*): Tell 'im? (*then scornfully*) Oh, you mean 'is bloomin' Majesty. What's the gaime, any'ow? What are you sneakin' away for? Been stealin' a bit, I s'pose. (*He taps her bundle with his riding whip significantly.*)

WOMAN (*shaking her head vehemently*): No, me no steal.

SMITHERS: Bloody liar! But tell me what's up. There's somethin' funny goin' on. I smelled it in the air first thing I got up this mornin'. You blacks are up to some devilment. This palace of 'is is like a bleedin' tomb. Where's all the 'ands? (*The woman keeps sullenly silent. Smithers raises his whip threateningly.*) Ow, yer won't, won't yer? I'll show yer what's what.

WOMAN (*coweringly*): I tell, Mister. You no hit. They go—all go. (*She makes a sweeping gesture toward the hills in the distance.*)

SMITHERS: Run away—to the 'ills?

WOMAN: Yes, Mister. Him Emperor—Great Father. (*She touches her forehead to the floor with a quick mechanical jerk.*) Him sleep after eat. Then they go—all go. Me old woman. Me left only. Now me go too.

SMITHERS (*his astonishment giving way to an immense, mean satisfaction*): Ow! So that's the ticket! Well, I know bloody well wot's in the air—when they runs orf to the 'ills. The tomtom 'll be thumping out there bloomin' soon. (*with extreme vindictiveness*) And I'm bloody glad of it, for one! Serve 'im right! Puttin' on airs, the stinkin' nigger! 'Is Majesty! Gawd blimey! I only 'opes I'm there when they takes 'im out to shoot 'im. (*suddenly*) 'E's still 'ere all right, ain't 'e?

WOMAN: Him sleep.

SMITHERS: 'E's bound to find out soon as 'e wakes up. 'E's cunnin' enough to know when 'is time's come. (*He goes to the doorway on right and whistles shrilly with his fingers in his mouth. The old woman springs to her feet and runs out of the doorway, rear. Smithers goes after her, reaching for his revolver.*) Stop or I'll shoot! (*then stopping—indifferently*) Pop orf then, if yer like, yer black cow. (*He stands in the doorway, looking after her.*)

(*Jones enters from the right. He is a tall, powerfully-built, full-blooded negro of middle age. His features are typically negroid, yet there is something decidedly distinctive about his face—an underlying strength of will, a hardy, self-reliant confidence in himself that inspires respect. His eyes are alive with a keen, cunning intelligence. In manner he is shrewd, suspicious, evasive. He wears a light blue uniform coat, sprayed with brass buttons, heavy gold chevrons on his shoulders, gold braid on the collar, cuffs, etc. His pants are bright red with a light blue stripe down the side. Patent leather laced boots with brass spurs, and a belt with a long-barrelled, pearl-handled revolver in a holster complete his make up. Yet there is something not altogether ridiculous about his grandeur. He has a way of carrying it off.*)

JONES (*not seeing anyone—greatly irritated and blinking sleepily—shouts*): Who dare whistle dat way in my palace? Who dare wake up de Emperor? I'll git de hide frayled off some o' you niggers sho'!

SMITHERS (*showing himself—in a manner half-afraid and half-defiant*): It was me whistled to yer. (*as Jones frowns angrily*) I got news for yer.

JONES (*putting on his suavest manner, which fails to cover up his contempt for the white man*): Oh, it's you, Mister Smithers. (*He sits down on his throne with easy dignity.*) What news you got to tell me?

SMITHERS (*coming close to enjoy his discomfiture*): Don't yer notice nothin' funny today?

JONES (*coldly*): Funny? No. I ain't perceived nothin' of de kind!

SMITHERS: Then yer ain't so foxy as I thought yer was. Where's all your court? (*sarcastically*) the Generals and the Cabinet Ministers and all?

JONES (*imperturbably*): Where dey mostly runs to minute I closes my eyes—drinkin' rum and talkin' big down in de town. (*sarcastically*) How come you don't know dat? Ain't you sousin' with 'em most every day?

SMITHERS (*stung but pretending indifference—with a wink*): That's part of the day's work. I got ter—ain't I—in my business?

JONES (*contemptuously*): Yo' business!

SMITHERS (*imprudently enraged*): Gawd blimey, you was glad enough for me ter take yer in on it when you landed here first. And didn' 'ave no 'igh and mighty airs in them days!

JONES (*his hand going to his revolver like a flash—menacingly*): Talk polite, white man! Talk polite, you heah me! I'm boss heah, now, is you fergettin'? (*The Cockney seems about to challenge this last statement with the facts but something in the other's eyes holds and cows him.*)

SMITHERS (*in a cowardly whine*): No 'arm meant, old top.

JONES (condescendingly): I accep͡t yo' apology. (*lets his hand fall from his revolver*) No use'n you rakin' up ole times. What I was den is one thing. What I is now 's another. You didn't let me in on yo' crooked work out o' no kind feelin's dat time. I done de dirty work fo' you—and most o' de brain work, too, fo' dat matter—and I was wu'th money to you, dat's de reason.

SMITHERS: Well, blimey, I give yer a start, didn't I?—when no one else would. I wasn't afraid to 'ire you like the rest was—'count of the story about your breakin' jail back in the States.

JONES: No, you didn't have no s'cuse to look down on me fo' dat. You been in jail you'self more'n once.

SMITHERS (*furiously*): It's a lie! (*then trying to pass it off by an attempt at scorn*) Garn! Who told yer that fairy tale?

JONES: Dey's some tings I ain't got to be tole. I kin see 'em in folk's eyes. (*then after a pause—meditatively*) Yes, you sho' give me a start. And it didn't take long from dat time to git dese fool, woods' niggers right where I wanted dem. (*with pride*) From stowaway to Emperor in two years! Dat's goin' some!

SMITHERS (*with curiosity*): And I bet you got yer pile o' money 'id safe some place.

JONES (*with satisfaction*): I sho' has! And it's in a foreign bank where no pusson don't ever git it out but me no matter what come. You didn't s'pose I was holdin' down dis Emperor job for de glory in it, did you? Sho'! De fuss and glory part of it, dat's only to turn de heads o' de low-flung, bush niggers dat's here. Dey wants de big circus show for deir money. I gives it to 'em an' I gits de money. (*with a grin*) De long green, dat's me every time! (*then rebukingly*) But you ain't got no kick agin me, Smithers. I'se paid you back all you done for me many times. Ain't I pertected you and winked at all de crooked tradin' you been doin' right out in de broad day? Sho' I has—and me makin' laws to stop it at de same time! (*He chuckles.*)

SMITHERS (*grinning*): But, meanin' no 'arm, you been grabbin' right and left yourself, ain't yer? Look at the taxes you've put on 'em! Blimey! You've squeezed 'em dry!

JONES (*chuckling*): No, dey ain't *all* dry yet. I'se still heah, ain't I?

SMITHERS (*smiling at his secret thought*): They're dry right now, you'll find out. (*changing the subject abruptly*) And as for me breakin' laws, you've broke 'em all yerself just as fast as yer made 'em.

JONES: Ain't I de Emperor? De laws don't go for him. (*judicially*) You heah what I tells you, Smithers. Dere's little stealin' like you does, and dere's big stealin' like I does. For de little stealin' dey gits you in jail soon or late. For de big stealin' dey makes you Emperor and puts you in de Hall o' Fame when you croaks. (*reminiscently*) If dey's one thing I learns in ten years on de Pullman ca's listenin' to de white quality talk, it's dat same fact. And when I gits a chance to use it I winds up Emperor in two years.

SMITHERS (*unable to repress the genuine admiration of the small fry for the large*): Yes, yer turned the bleedin' trick, all right. Blimey, I never seen a bloke 'as 'ad the bloomin' luck you 'as.

JONES (*severely*): Luck? What you mean—luck?

SMITHERS: I suppose you'll say as that swank about the silver bullet ain't luck—and that was what first got to the fool blacks on yer side the time of the revolution, wasn't it?

JONES (*with a laugh*): Oh, dat silver bullet! Sho' was luck! But I makes dat luck, you heah? I loads de dice! Yessuh! When dat murderin' nigger ole Lem hired to kill me takes aim ten feet away and his gun misses fire and I shoots him dead, what you heah me say?

SMITHERS: You said yer'd got a charm so's no lead bullet'd kill yer. You was so strong only a silver bullet could kill yer, you told 'em. Blimey, wasn't that swank for yer—and plain, fat-'eaded luck?

JONES (*proudly*): I got brains and I uses 'em quick. Dat ain't luck.

SMITHERS: Yer know they wasn't 'ardly liable to get no silver bullets. And it was luck 'e didn't 'it you that time.

JONES (*laughing*): And dere all dem fool bush niggers

was kneelin' down and bumpin' deir head on de ground like I was a miracle out o' de Bible. Oh Lawd, from dat time on I has dem all eatin' out of my hand. I cracks de whip and dey jumps through.

SMITHERS (*with a sniff*): Yankee bluff done it.

JONES: Ain't a man's talkin' big what makes him big— long as he makes folks believe it? Sho', I talks large when I ain't got nothin' to back it up, but I ain't talkin' wild just de same. I knows I kin fool 'em— I *know* it—and dat's backin' enough fo' my game. And ain't I got to learn deir lingo and teach some of dem English befo' I kin talk to 'em? Ain't dat wuk? You ain't never learned ary word er it, Smithers, in de ten years you been heah, dough you knows it's money in you' pocket tradin' wid 'em if you does. But you'se too shiftless to take de trouble.

SMITHERS (*flushing*): Never mind about me. What's this I've 'eard about yer really 'avin' a silver bullet moulded for yourself?

JONES: It's playin' out my bluff. I has de silver bullet moulded and I tells 'em when de time comes I kills myself wid it. I tells 'em dat's 'cause I'm de on'y man in de world big enuff to git me. No use'n deir tryin'. And dey falls down and bumps deir heads. (*He laughs.*) I does dat so's I kin take a walk in peace widout no jealous nigger gunnin' at me from behind de trees.

SMITHERS (*astonished*): Then you 'ad it made—'onest?

JONES: Sho' did. Heah she be. (*He takes out his revolver, breaks it and takes the silver bullet out of one chamber.*) Five lead an' dis silver baby at de last. Don't she shine pretty? (*He holds it in his hand, looking at it admiringly, as if strangely fascinated.*)

SMITHERS: Let me see. (*reaches out his hand for it*)

JONES (*harshly*): Keep yo' hands whar dey b'long,

white man. (*He replaces it in the chamber and puts the revolver back on his hip.*)

SMITHERS (*snarling*): Gawd blimey! Think I'm a bleedin' thief, you would.

JONES: No, 'tain't dat. I knows you'se scared to steal from me. On'y I ain't 'lowin' nary body to touch dis baby. She's my rabbit's foot.

SMITHERS (*sneering*): A bloomin' charm, wot? (*venomously*) Well, you'll need all the bloody charms you 'as before long, s' 'elp me!

JONES (*judicially*): Oh, I'se good for six months yit 'fore dey gits sick o' my game. Den, when I sees trouble comin', I makes my getaway.

SMITHERS: Ho! You got it all planned, ain't ycr?

JONES: I ain't no fool. I knows dis Emperor's time is sho't. Dat why I make hay when de sun shine. Was you thinkin' I'se aimin' to hold down dis job for life? No, suh! What good is gittin' money if you stays back in dis raggedy country? I wants action when I spends. And when I sees dese niggers gittin' up deir nerve to tu'n me out, and I'se got all de money in sight, I resigns on de spot and beats it quick.

SMITHERS: Where to?

JONES: None o' yo' business.

SMITHERS: Not back to the bloody States, I'll lay my oath.

JONES (*suspiciously*): Why don't I? (*then with an easy laugh*) You mean 'count of dat story 'bout me breakin' from jail back dere? Dat's all talk.

SMITHERS (*skeptically*): Ho, yes!

JONES (*sharply*): You ain't 'sinuatin' I'se a liar, is you?

SMITHERS (*hastily*): No, Gawd strike me! I was only thinkin' o' the bloody lies you told the blacks 'ere about killin' white men in the States.

JONES (*angered*): How come dey're lies?

SMITHERS: You'd 'ave been in jail if you 'ad, wouldn't yer then? (*with venom*) And from what I'd 'eard, it ain't 'ealthy for a black to kill a white man in the States. They burns 'em in oil, don't they?

JONES (*with cool deadliness*): You mean lynchin' 'd scare me? Well, I tells you, Smithers, maybe I does kill one white man back dere. Maybe I does. And maybe I kills another right heah 'fore long if he don't look out.

SMITHERS (*trying to force a laugh*): I was on'y spoofin' yer. Can't yer take a joke? And you was just sayin' you'd never been in jail.

JONES (*in the same tone—slightly boastful*): Maybe I goes to jail dere for gettin' in an argument wid razors ovah a crap game. Maybe I gits twenty years when dat colored man die. Maybe I gits in 'nother argument wid de prison guard was overseer ovah us when we're wukin' de road. Maybe he hits me wid a whip and I splits his head wid a shovel and runs away and files de chain off my leg and gits away safe. Maybe I does all dat an' maybe I don't. It's a story I tells you so's you knows I'se de kind of man dat if you evah repeats one word of it, I ends you' stealin' on dis yearth mighty damn quick!

SMITHERS (*terrified*): Think I'd peach on yer? Not me! Ain't I always been yer friend?

JONES (*suddenly relaxing*): Sho' you has—and you better be.

SMITHERS (*recovering his composure—and with it his malice*): And just to show yer I'm yer friend, I'll tell yer that bit o' news I was goin' to.

JONES: Go ahead! Shoot de piece. Must be bad news from de happy way you look

SMITHERS (*warningly*): Maybe it's gettin' time for you to resign—with that bloomin' silver bullet, wot? (*He finishes with a mocking grin.*)

JONES (*puzzled*): What's dat you say? Talk plain.

SMITHERS: Ain't noticed any of the guards or servants about the place today, I 'aven't.

JONES (*carelessly*): Dey're all out in de garden sleepin' under deir trees. When I sleeps, dey sneaks a sleep, too, and I pretends I never suspicions it. All I got to do is ring de bell and dey come flyin', makin' a bluff dey was wukin' all de time.

SMITHERS (*in the same mocking tone*): Ring the bell now an' you'll bloody well see what I means.

JONES (*startled to alertness, but preserving the same careless tone*): Sho' I rings. (*He reaches below the throne and pulls out a big, common dinner bell which is painted the same vivid scarlet as the throne. He rings this vigorously—then stops to listen. Then he goes to both doors, rings again, and looks out.*)

SMITHERS (*watching him with malicious satisfaction, after a pause—mockingly*): The bloody ship is sinkin' an' the bleedin' rats 'as slung their 'ooks.

JONES (*in a sudden fit of anger flings the bell clattering into a corner*): Low-flung, woods' niggers! (*Then catching Smithers' eye on him, he controls himself and suddenly bursts into a low chuckle laugh.*) Reckon I overplays my hand dis once! A man can't take de pot on a bob-tailed flush all de time. Was I sayin' I'd sit in six months mo'? Well, I'se changed my mind den. I cashes in and resigns de job of Emperor right dis minute.

SMITHERS (*with real admiration*): Blimey, but you're a cool bird, and no mistake.

JONES: No use'n fussin'. When I knows de game's up I kisses it good-by widout no long waits. Dey've all run off to de hills, ain't dey?

SMITHERS: Yes—every bleedin' man jack of 'em.

JONES: Den de revolution is at de post. And de Em-

peror better git his feet smokin' up de trail. (*He
starts for the door in rear.*)

SMITHERS: Goin' out to look for your 'orse? Yer won't
find any. They steals the 'orses first thing. Mine was
gone when I went for 'im this mornin'. That's wot
first give me a suspicion of wot was up.

JONES (*alarmed for a second, scratches his head, then
philosophically*) Well, den I hoofs it. Feet, do yo'
duty! (*He pulls out a gold watch and looks at it.*)
Three-thuty. Sundown's at six-thuty or dereabouts.
(*puts his watch back—with cool confidence*) I got
plenty o' time to make it easy.

SMITHERS: Don't be so bloomin' sure of it. They'll be
after you 'ot and 'eavy. Ole Lem is at the bottom
o' this business an' 'e 'ates you like 'ell. 'E'd rather
do for you than eat 'is dinner, 'e would!

JONES (*scornfully*): Dat fool no-count nigger! Does
you think I'se scared o' him? I stands him on his
thick head more'n once befo' dis, and I does it again
if he comes in my way— (*fiercely*) And dis time I
leave him a dead nigger fo' sho'!

SMITHERS: You'll 'ave to cut through the big forest—
an' these blacks 'ere can sniff and follow a trail in
the dark like 'ounds. You'd 'ave to 'ustle to get
through that forest in twelve hours even if you knew
all the bloomin' trails like a native.

JONES (*with indignant scorn*): Look-a-heah, white man!
Does you think I'se a natural bo'n fool? Give me
credit fo' havin' some sense, fo' Lawd's sake! Don't
you s'pose I'se looked ahead and made so' of all de
chances? I'se gone out in dat big forest, pretendin'
to hunt, so many times dat I knows it high an' low
like a book. I could go through on dem trails wid
my eyes shut. (*with great contempt*) Think dese ign'-
rent bush niggers dat ain't got brains enuff to make
deir own names even can catch Brutus Jones? Huh,

I s'pects not! Not on yo' life! Why, man, de whit men went after me wid bloodhounds where I come from an' I jes' laughs at 'em. It's a shame to fool dese black trash around heah, dey're so easy. You watch me, man. I'll make dem look sick, I will. I'll be 'cross de plain to de edge of de forest by time dark comes. Once in de woods in de night, dey got a swell chance o' findin' dis baby! Dawn tomorrow I'll be out at de oder side and on de coast whar dat French gunboat is stayin'. She picks me up, takes me to Martinique when she go dar, and dere I is safe wid a mighty big bankroll in my jeans. It's easy as rollin' off a log.

SMITHERS (*maliciously*): But s'posin' somethin' 'appens wrong 'an they do nab yer?

JONES (*decisively*): Dey don't—dat's de answer.

SMITHERS: But, just for agyment's sake—what'd you do?

JONES (*frowning*): I'se for five lead bullets in dis gun good enuff fo' common bush niggers—and after dat I got de silver bullet left to cheat 'em out o' gittin' me.

SMITHERS (*jeeringly*): Ho, I was fergettin' that silver bullet. You'll bump yourself orf in style, won't yer? Blimey!

JONES (*gloomily*): You kin bet yo' whole roll on one thing, white man. Dis baby plays out his string on de end and when he quits, he quits wid a bang de way he ought. Silver bullet ain't none too good for him when he go, dat's a fac'! (*then shaking off his nervousness—with a confident laugh*) Sho'! What is I talkin' about? Ain't come to dat yit and I never will—not wid trash niggers like dese yere. (*boastfully*) Silver bullet bring me luck anyway. I kin outguess, outrun, an' outplay de whole lot o' dem all ovah de board any time o' de day er night! You watch me! (*From the distant hills comes the faint, steady thump of a tom-tom, low and vibrating. It starts at a rate exactly corresponding to normal pulse beat—72 to the minute—and continues at a gradually accelerating rate from this point uninterruptedly to the very end of the play. Jones starts at the sound. A strange look of apprehension creeps into his face for a moment as he listens. Then he asks, with an attempt to regain his most casual manner*) What'd dat drum beatin' fo'?

SMITHERS (*with a mean grin*): For you. That means the bleedin' ceremony 'as started. I've 'eard it before and I knows.

JONES: Cer'mony? What cer'mony?

SMITHERS: The blacks is 'oldin' a bloody meetin', 'avin' a war dance, gettin' their courage worked up b'fore they starts after you.

JONES: Let dem! Dey'll sho' need it!

SMITHERS: And they're there 'oldin' their 'eathen religious service—makin' no end of devil spells and charms to 'elp 'em against your silver bullet. (*He guffaws loudly.*) Blimey, but they're balmy as 'ell!

JONES (*a tiny bit awed and shaken in spite of himself*): Huh! Takes more'n dat to scare dis chicken!

SMITHERS (*scenting the other's feeling—maliciously*): Ternight when it's pitch black in the forest, they'll 'ave their pet devils and ghosts 'oundin' after you. You'll find yer bloody 'air 'll be standin' on end before termorrow mornin'. (*seriously*) It's a bleedin' queer place, that stinkin' forest, even in daylight. Yer don't know what might 'appen in there, it's that rotten still. Always sends the cold shivers down my back minute I gets in it.

JONES (*with a contemptuous sniff*): I ain't no chicken-liver like you is. Trees an' me, we'se friends, and dar's a full moon comin' bring me light. And let dem po' niggers make all de fool spells dey'se a min' to. Does yo' s'pect I'se silly enuff to b'lieve in ghosts an' ha'nts an' all dat ole woman's talk? G'long, white man! You ain't talkin' to me. (*with a chuckle*) Doesn't you know dey's got to do wid a man was member in good standin' o' de Baptist Church? Sho' I was dat when I was porter on de Pullmans, befo' I gits into my little trouble. Let dem try der heathen tricks. De Baptist Church done perfect me and land dem all in hell. (*then with more confident satisfaction*) And I'se got little silver bullet o' my own don't forgit!

SMITHERS: Ho! You 'aven't give much 'eed to your Baptist Church since you been down 'ere. I've 'eard myself you 'ad turned yer coat an' was takin' up with their blarsted witch-doctors, or whatever the 'ell yer calls the swine.

JONES (*vehemently*): I pretends to! Sho' I pretends! Dat's part o' my game from de fust. If I finds out dem niggers believes dat black is white, den I yells it out louder 'n deir loudest. It don't git me nothin' to do missionary work for de Baptist Church. I'se after de coin, an' I lays me Jesus on de shelf for de time bein'. (*stops abruptly to look at his watch—alertly*) But I ain't got de time to waste on no more fool talk wid you. I'se gwine away from heah dis secon'. (*He reaches in under the throne and pulls out an expensive Panama hat with a bright multi-colored band and sets it jauntily on his head.*) So long, white man! (*with a grin*) See you in jail sometime, maybe!

SMITHERS: Not me, you won't. Well, I wouldn't be in yer bloody boots for no bloomin' money, but 'ere's wishin' yer luck just the same.

JONES (*contemptuously*): You're de frightenedest man evah I see! I tells you I'se safe's 'f I was in New York City. It takes dem niggers from now to dark to git up de nerve to start somethin'. By dat time, I'se got a head start dey never kotch up wid.

SMITHERS (*maliciously*): Give my regards to any ghosts yer meets up with.

JONES (*grinning*): If dat ghost got money, I'll tell him never ha'nt you less'n he wants to lose it.

SMITHERS (*flattered*): Garn! (*then curiously*) Ain't yer takin' no luggage with yer?

JONES: I travels light when I wants to move fast. And I got tinned grub buried on de edge o' de forest. (*boastfully*) Now say dat I don't look ahead an' use my brains! (*with a wide, liberal gesture*) I will all dat's left in de palace to you—and you better grab all you kin sneak away wid befo' dey gits here.

SMITHERS (*gratefully*): Righto—and thanks ter yer. (*as Jones walks toward the door in rear—cautiously*) Say! Look 'ere, you ain't goin' out that way, are yer?

JONES: Does you think I'd slink out de back door like a common nigger? I'se Emperor yit, ain't I? And de Emperor Jones leaves de way he comes, and dat black trash don't dare stop him—not yit, leastways. (*He stops for a moment in the doorway, listening to the far-off but insistent beat of the tom-tom.*) Listen to dat roll-call, will you? Must be mighty big drum carry dat far. (*then with a laugh*) Well, if dey ain't no whole brass band to see me off, I sho' got de drum part of it. So long, white man. (*He puts his hands in his pockets and with studied carelessness, whistling a tune, he saunters out of the doorway and off to the left.*)

SMITHERS (*looks after him with a puzzled admiration*):

'E's got 'is bloomin' nerve with 'im, s'elp me! (*then angrily*) Ho—the bleedin' nigger—puttin' on 'is bloody airs! I 'opes they nabs 'im an' gives 'im what's what!

(*Curtain*)

SCENE TWO

*The end of the plain where the Great Forest begins.
The foreground is sandy, level ground dotted by a few
stones and clumps of stunted bushes cowering close
against the earth to escape the buffeting of the trade
wind. In the rear of the forest is a wall of darkness
dividing the world. Only when the eye becomes accustomed to the gloom can the outlines of separate trunks
of the nearest trees be made out, enormous pillars of
deeper blackness. A somber monotone of wind lost in
the leaves moans in the air. Yet this sound serves but
to intensify the impression of the forest's relentless im-
mobility, to form a background throwing into relief its
brooding, implacable silence.*

*Jones enters from the left, walking rapidly. He stops
as he nears the edge of the forest, looks around him
quickly, peering into the dark as if searching for some
familiar landmark. Then, apparently satisfied that he is
where he ought to be, he throws himself on the ground,
dog-tired.*

Well, heah I is. In de nick o' time, too! Little mo'
an' it'd be blacker'n de ace of spades heahabouts. (*He
pulls a bandana handkerchief from his hip pocket and
mops off his perspiring face.*) Sho'! Gimme air! I'se
tuckered out sho' 'nuff. Dat soft Emperor job ain't no
trainin' fo' a long hike ovah dat plain in de brilin' sun
(*then with a chuckle*) Cheer up, nigger, de worst is yet

to come. (*He lifts his head and stares at the forest. His chuckle peters out abruptly. In a tone of awe*) My goodness, look at dem woods, will you? Dat no-count Smithers said dey'd be black an' he sho' called de turn. (*Turning away from them quickly and looking down at his feet, he snatches at a chance to change the subject—solicitously*) Feet, you is holdin' up yo' end fine an' I sutinly hopes you ain't blistern' none. It's time you git a rest. (*He takes off his shoes, his eyes studiously avoiding the forest. He feels of the soles of his feet gingerly.*) You is still in de pink—on'y a little mite feverish. Cool yo'selfs. Remember you done got a long journey yit befo' you. (*He sits in a weary attitude, listening to the rhythmic beating of the tom-tom. He grumbles in a loud tone to cover up a growing uneasiness*) Bush niggers! Wonder dey wouldn't git sick o' beatin' dat drum. Sound louder, seem like. I wonder if dey's startin' after me? (*He scrambles to his feet, looking back across the plain.*) Couldn't see dem now, nohow, if dey was hundred feet away. (*then shaking himself like a wet dog to get rid of these depressing thoughts*) Sho', dey's miles an' miles behind. What you gittin' fidgety about? (*But he sits down and begins to lace up his shoes in great haste, all the time muttering reassuringly.*) You know what? Yo' belly is empty, dat's what's de matter wid you. Come time to eat! Wid nothin' but wind on yo' stumach, o' course you feels jiggedy. Well, we eats right heah an' now soon's I gits dese pesky shoes laced up. (*He finishes lacing up his shoes.*) Dere! Now le's see! (*gets on his hands and knees and searches the ground around him with his eyes*) White stone, white stone, where is you? (*He sees the first white stone and crawls to it—with satisfaction*) Heah you is! I knowed dis was de right place. Box of grub, come to me. (*He turns over the stone and feels in under it—in a tone of dismay*) Ain't heah!

Gorry, is I in de right place or isn't I? Dere's 'nother stone. Guess dat's it. (*He scrambles to the next stone and turns it over.*) Ain't heah, neither! Grub, whar is you? Ain't heah. Gorry, has I got to go hungry into dem woods—all de night? (*While he is talking he scrambles from one stone to another, turning them over in frantic haste. Finally, he jumps to his feet excitedly.*) Is I lost de place? Must have! But how dat happen when I was followin' de trail across de plain in broad daylight? (*almost plaintively*) I'se hungry, I is! I gotta git my feed. Whar's my strength gonna come from if I doesn't? Gorry, I gotta find dat grub high an' low somehow! Why it come dark so quick like dat? Can't see nothing'. (*He scratches a match on his trousers and peers about him. The rate of the beat of the far-off tom-tom increases perceptibly as he does so. He mutters in a bewildered voice*) How come all dese white stones come heah when I only remembers one? (*Suddenly, with a frightened gasp, he flings the match on the ground and stamps on it.*) Nigger, is you gone crazy mad? Is you lightin' matches to show dem whar you is? Fo' Lawd's sake, use yo' haid. Gorry, I'se got to be careful! (*He stares at the plain behind him apprehensively, his hand on his revolver.*) But how come all dese white stones? And whar's dat tin box o' grub I hid all wrapped up in oilcloth?

(*While his back is turned, the Little Formless Fears creep out from the deeper blackness of the forest. They are black, shapeless, only their glittering little eyes can be seen. If they have any describable form at all it is that of a grubworm about the size of a creeping child. They move noiselessly, but with deliberate, painful effort, striving to raise themselves on end, failing and sinking prone again. Jones turns about to face the forest. He stars up to the tops of the trees, seeking vainly to discover his whereabouts by their conformation.*)

Can't tell nothin' from dem trees! Gorry, nothin' 'round heah looks like I ev*ah* seed it befo'. I'se done lost de place sho' 'uff! (*with mournful foreboding*) It's mighty queer! It's mighty queer! (*with sudden forced defiance—in an angry tone*) Woods, is you tryin' to put somethin' ovah on me?

(*From the formless creatures on the ground in front of him comes a tiny gale of low mocking laughter like a rustling of leaves. They squirm upward toward him in twisted attitudes. Jones looks down, leaps backward with a yell of terror, yanking out his revolver as he does so—in a quavering voice*) What's dat? Who's dar? What is you? Git away from me befo' I shoots you up! You don't?—

(*He fires. There is a flash, a loud report, then silence broken only by the far-off, quickened throb of the tom-tom. The formless creatures have scurried back into the forest. Jones remains fixed in his position, listening intently. The sound of the shot, the reassuring feel of the revolver in his hand, have somewhat restored his shaken nerve. He addresses himself with renewed confidence.*)

Dey're gone. Dat shot fix 'em. Dey was only little animals—little wild pigs, I reckon. Dey've maybe rooted out yo' grub an' eat it. Sho', you fool nigger, what you think dey is—ha'nts? (*excitedly*) Gorry, you give de game away when you fire dat shot. Dem niggers heah dat fo' su'tin! Time you beat it in de woods widout no long waits. (*He starts for the forest—hesitates before the plunge—then urging himself in with manful resolution*) Git in, nigger! What you skeered at? Ain't nothin' dere but de trees! Git in! (*He plunges boldly into the forest.*)

SCENE THREE

In the forest. The moon has just risen. Its beams, drift-ing through the canopy of leaves, make a barely percep-tibly, suffused, eerie glow. A dense low wall of underbrush and creepers is in the nearest foreground, fencing in a small triangular clearing. Beyond this is the massed blackness of the forest like an encompassing barrier. A path is dimly discerned leading down to the clearing from left, rear, and wind away from it again toward the right. As the scene opens nothing can be distinctly made out. Except for the beating of the tom-tom, which is a trifle louder and quicker than at the close of the previous scene, there is silence, broken every few seconds by a queer, clicking sound. Then gradually the figure of the negro, Jeff, can be discerned crouching on his haunches at the rear of the triangle. He is middle-aged, thin, brown in color, is dressed in a Pullman porter's uniform and cap. He is throwing a pair of dice on the ground before him, picking them up, shaking them, casting them out with the regular, rigid, mechanical movements of an automaton. The heavy, plodding footsteps of someone approaching along the trail from the left are heard and Jones' voice, pitched on a slightly higher key and strained in a cheery effort to overcome its own tremors.

De moon's rizen. Does you heah dat, nigger? You gits more light from dis out. No mo' buttin' yo' fool head agin' de trunks an' scratchin' de hide off yo' legs in de bushes. Now you sees whar yo'se gwine. So cheer up! From now on you has a snap. (*He steps just to the rear of the triangular clearing and mops off his face on his sleeve. He has lost his Panama hat. His face is scratched, his brilliant uniform shows several large rents.*) What time's it gittin to be, I wonder? I dassent light no match to find out. Phoo'. It's wa'm an' dat's a fac'! (*wearily*) How long I been makin' tracks in dese woods? Must be hours an' hours. Seems like fo'evah! Yit can't be, when de moon's jes' riz. Dis am a long night fo' yo', yo' Majesty! (*with a mournful chuckle*) Majesty! Der ain't much majesty 'bout dis baby now. (*with attempted cheerfulness*) Never min'. It's all part o' de game. Dis night come to an end like everything else. And when you gits dar safe and has dat bankroll in yo' hands you laughs at all dis. (*He starts to whistle but checks himself abruptly.*) What yo' whistlin' for, you po' dope! Want all de worl' to heah you? (*He stops talking to listen.*) Heah dat ole drum! Sho' gits nearer from de sound. Dey's packin' it along wid 'em. Time fo' me to move. (*He takes a step forward, then stops—worriedly.*) What's dat odder queer clickety sound I heah? Dere it is! Sound close! Sound like—sound like—Fo' God sake, sound like some nigger was shootin' crap! (*frightenedly*) I better beat it quick when I gits dem notions. (*He walks quickly into the clear space—then stands transfixed as he sees Jeff— in a terrified gasp*) Who dar? Who dat? Is dat you, Jeff? (*starting toward the others, forgetful for a moment of his surroundings and really believing it is a living man that he sees—in a tone of happy relief*) Jeff! I'se sho' mighty glad to see you! Dey tol' me you done died from dat razor cut I gives you. (*stopping suddenly, bewilderedly*) But how you come to be heah, nigger? (*He stares fascinatedly at the other who contin-*

ues his mechanical play with the dice. Jones' eyes begin to roll wildly. He stutters) Ain't you gwine—look up— can't you speak to me? Is you—is you—a ha'nt? (*He jerks out his revolver in a frenzy of terrified rage.*) Nigger, I kills you dead once. Has I got to kill you ag'in? You take it den. (*He fires. When the smoke clears away Jeff has disappeared. Jones stands trembling—then with a certain reassurance*) He's gone, anyway. Ha'nt or not ha'nt, dat shot fix him. (*The beat of the far-off tom-tom is perceptibly louder and more rapid. Jones becomes conscious of it—with a start, looking back over his shoulder*) Dey's gittin' near! Dey's comin' fast! And heah I is shootin' shots to let 'em knows jes' whar I is! Oh, Gorry, I'se got to run. (*Forgetting the path he plunges wildly into the underbrush in the rear and disappears in the shadow.*)

SCENE FOUR

In the forest. A wide dirt road runs diagonally from right, front, to left, rear. Rising sheer on both sides the forest walls it in. The moon is now up. Under its light the road glimmers ghastly and unreal. It is as if the forest had stood aside momentarily to let the road pass through and accomplish its veiled purpose. This done, the forest will fold in upon itself again and the road will be no more. Jones stumbles in from the forest on the right. His uniform is ragged and torn. He looks about him with numbed surprise when he sees the road, his eyes blinking in the bright moonlight. He flops down exhaustedly and pants heavily for a while. Then with sudden anger

I'm meltin' wid heat! Runnin' an' runnin' an' runnin'! Damn dis heah coat! Like a straitjacket! (*He tears off his coat and flings it away from him, revealing himself stripped to the waist.*) Dere! Dat's better! Now I kin breathe! (*looking down at his feet, the spurs catch his eye*) And to hell wid dese high-fangled spurs. Dey're what's been a-trippin' me up an' breakin' my neck. (*He unstraps them and flings them away disgustedly.*) Dere! I gits rid o' dem frippety Emperor trappin's an' I travels lighter. Lawd! I'se tired! (*after a pause, listening to the insistent beat of the tom-tom in the distance*) I must 'a' put some distance between myself an' dem—runnin' like dat—and yit—dat damn

137

drum sounds jes' de same—nearer, even. Well, I guess
I a'most holds my lead anyhow. Dey won't never catch
up. (*with a sigh*) If on'y my fool legs stands up. Oh,
I'se sorry I evah went in for dis. Dat Emperor job is
sho' hard to shake. (*He looks around him suspiciously.*) How'd dis road evah git heah? Good level
road, too. I never remembers seein' it befo'. (*shaking
his head apprehensively*) Dese woods is sho' full o' de
queerest things at night. (*with a sudden terror*) Lawd
God, don't let me see no more o' dem ha'nts! Dey
gits my goat! (*then trying to talk himself into confidence*) Ha'nts! You fool nigger, dey ain't no such
things! Don't de Baptist parson tell you dat many
time? Is you civilized, or is you like dese ign'rent black
niggers heah? Sho'! Dat was all in yo' own head.
Wasn't nothin' dere. Wasn't no Jeff! Know what? You
jus' get seein' dem things 'cause yo' belly's empty and
yo's sick wid hunger inside. Hunger 'fects yo' head
and yo' eyes. Any fool know dat. (*then pleading fer-
vently*) But bless God, I don't come across no more
o' dem, whatever dey is! (*then cautiously*) Rest! Don't
talk! Rest! You needs it. Den you gits on yo' way
again. (*looking at the moon*) Night's half gone a'most.
You hit de coast in de mawning! Den you's all safe.

(*From the right forward a small gang of negroes
enter. They are dressed in striped convict suits, their
heads are shaven, one leg drags limpingly, shackled to
a heavy ball and chain. Some carry picks, the others
shovels. They are followed by a white man dressed in
the uniform of a prison guard. A Winchester rifle is
slung across his shoulders and he carries a heavy whip.
At a signal from the guard they stop on the road opposite where Jones is sitting. Jones, who has been staring
up at the sky, unmindful of their noiseless approach,
suddenly looks down and sees them. His eyes pop out,
he tries to get to his feet and fly, but sinks back, too*

*numbed by fright to move. His voice catches in a chok-
ing prayer.)*

Lawd Jesus!

*(The prison guard cracks his whip—noiselessly—and
at that signal all the convicts start to work on the road.
They swing their picks, they shovel, but not a sound
comes from their labor. Their movements, like those of
Jeff in the preceding scene, are those of automatons,—
rigid, slow, and mechanical. The prison guard points
sternly at Jones with his whip, motions him to take his
place among the other shovelers. Jones gets to his feet
in a hypnotized stupor. He mumbles subserviently)*

Yes, suh! Yes, suh! I'se comin'.

*(As he shuffles, dragging one foot, over to his place,
he curses under his breath with rage and hatred.)*

God damn yo' soul, I gits even wid you yit,
sometime.

*(As if there were a shovel in his hands he goes
through weary, mechanical gestures of digging up dirt,
and throwing it to the roadside. Suddenly the guard
approaches him angrily, threateningly. He raises his
whip and lashes Jones viciously across the shoulders
with it. Jones winces with pain and cowers abjectly. The
guard turns his back on him and walks away contemptuously. Instantly Jones straightens up. With arms up-
raised as if his shovel were a club in his hands he
springs murderously at the unsuspecting guard. In the
act of crashing down his shovel on the white man's
skull, Jones suddenly become aware that his hands are
empty. He cries despairingly)*

Whar's my shovel? Gimme my shovel 'til I splits his
damn head! *(appealing to his fellow convicts)* Gimme
a shovel, one o' you, fo' God's sake!

*(They stand fixed in motionless attitudes, their eyes
on the ground. The guard seems to wait expectantly, his*

*back turned to the attacker. Jones bellows with baffled,
terrified rage, tugging frantically at his revolver.)*

I kills you, you white debil, if it's de last thing I
evah does! Ghost or debil, I kill you again!

*(He fires the revolver and fires point blank at the
guard's back. Instantly the walls of the forest close in
from both sides, the road and the figures of the convict
gang are blotted out in an enshrouding darkness. The
only sounds are a crashing in the underbrush as Jones
leaps away in mad flight and the throbbing of the tom-
tom, still far distant, but increased in volume of sound
and rapidity of beat.)*

SCENE FIVE

A large circular clearing, enclosed by the serried ranks of gigantic trunks of tall trees whose tops are lost to view. In the center is a big dead stump worn by time into a curious resemblance to an auction block. The moon floods the clearing with a clear light. Jones forces his way in through the forest on the left. He looks wildly about the clearing with hunted, fearful glances. His pants are in tatters, his shoes are cut and misshapen, flapping about his feet. He slinks cautiously to the stump in the center and sits down in a tense position, ready for instant flight. Then he holds his head in his hands and rocks back and forth, moaning to himself miserably.

Oh Lawd, Lawd! Oh Lawd, Lawd! (*Suddenly he throws himself on his knees and raises his clasped hands to the sky—in a voice of agonized pleading*) Lawd Jesus, heah my prayer! I'se a po' sinner, a po' sinner! I knows I done wrong, I knows it! When I cotches Jeff cheatin' wid loaded dice my anger overcomes me and I kills him dead! Lawd, I done wrong! When dat guard hits me wid de whip, my anger overcomes me, and I kills him dead. Lawd, I done wrong! And down heah whar dese fool bush niggers raises me up to the seat o' de mighty, I steals all I could grab. Lawd, I done wrong! I knows it! I'se sorry! Forgive me, Lawd! Forgive dis po' sinner! (*then beseech-*

ing terrifiedly) And keep dem away, Lawd! Keep dem away from me! And stop dat drum soundin' in my ears! Dat begin to sound ha'nted, too. (*He gets to his feet, evidently slightly reassured by his prayer—with attempted confidence*) De Lawd'll preserve me from dem ha'nts after dis. (*sits down on the stump again*) I ain't skeered o' real men. Let dem come. But dem odders— (*He shudders—then looks down at his feet, working his toes inside the shoes—with a groan*) Oh, my po' feet! Dem shoes ain't no use no more 'ceptin' to hurt. I'se better off widout dem. (*He unlaces them and pulls them off—holds the wrecks of the shoes in his hands and regards them mournfully.*) You was real, A-one patin' leather, too. Look at you now. Emperor, you'se gittin' mighty low!

(*He sighs dejectedly and remains with bowed shoulders, staring down at the shoes in his hands as if reluctant to throw them away. While his attention is thus occupied, a crowd of figures silently enter the clearing from all sides. All are dressed in Southern costumes of the period of the fifties of the last century. There are middle-aged men who are evidently well-to-do planters. There is one spruce, authoritative individual—the auctioneer. There is a crowd of curious spectators, chiefly young belles and dandies who have come to the slave-market for diversion. All exchange courtly greetings in dumb show and chat silently together. There is something stiff, rigid, unreal, marionettish about their movements. They group themselves about the stump. Finally a batch of slaves is led in from the left by an attendant—three men of different ages, two women, one with a baby in her arms, nursing. They are placed to the left of the stump, beside Jones.*

(*The white planters look them over appraisingly as if they were cattle, and exchange judgments on each.*

The dandies point with their fingers and make witty remarks. The belles titter bewitchingly. All this is in silence save for the ominous throb of the tom-tom. The auctioneer holds up his hand, taking his place at the stump. The groups strain forward attentively. He touches Jones on the shoulder peremptorily, motioning for him to stand on the stump—the auction block.

(Jones looks up, sees the figures on all sides, looks wildly for some opening to escape, sees none, screams and leaps madly to the top of the stump to get as far away from them as possible. He stands there, cowering, paralyzed with horror. The auctioneer begins his silent spiel. He points to Jones, appeals to the planters to see for themselves. Here is a good field hand, sound in wind and limb as they can see. Very strong still in spite of his being middle-aged. Look at that back. Look at those shoulders. Look at the muscles in his arms and his sturdy legs. Capable of any amount of hard labor. Moreover, of a good disposition, intelligent and tractable. Will any gentleman start the bidding? The planters raise their fingers, make their bids. They are apparently all eager to possess Jones. The bidding is lively, the crowd interested. While this has been going on, Jones has been seized by the courage of desperation. He dares to look down and around him. Over his face abject terror gives way to mystification, to gradual realization—stutteringly)

What you all doin', white folks? What's all dis? What you all lookin' at me fo'? What you doin' wid me, anyhow? *(suddenly convulsed with raging hatred and fear)* Is dis a auction? Is you sellin' me like dey uster befo' de war? *(jerking out his revolver just as the auctioneer knocks him down to one of the planters—glaring from him to the purchaser)* And *you* sells me? And *you* buys me? I shows you I'se a free nigger,

damn yo' souls! (*He fires at the auctioneer and at the planter with such rapidity that the two shots are almost simultaneous. As if this were a signal the walls of the forest fold in. Only blackness remains and silence broken by Jones as he rushes off, crying with fear—and by the quickened, ever louder beat of the tom-tom.*)

SCENE SIX

A cleared space in the forest. The limbs of the trees meet over it forming a low ceiling about five feet from the ground. The interlocked ropes of creepers reaching upward to entwine the tree trunks give an arched appearance to the sides. The space thus enclosed is like the dark, noisome hold of some ancient vessel. The moonlight is almost completely shut out and only a vague wan light filters through. There is the noise of someone approaching from the left, stumbling and crawling through the undergrowth. Jones' voice is heard between chattering moans.

Oh, Lawd, what I gwine do now? Ain't got no bullet left on'y de silver one. If mo' o' dem ha'nts come after me, how I gwine skeer dem away? Oh, Lawd, on'y de silver one left—an' I gotta save dat fo' luck. If I shoots dat one I'm a goner sho'! Lawd, it's black heah! What's de moon? Oh, Lawd, don't dis night evah come to an end! (*By the sounds, he is feeling his way cautiously forward.*) Dere! Dis feels like a clear space. I gotta lie down an' rest. I don't care if dem niggers does cotch me. I gotta rest.

(*He is well forward now when his figure can be dimly made out. His pants have been so torn away that what is left of them is no better than a breech cloth. He flings himself full length, face downward, on the ground, panting with exhaustion. Gradually it seems to*

145

grow lighter in the enclosed space and two rows of seated figures can be seen behind Jones. They are sitting in crumpled, despairing attitudes, hunched, facing one another with their backs touching the forest walls as if they were shackled to them. All are negroes, naked save for loin cloths. At first they are silent and motionless. Then they begin to sway slowly forward toward each other and back again in unison, as if they were laxly letting themselves follow the long roll of a ship at sea. At the same time, a low, melancholy murmur rises among them, increasing gradually by rhythmic degrees which seem to be directed and controlled by the throb of the tom-tom in the distance, to a long, tremulous wail of despair that reaches a certain pitch, unbearably acute, then falls by slow gradations of tone into silence and is taken up again. Jones starts, looks up, sees the figures, and throws himself down again to shut out the sight. A shudder of terror shakes his whole body as the wail rises up about him again. But the next time, his voice, as if under some uncanny compulsion, starts with the others. As their chorus lifts he rises to a sitting posture similar to the others, swaying back and forth. His voice reaches the highest pitch of sorrow, of desolation. The light fades out, the other voices cease, and only darkness is left. Jones can be heard scrambling to his feet and running off, his voice sinking down the scale and receding as he moves farther and farther away in the forest. The tom-tom beats louder, quicker, with a more insistent, triumphant pulsation.)

SCENE SEVEN

The foot of a gigantic tree by the edge of a great river. A rough structure of boulders, like an altar, is by the tree. The raised river bank is in the nearer background. Beyond this the surface of the river spreads out, brilliant and unruffled in the moonlight, blotted out and merged into a veil of bluish mist in the distance. Jones' voice is heard from the left rising and falling in the long, despairing wail of the chained slaves, to the rhythmic beat of the tom-tom. As his voice sinks into silence, he enters the open space. The expression of his face is fixed and stony, his eyes have an obsessed glare, he moves with a strange deliberation like a sleep-walker or one in a trance. He looks around at the tree, the rough stone altar, the moonlight surface of the river beyond, and passes his hand over his head with a vague gesture of puzzled bewilderment. Then, as if in obedience to some obscure impulse, he sinks into a kneeling, devotional posture before the altar. Then he seems to come to himself partly, to have an uncertain realization of what he is doing, for he straightens up and stares about him horrifiedly—in an incoherent mumble

What—what is I doin'? What is—dis place? Seems like I know dat tree—an' dem stones—an' de river. I remember—seems like I been heah befo'. (*trembling*) Oh, Gorry, I'se skeered in dis place! I'se skeered. Oh, Lawd, pertect dis sinner!

(*Crawling away from the altar, he cowers close to the ground, his face hidden, his shoulders heaving with sobs of hysterical fright. From behind the trunk of the tree, as if he had sprung out of it, the figure of the Congo witch-doctor appears. He is wizened and old, naked except for the fur of some small animal tied about his waist, is bushy tail hanging down in front. His body is stained all over a bright red. Antelope horns are on each side of his head, branching upward. In one hand he carries a bone rattle, in the other a charm stick with a bunch of white cockatoo feathers tied to the end. A great number of glass beads and bone ornaments are about his neck, ears, wrists, and ankles. He struts noiselessly with a queer prancing step to a position in the clear ground between Jones and the altar. Then with a preliminary, summoning stamp of his foot on the earth, he begins to dance and to chant. As if in response to his summons the beating of the tom-tom grows to a fierce, exultant boom whose throbs seem to fill the air with vibrating rhythm. Jones looks up, starts to spring to his feet, reaches a half-kneeling, half-squatting position and remains rigidly fixed there, paralyzed with awed fascination by this new apparition. The witch-doctor sways, stamping with his foot, his bone rattle clicking the time. His voice rises and falls in a weird, monotonous croon, without articulate word divisions. Gradually his dance becomes clearly one of a narrative in pantomime, his croon is an incantation, a charm to allay the fierceness of some impalpable deity damaging sacrifice. He flees, he is pursued by devils, he hides, he flees again. Ever wilder and wilder becomes his flight, nearer and nearer draws the pursuing evil, more and more the spirit of terror gains possession of him. His croon, rising to intensity, is punctuated by shrill cries. Jones has become completely hypnotized. His voice joins in the incantation, in the cries, he beats time with*

*his hands and sways his body to and fro from the waist.
The whole spirit and meaning of the dance has entered
into him, has become his spirit. Finally the theme of
the pantomime halts on a howl of despair, and is taken
up again in a note of savage hope. There is a salvation.
The forces of evil demand sacrifice. They must be appeased. The witch-doctor points with his wand to the
sacred tree, to the river beyond, to the altar, and finally
to Jones with a ferocious command. Jones seems to
sense the meaning of this. It is he who must offer himself for sacrifice. He beats his forehead abjectly to the
ground, moaning hysterically)*

Mercy, Oh Lawd! Mercy! Mercy on dis po' sinner.

*(The witch-doctor springs to the river bank. He
stretches out his arms and calls to some God within
its depths. Then he starts backward slowly, his arms
remaining out. A huge head of a crocodile appears over
the bank and its eyes, glittering greenly, fasten upon
Jones. He stares into them fascinatedly. The witch-
doctor prances up to him, touches him with his wand,
motions with hideous command toward the waiting
monster. Jones squirms on his belly nearer and nearer,
moaning continually)*

Mercy, Lawd! Mercy!

*(The crocodile heaves more of his enormous hulk
onto the land. Jones squirms toward him. The witch-
doctor's voice shrills out in furious exultation, the tom-
tom beats madly. Jones cries out in a fierce, exhausted
spasm of anguished pleading)*

Lawd, save me! Lawd Jesus, heah my prayer!

*(Immediately, in answer to his prayer, comes the
thought of the one bullet left him. He snatches at his
hip, shouting defiantly)*

De silver bullet! You don't git me yit!

*(He fires at the green eyes in front of him. The head
of the crocodile sinks back behind the river bank, the*

witch-doctor springs behind the sacred tree and disappears. Jones lies with his face to the ground, his arms outstretched, whimpering with fear as the throb of the tom-tom fills the silence about him with a somber pulsation, a baffled but revengeful power.)

SCENE EIGHT

Dawn. Same as Scene Two, the dividing line of forest and plain. The nearest tree trunks are dimly revealed but the forest behind them is still a mass of glooming shadow. The tom-tom seems on the very spot, so loud and continuously vibrating are its beats. Lem enters from the left, followed by a small squad of his soldiers, and by the Cockney trader, Smithers. Lem is a heavy-set, ape-faced old savage of the extreme African type, dressed only in a loin cloth. A revolver and cartridge belt are about his waist. His soldiers are in different degrees of rag-concealed nakedness. All wear broad palm-leaf hats. Each one carries a rifle. Smithers is the same as in Scene One. One of the soldiers, evidently a tracker, is peering about keenly on the ground. He points to the spot where Jones entered the forest. Lem and Smithers come to look.

SMITHERS (*after a glance, turns away in disgust*): That's where 'e went in right enough. Much good it'll do yer. 'E's miles orf by this an' safe to the Coast, damn 's 'ide! I tole yer yer'd lose 'im, didn't I?—wastin' the 'ole bloomin' night beatin' yer bloody drum and castin' yer silly spells! Gawd blimey, wot a pack!

LEM (*gutturally*): We cotch him. (*He makes a motion to his soldiers who squat down on their haunches in a semi-circle.*)

SMITHERS (*exasperatedly*) Well, ain't yer goin' in an' 'unt 'im in the woods? What the 'ell's the good of waitin'?

LEM (*imperturbably—squatting down himself*) We cotch him.

SMITHERS (*turning away from him contemptuously*) Aw! Garn! 'E's a better man than the lot o' you put together. I 'ates the sight o' 'im but I'll say that for 'im. (*A sound comes from the forest. The soldiers jump to their feet, cocking their rifles alertly. Lem remains sitting with an imperturbable expression, but listening intently. He makes a quick signal with his hand. His followers creep quickly into the forest, scattering so that each enters at a different spot.*)

SMITHERS: You ain't thinkin' that would be 'im, I 'ope?

LEM (*calmly*): We cotch him.

SMITHERS: Blarsted fat 'eads! (*then after a second's thought—wonderingly*) Still an' all, it might 'appen. If 'e lost 'is bloody way in these stinkin' woods 'e'd likely turn in a circle without 'is knowin' it.

LEM (*peremptorily*) Sssh! (*The reports of several rifles sound from the forest, followed a second later by savage, exultant yells. The beating of the tom-tom abruptly ceases. Lem looks up at the white man with a grin of satisfaction.*) We cotch him. Him dead.

SMITHERS (*with a snarl*) 'Owd d'yer know it's 'im an' 'ow d'yer know 'e's dead?

LEM: My mens dey got um silver bullets. Lead bullet no kill him. He got um strong charm. I cook um money, make um silver bullet, make um strong charm, too.

SMITHERS (*astonished*): So that's wot you was up to all night, wot? You was scared to put after 'im till yo'd moulded silver bullets, eh?

LEM (*simply stating a fact*): Yes. Him got strong charm. Lead no good.

SMITHERS (*slapping his thigh and guffawing*) Haw-haw! If yer don't beat all 'ell! (*then recovering himself—scornfully*) I'll bet yer it ain't 'im they shot at all, yer bleedin' looney!

LEM (*calmly*) Dey come bring him now. (*The soldiers come out of the forest, carrying Jones' limp body. He is dead. They carry him to Lem, who examines his body with great satisfaction.*)

SMITHERS (*leans over his shoulder—in a tone of frightened awe*) Well, they did for yer right enough, Jonesey, me lad! Dead as a 'erring! (*mockingly*) Where's yer 'igh an' mighty airs now, yer bloomin' Majesty? (*then with a grin*) Silver bullets! Gawd blimey, but yer died in the 'eighth o' style, any'ow!

(*Curtain*)

ANNA CHRISTIE

A Play in Four Acts

CHARACTERS

"JOHNNY-THE-PRIEST"
TWO LONGSHOREMEN
A POSTMAN
LARRY, *bartender*
CHRIS. CHRISTOPHERSON, *captain of the barge*
Simeon Winthrop
MARTHY OWEN
ANNA CHRISTOPHERSON, *Chris's daughter*
THREE MEN OF A STEAMER'S CREW
MAT BURKE, *a stoker*
JOHNSON, *deckhand on the barge*

SCENES

Act One

"Johnny-the-Priest's" saloon near the waterfront, New York City

Act Two

The barge, *Simeon Winthrop*, at anchor in the harbor of Provincetown, Mass. Ten days later.

Act Three

Cabin of the barge, at dock in Boston. A week later.

Act Four

The same. Two days later.

Time of the Play—About 1910.

ACT ONE

SCENE—*"Johnny-the-Priest's"* saloon near South Street, New York City. The stage is divided into two sections, showing a small back room on the right. On the left, forward, of the barroom, a large window looking out on the street. Beyond it, the main entrance—a double swinging door. Farther back, another window. The bar runs from left to right nearly the whole length of the rear wall. In back of the bar, a small showcase displaying a few bottles of case goods, for which there is evidently little call. The remainder of the rear space in front of the large mirrors is occupied by half-barrels of cheap whiskey of the "nickel-a-shot" variety, from which the liquor is drawn by means of spigots. On the right is an open doorway leading to the back room. In the back room are four round wooden tables with five chairs groped about each. In the rear, a family entrance opening on a side street.

It is late afternoon of a day in fall.

As the curtain rises, Johnny is discovered. "Johnny-the-Priest" deserves his nickname. With his pale, thin clean-shaven face, mild blue eyes and white hair, a cassock would seem more suited to him than the apron he wears. Neither his voice nor his general manner dispel this illusion which has made him a personage of the waterfront. They are soft and bland. But beneath all his mildness one senses the man behind the mask—cynical, callous, hard as nails. He is lounging at ease *behind the bar, a pair of spectacles on his nose, reading an evening paper.*

Two longshoremen enter from the street, wearing their working aprons, the button of the union pinned conspicuously on the caps pulled sideways on their heads at an aggressive angle.

FIRST LONGSHOREMAN (*as they range themselves at the bar*): Gimme a shock. Number Two. (*He tosses a coin on the bar.*)

SECOND LONGSHOREMAN: Same here. (*Johnny sets two glasses of barrel whiskey before them.*)

FIRST LONGSHOREMAN: Here's luck! (*The other nods. They gulp down their whiskey.*)

SECOND LONGSHOREMAN (*putting money on the bar*): Give us another.

FIRST LONGSHOREMAN: Gimme a scoop this time— lager and porter. I'm dry.

SECOND LONGSHOREMAN: Same here. (*Johnny draws the lager and porter and sets the big, foaming schooners before them. They drink down half the contents and start to talk together hurriedly in low tones. The door on the left is swung open and Larry enters. He is boyish, red-cheeked, rather good-looking young fellow of twenty or so.*)

LARRY (*nodding to Johnny—cheerily*): Hello, boss.

JOHNNY: Hello, Larry. (*with a glance at his watch*) Just on time. (*Larry goes to the right behind the bar, takes off his coat, and puts on an apron.*)

FIRST LONGSHOREMAN (*abruptly*): Let's drink up and get back to it. (*They finish their drinks and go out left. The postman enters as they leave. He exchanges nods with Johnny and throws a letter on the bar.*)

THE POSTMAN: Addressed care of you, Johnny. Know him?

JOHNNY (*picks up the letter, adjusting his spectacles.*

Larry comes and peers over his shoulder. Johnny reads very slowly) Christopher Christopherson.

THE POSTMAN (*helpfully*): Square-head name.

LARRY: Old Chris—that's who.

JOHNNY: Oh, sure. I was forgetting Chris carried a hell of a name like that. Letters come here for him sometimes before, I remember now. Long time ago, though.

THE POSTMAN: It'll get him all right then?

JOHNNY: Sure thing. He comes here whenever he's in port.

THE POSTMAN (*turning to go*): Sailor, eh?

JOHNNY (*with a grin*): Captain of a coal barge.

THE POSTMAN (laughing): Some job! Well, s'long.

JOHNNY: S'long. I'll see he gets it. (*The postman goes out. Johnny scrutinizes the letter.*) You got good eyes, Larry. Where's it from?

LARRY (*after a glance*): St. Paul. That'll be in Minnesota, I'm thinkin'. Looks like a woman's writing, too, the old divil!

JOHNNY: He's got a daughter somewheres out West, I think he told me once. (*He puts the letter on the cash register.*) Come to think of it, I ain't seen old Chris in a dog's age. (*Putting his overcoat on, he comes around the end of the bar.*) Guess I'll be gettin' home. See you to-morrow.

LARRY: Good-night to ye, boss. (*As Johnny goes toward the street door, it is pushed open and Christopher Christopherson enters. He is a short, squat, broad-shouldered man of about fifty, with a round, weather-beaten, red face from which his light blue eyes peer short-sightedly, twinkling with a simple good humor. His large mouth, over-hung by a thick, drooping, yellow mustache, is childishly self-willed and weak, of an obstinate kindliness. A thick neck is jammed like a post into the heavy trunk of his*

*body. His arms with their big, hairy, freckled hands,
and his stumpy legs terminating in large flat feet, are
awkwardly short and muscular. He walks with a
clumsy, rolling gait. His voice, when not raised in a
hollow boom, is toned down to a sly, confidential
half-whisper with something vaguely plaintive in its
quality. He is dressed in a wrinkled, ill-fitting dark
suit of shore clothes, and wears a faded cap of gray
cloth over his mop of grizzled, blond hair. Just now
his face beams with a too-blissful happiness, and he
has evidently been drinking. He reaches his hand out
to Johnny.)*

CHRIS: Hello, Yohnny! Have drink on me. Come on,
Larry. Give us drink. Have one yourself. (*putting his
hand in his pocket*) Ay gat money—plenty money.

JOHNNY (*shakes Chris by the hand*): Speak of the devil.
We was just talkin' about you.

LARRY (*coming to the end of the bar*): Hello, Chris.
Put it there. (*They shake hands.*)

CHRIS (*beaming*): Give us drink.

JOHNNY (*with a grin*): You got a half-snootful now.
Where'd you get it?

CHRIS (*grinning*): Oder fallar on oder barge—Irish fallar—he gat bottle vhiskey and we drank it, just us
two. Dot vhiskey gat kick, by yingo! Ay yust come
ashore. Give us drink, Larry. Ay vas little drunk,
not much. Yust feel good. (*He laughs and commences to sing in a nasal, high-pitched quaver.*)

"My Yosephine, come board de ship. Long time Ay
vait for you.

De moon, she shi-i-i-ine. She looka yust like you.

Tchee-tchee, tchee-tchee, tchee-tchee, tchee-tchee."

(*To the accompaniment of this last he waves his hand
as if he were conducting an orchestra.*)

JOHNNY (*with a laugh*): Same old Yosie, eh, Chris?

CHRIS: You don't know good song when you hear him.

Italian fallar on oder barge, he learn me dat. Give us drink. (*He throws change on the bar.*)

LARRY (*with a professional air*): What's your pleasure, gentlemen?

JOHNNY: Small beer, Larry.

CHRIS: Vhiskey—Number Two.

LARRY (*as he gets their drinks*): I'll take a cigar on you.

CHRIS (*lifting his glass*): Skoal! (*He drinks.*)

JOHNNY: Drink hearty.

CHRIS (*immediately*): Have oder drink.

JOHNNY: No. Some other time. Got to go home now. So you've just landed? Where are you in from this time?

CHRIS: Norfolk. Ve make slow voyage—dirty vedder—yust fog, fog, fog, all bloody time! (*There is an insistent ring from the doorbell at the family entrance in the back room. Chris gives a start—hurriedly*) Ay go open, Larry. Ay forgat. It vas Marthy. She come with me. (*He goes into the back room.*)

LARRY (*with a chuckle*): He's still got that same cow livin' with him, the old fool!

JOHNNY (*with a grin*): A sport, Chris is. Well, I'll beat it home. S'long. (*He goes to the street door.*)

LARRY: So long, boss.

JOHNNY: Oh—don't forget to give him his letter.

LARRY: I won't. (*Johnny goes out. In the meantime, Chris has opened the family entrance door, admitting Marthy. She might be forty or fifty. Her jowly, mottled face, with its thick red nose, is streaked with interlacing purple veins. Her thick, gray hair is piled anyhow in a greasy mop on top of her round head. Her figure is flabby and fat; her breath comes in wheezy gasps; she speaks in a loud, mannish voice, punctuated by explosions of hoarse laughter. But there still twinkles in her blood-shot blue eyes a youthful lust for life which hard usage has failed to*) *stifle, a sense of humor mocking, but good-tempered. She wears a man's cap, double-breasted man's jacket, and a grimy, calico skirt. Her bare feet are encased in a man's brogans several sizes too large for her, which gives her a shuffling, wobbly gait.*)

MARTHY (*grumbling*): What yuh tryin' to do, Dutchy—keep me standin' out there all day? (*She comes forward and sits at the table in the right corner, front.*)

CHRIS (*mollifyingly*): Ay'm sorry, Marthy. Ay talk to Yohnny. Ay forgat. What you goin' take for drink?

MARTHY (*appeased*): Gimme a scoop of lager an' ale.

CHRIS: Ay go bring him back. (*He returns to the bar.*) Lager and ale for Marthy, Larry. Vhiskey for me. (*He throws change on the bar.*)

LARRY: Right you are. (*Then remembering, he takes the letter from in back of the bar.*) Here's a letter for you—from St. Paul, Minnesota—and a lady's writin'. (*He grins.*)

CHRIS (*quickly—taking it*): Oh, den it come from my daughter, Anna. She live dere. (*He turns the letter over in his hands uncertainly.*) Ay don't gat letter from Anna—must be a year.

LARRY (*jokingly*): That's a fine fairy tale to be tellin'—your daughter! Sure I'll bet it's some bum.

CHRIS (*soberly*): No. Dis come from Anna. (*engrossed by the letter in his hand—uncertainly*) By golly, Ay tank Ay'm too drunk for read dis letter from Anna. Ay tank Ay sat down for a minute. You bring drinks in back room, Larry. (*He goes into the room on right.*)

MARTHY (*angrily*): Where's my larger an' ale, yuh big stiff?

CHRIS (*preoccupied*): Larry bring him. (*He sits down opposite her. Larry brings in the drinks and sets them on the table. He and Marthy exchange nods of recog-*

nition. Larry stands looking at Chris curiously. Marthy takes a long draught of her schooner and heaves a huge sigh of satisfaction, wiping her mouth with the back of her hand. Chris stares at the letter for a moment—slowly opens it, squinting his eyes, commences to read laboriously, his lips moving as he spells out the words. As he reads his face lights up with an expression of mingled joy and bewilderment.)

LARRY: Good news?

MARTHY (*her curiosity also aroused*): What's that yuh got—a letter, fur Gawd's sake?

CHRIS (*pauses for a moment, after finishing the letter as if to let the news sink in—then suddenly pounds his fist on the table with happy excitement*): Py yiminy! Yust tank, Anna say she's comin' here right avay! She gat sick on yob in St. Paul, she say. It's short letter, don't tal me much more'n dat. (*beaming*) Py golly, dat's good news all at one time for ole fallar! (*then turning to Marthy, rather shamefacedly*) You know, Marthy, Ay've tole you Ay don't see my Anna since she vas little gel in Sveden five year ole.

MARTHY: How old'll she be now?

CHRIS: She must be—lat me see—she must be twenty year ole, py Yo!

LARRY (*surprised*): You've not seen her in fifteen years?

CHRIS (*suddenly growing somber—in a low tone*): No. Ven she vas little gel, Ay vas bo'sun on vindjammer. Ay never gat home only few time dem year. Ay'm fool sailor fallar. My voman—Anna's mother—she gat tired vait all time Sveden for me ven Ay don't never come. She come dis country, bring Anna, dey go out Minnesota, live with her cousins on farm. Den ven her mo'der die ven Ay vas on voyage, Ay tank it's better dem cousins keep Anna. Ay tank it's better Anna live on farm, den she don't know dat ole davil, sea, she don't know fader like me.

LARRY (*with a wink at Marthy*): This girl, now, 'll be marryin' a sailor herself, likely. It's in the blood.

CHRIS (*suddenly springing to his feet and smashing his fist on the table in a rage*): No, py God! She don't do dat!

MARTHY (*grasping her schooner hastily—angrily*): Hey, look out, yuh nut! Wanta spill my suds for me?

LARRY (*amazed*): Oho, what's up with you? Ain't you a sailor yourself now, and always been?

CHRIS (*slowly*): Dat's yust vhy Ay say it. (*forcing a smile*) Sailor vas all right fallar, but not for marry gel. No. Ay know dat. Anna's mo'der, she know it, too. •

LARRY (*as Chris remains sunk in gloomy reflection*): When is your daughter comin'? Soon?

CHRIS (*roused*): Py yiminy, Ay forgat. (*reads through the letter hurriedly*) She say she come right avay, dat's all.

LARRY: She'll maybe be comin' here to look for you, I s'pose (*He returns to the bar, whistling. Left alone with Marthy, who stares at him with a twinkle of malicious humor in her eyes, Chris suddenly become desperately ill-at-ease. He fidgets, then gets up hurriedly.*)

CHRIS: Ay gat speak with Larry. Ay be right back. (*mollifyingly*) Ay bring you oder drink.

MARTHY (*emptying her glass*): Sure. That's me. (*As he retreats with the glass she guffaws after him derisively.*)

CHRIS (*to Larry in an alarmed whisper*): Py yingo, Ay gat gat Marthy shore off barge before Anna come! Anna raise hell if she find dat out. Marthy raise hell, too, for go, py golly!

LARRY (*with a chuckle*): Serve ye right, ye old divil—havin' a woman at your age!

CHRIS (*scratching his head in a quandary*): You tal me lie for tal Marthy, Larry, so's she gat off barge quick.

LARRY: She knows your daughter's comin'. Tell her to get the hell out of it.

CHRIS: No. Ay don't like make her feel bad.

LARRY: You're an old mush! Keep your girl away from the barge, then. She'll likely want to stay ashore anyway. (*curiously*) What does she work at, your Anna?

CHRIS: She stay on dem cousins' farm 'till two year ago. Dan she gat yob nurse gel in St. Paul. (*then shaking his head resolutely*) But Ay don't vant for her gat yob now. Ay vant for her stay with me.

LARRY (*scornfully*): On a coal barge! She'll not like that, I'm thinkin'.

MARTHY (*shouts from next room*): Don't I get that bucket o'suds, Dutchy?

CHRIS (*startled—in apprehensive confusion*): Yes, Ay come, Marthy.

LARRY (*drawing the lager and ale, hands it to Chris—laughing*) Now you're in for it! You'd better tell her straight to get out!

CHRIS (*shaking in his boots*): Py golly. (*He takes her drink in to Marthy and sits down at the table. She sips it in silence. Larry moves quietly close to the partition to listen, grinning with expectation. Chris seems on the verge of speaking, hesitates, gulps down his whiskey desperately as if seeking for courage. He attempts to whistle a few bars of "Yosephine" with careless bravado, but the whistle peters out futility. Marthy stares at him keenly, taking in his embarrassment with a malicious twinkle of amusement in her eye. Chris clears his throat.*) Marthy—

MARTHY (*aggressively*): What's that? (*then, pretending to fly into a rage, her eyes enjoying Chris' misery*) I'm wise to what's in back of your nut, Dutchy. Yuh want to git rid o' me, huh?—now she's comin'. Gimme the bum's rush ashore, huh? Lemme tell yuh, Dutchy, there ain't a square-head workin' on a boat man enough to git away with that. Don't start nothin' yuh can't finish!

CHRIS (*miserably*): Ay don't start nutting, Marthy.

MARTHY (*glares at him for a second—then cannot control a burst of laughter*): Ho-ho! Yuh're a scream, Square-head—an honest-ter-Gawd knockout! Ho-ho! (*She wheezes, panting for breath.*)

CHRIS (*with childish pique*): Ay don't see nutting for laugh at.

MARTHY: Take a slant in the mirror and yuh'll see. Ho-ho! (*recovering from her mirth—chuckling, scornfully*) A square-head tryin' to kid Marthy Owen at this late day!—after me campin' with barge men the last twenty years. I'm wise to the game, up, down, and sideways. I ain't been born and dragged up on the water front for nothin'. Think I'd make trouble, huh? Not me! I'll pack up me duds an' beat it. I'm quittin' yuh, get me? I'm tellin' yuh I'm sick of stickin' with yuh, and I'm leavin' yuh flat, see? There's plenty of other guys on other barges waitin' for me. Always was, I always found. (*She claps the astonished Chris on the back.*) So cheer up, Dutchy! I'll be offen the barge before she comes. You'll be rid o' me for good—and me o' you—good riddance for both of us. Ho-ho!

CHRIS (*seriously*): Ay don't tank dat. You vas good gel, Marthy.

MARTHY (*grinning*): Good girl? Aw, can the bull! Well, yuh treated me square, yuhself. So it's fifty-

fifty. Nobody's sore at nobody. We're still good frien's, huh? (*Larry returns to bar.*)

CHRIS (*beaming now that he sees his troubles disappearing*): Yes, py golly.

MARTHY: That's the talkin'! In all my time I tried never to split with a guy with no hard feelin's. But what was yuh so scared about—that I'd kick up a row? That ain't Marthy's way. (*scornfully*) Think I'd break my heart to loose yuh? Commit suicide, huh? Ho-ho! Gawd! The world's full o' men if that's all I'd worry about! (*then with a grin, after emptying her glass*) Blow me to another scoop, huh? I'll drink your kid's health for yuh.

CHRIS (*eagerly*): Sure tang. Ay go gat him. (*He takes the two glasses into the bar.*) Oder drink. Same for both.

LARRY (*getting the drinks and putting them on the bar*) She's not such a bad lot, that one.

CHRIS (*jovially*): She's good gel Ay tal you! Py golly, Ay calabrate now! Give me vhiskey here at bar, too. (*He puts down money. Larry serves him.*) You have drink, Larry.

LARRY (*virtuously*): You know I never touch it.

CHRIS: You don't know what you miss. Skoal! (*He drinks—then begins to sing loudly*)
"My Yosephine, come board de ship—"
(*He picks up the drinks for Marthy and himself and walks unsteadily into the back room, singing.*)
"De moon, she shi-i-i-ine. She looks yust like you. Tche-tchee, tchee-tchee, tchee-tchee, tchee-tchee."

MARTHY (*grinning, hands to ears*): Gawd!

CHRIS (*sitting down*): Ay'm good singer, yes? Ve drink, eh? Skoal! Ay calabrate! (*He drinks.*) Ay calabrate 'cause Anna's coming home. You know, Marthy, Ay never write for her to come, 'cause Ay tank Ay'm no good for her. But all time Ay hope like hell some day she vant for see me and den she come. And dat's vay it happen now, py yiminy! (*his face beaming*) What you tank she look like, Marthy? Ay bet you she's fine, good, strong gel, pooty like hell! Living on farm made her like dat. And Ay bet you some day she marry good, steady land fallar here in East, have home all her own, have kits— and dan Ay'm ole grandfader, py golly! And Ay go visit dem every time Ay gat in port near! (*bursting with joy*) By yiminy crickets, Ay calabrate dat! (*shouts*) Bring oder drink, Larry! (*He smashes his fist on the table with a bang.*)

LARRY (*coming in from bar—irritably*): Easy there! Don't be breakin' the table, you old goat!

CHRIS (*by way of reply, grins foolishly and begins to sing*): "My Yosephine comes board de ship—"

MARTHY (*touching Chris' arm persuasively*): You're soused to the ears, Dutchy. Go out and put a feed into you. It'll sober you up. (*then as Chris shakes his head obstinately*) Listen, yuh old nut! Yuh don't know what time your kid's liable to show up. Yuh want to be sober when she comes, don't yuh?

CHRIS (*aroused—gets unsteadily to his feet*): Py golly, yes.

LARRY: That's good sense for you. A good beef stew'll fix you. Go round the corner.

CHRIS: All right. Ay be back soon, Marthy. (*Chris goes through the bar and out the street door.*)

LARRY: He'll come round all right with some grub in him.

MARTHY: Sure. (*Larry goes back to the bar and resumes his newspaper. Marthy sips what is left of her schooner reflectively. There is the ring of the family entrance bell. Larry comes to the door and opens it a trifle—then, with a puzzled expression, pulls it wide. Anna Christopherson enters. She is a tall,*

*blond, fully-developed girl of twenty, handsome after
a large, Viking-daughter fashion but now run down
in health and plainly showing all the outward evi-
dences of belonging to the world's oldest profession.
Her youthful face is already hard and cynical beneath its layer of make-up. Her clothes are the tawdry
finery of peasant stock turned prostitute. She comes
and sinks wearily in a chair by the table, left front.)*

ANNA: Gimme a whiskey—ginger ale on the side.
*(then, as Larry turns to go, forcing a winning smile
at him)* And don't be stingy, baby.

LARRY *(sarcastically)*: Shall I serve it in a pail?

ANNA *(with a hard laugh)*: That suits me down to the
ground. *(Larry goes into the bar. The two women
size each other up with frank stares. Larry comes
back with the drink which he sets before Anna and
returns to the bar again. Anna downs her drink at a
gulp. Then, after a moment, as the alcohol begins to
rouse her, she turns to Marthy with a friendly smile.)*
Gee, I needed that bad, all right, all right!

MARTHY *(nodding her head sympathetically)* Sure, yuh
look all in. Been on a bat?

ANNA: No—travelling—day and a half on the train.
Had to sit up all night in the dirty coach, too. Gawd,
I thought I'd never get here!

MARTHY *(with a start—looking at her intently)*:
Where'd yuh come from, huh?

ANNA: St. Paul—out in Minnesota.

MARTHY *(staring at her in amazement—slowly)*: So—
yuh're— *(She suddenly bursts out into hoarse, ironical laughter.)* Gawd!

ANNA: All the way from Minnesota, sure. *(flaring up)*
What you laughing at? Me?

MARTHY *(hastily)*: No, honest, kid. I was thinkin' of
somethin' else.

ANNA *(mollified—with a smile)*: Well, I wouldn't

blame you, at that. Guess I do look rotten—yust
out of the hospital two weeks. I'm going to have
another 'ski. What d'you say? Have something on
me?

MARTHY: Sure I will. T'anks. (*She calls.*) Hey, Larry!
Little service! (*He comes in.*)

ANNA: Same for me.

MARTHY: Same here. (*Larry takes their glasses and
goes out.*)

ANNA: Why don't you come sit over here, be sociable.
I'm a dead stranger in this burg—and I ain't spoke
a word with no one since day before yesterday.

MARTHY: Sure thing. (*She shuffles over to Anna's table
and sits down opposite her. Larry brings the drinks
and Anna pays him.*)

ANNA: Skoal! Here's how! (*She drinks.*)

MARTHY: Here's luck! (*She takes a gulp from her
schooner.*)

ANNA (*taking a package of Sweet Caporal cigarettes
from her bag*) Let you smoke in here, won't they?

MARTHY (*doubtfully*): Sure. (*then with evident anxiety*)
On'y trow it away if yuh hear someone comin'.

ANNA (*lighting one and taking a deep inhale*): Gee,
they're fussy in this dump, ain't they? (*She puffs,
staring at the table top. Marthy looks her over with
a new penetrating interest, taking in every detail of
her face. Anna suddenly becomes conscious of this
appraising stare—resentfully*) Ain't nothing wrong
with me, is there? You're looking hard enough.

MARTHY (*irritated by the other's tone—scornfully*):
Ain't got to look much. I got your number the minute you stepped in the door.

ANNA (*her eyes narrowing*): Ain't you smart! Well, I
got yours, too, without no trouble. You're me forty
years from now. That's you! (*She gives a hard little laugh.*)

MARTHY (*angrily*): Is that so? Well, I'll tell you straight kiddo, that Marthy Owen never—(*She catches herself up short—with a grin*) What are you and me scrappin' over? Let's cut it out, huh? Me, I don't want no hard feelin's with no one. (*extending her hand*) Shake and forget it, huh?

ANNA (*shakes her hand gladly*): Only too glad to. I ain't looking for trouble. Let's have 'nother. What d'you say?

MARTHY (*shaking her head*) Not for mine. I'm full up. And you— Had anythin' to eat lately?

ANNA: Not since this morning on the train.

MARTHY: Then yuh better go easy on it, hadn't yuh?

ANNA (*after a moment's hesitation*): Guess you're right. I got to meet someone, too. But my nerves is on edge after that rotten trip.

MARTHY: Yuh said yuh was just outa the hospital?

ANNA: Two weeks ago. (*leaning over to Marthy confidentially*) The joint I was in out in St. Paul got raided. That was the start. The judge give all us girls thirty days. The others didn't seem to mind being in the cooler much. Some of 'em was used to it. But me, I couldn't stand it. It got my goat right— couldn't eat or sleep or nothing. I never could stand being caged up nowheres. I got good and sick and they had to send me to the hospital. It was nice there. I was sorry to leave it, honest!

MARTHY (*after a slight pause*): Did yuh say yuh got to meet someone here?

ANNA: Yes. Oh, not what you mean. It's my Old Man. I got to meet. Honest! It's funny, too. I ain't seen him since I was a kid—don't even know what he looks like—yust had a letter every now and then. This was always the only address he give me to write him back. He's yanitor of some building here now—used to be a sailor.

MARTHY (*astonished*): Janitor!

ANNA: Sure. And I was thinking maybe, seeing he ain't never done a thing for me in my life, he might be willing to stake me to a room and eats till I get rested up. (*wearily*) Gee, I sure need that rest! I'm knocked out. (*then resignedly*) But I ain't expecting much from him. Give you a kick when you're down, that's what all men do. (*with sudden passion*) Men, I hate 'em—all of 'em! And I don't expect he'll turn out no better than the rest. (*then with sudden interest*) Say, do you hang out around this dump much?

MARTHY: Oh, off and on.

ANNA: Then maybe you know him—my Old Man—or at least seen him?

MARTHY: It ain't old Chris, is it?

ANNA: Old Chris?

MARTHY: Chris Christopherson, his full name is.

ANNA (*excitedly*) Yes, that's him! Anna Christopherson—that's my real name—only out there I called myself Anna Christie. So you know him, eh?

MARTHY (*evasively*): Seen him about for years.

ANNA: Say, what's he like, tell me, honest?

MARTHY: Oh, he's short and—

ANNA (*impatiently*): I don't care what he looks like. What kind is he?

MARTHY (*earnestly*): Well, yuh can bet your life, kid, he's as good an old guy as ever walked on two feet. That goes!

ANNA (*pleased*): I'm glad to hear it. Then you think's he'll stake me to that rest cure I'm after?

MARTHY (*emphatically*): Surest thing you know. (*disgustedly*) But where'd yuh get the idea he was a janitor?

ANNA: He wrote me he was himself.

MARTHY: Well, he was lyin'. He ain't. He's captain of a barge—five men under him.

ANNA (*disgusted in her turn*): A barge? What kind of a barge?

MARTHY: Coal, mostly.

ANNA: A coal barge! (*with a harsh laugh*) If that ain't a swell job to find your long lost Old Man working at! Gee, I knew something'd be bound to turn out wrong—always does with me. That puts my idea of his giving me a rest on the bum.

MARTHY: What d'yuh mean?

ANNA: I s'pose he lives on the boat, don't he?

MARTHY: Sure. What about it? Can't you live on it, too?

ANNA (*scornfully*): Me? On a dirty coal barge! What d'you think I am?

MARTHY (*resentfully*): What d'yuh know about barges, huh? Bet yuh ain't never seen one. That's what comes of his bringing yuh up inland—away from the old devil sea—where yuh'd be safe—Gawd! (*The irony of it strikes her sense of humor and she laughs hoarsely.*)

ANNA (*angrily*): His bringing me up! Is that what he tells people! I like his nerve! He let them cousins of my Old Woman's keep me on their farm and work me to death like a dog.

MARTHY: Well, he's got queer notions on some things. I've heard him say a farm was the best place for a kid.

ANNA: Sure. That's what he'd always answer back—and a lot of crazy stuff about staying away from the sea—stuff I couldn't make head or tail to. I thought he must be nutty.

MARTHY: He is on that one point. (*casually*) So yuh didn't fall for life on the farm, huh?

ANNA: I should say not! The old man of the family, his wife, and four sons—I had to slave for all of 'em. I was only a poor relation, and they treated me worse than they dare treat a hired girl. (*after a moment's hesitation—somberly*) It was one of the sons—the youngest—started me—when I was sixteen. After that I hated 'em so I'd killed 'em all if I'd stayed. So I run away—to St. Paul.

MARTHY (*who has been listening sympathetically*): I've heard Old Chris talkin' about your bein' a nurse girl out there. Was that all a bluff yuh put up when yuh wrote him?

ANNA: Not on your life, it wasn't. It was true for two years. I didn't go wrong all at one jump. Being a nurse girl was yust what finished me. Taking care of other people's kids, always listening to their bawling and crying, caged in, when you're only a kid yourself and want to go out and see things. At last I got the chance—to get into that house. And you bet your life I took it! (*defiantly*) And I ain't sorry neither. (*after a pause—with bitter hatred*) It was all men's fault—the whole business. It was men on the farm ordering and beating me—and giving me the wrong start. Then when I was a nurse, it was men again hanging around, bothering me, trying to see what they could get. (*She gives a hard laugh*) And now it's men all the time. Gawd, I hate 'em all, every mother's son of 'em. Don't you?

MARTHY: Oh, I dunno. There's good ones and bad ones, kid. You've just had a run of bad luck with 'em, that's all. Your Old Man, now—old Chris—he's a good one.

ANNA (*sceptically*): He'll have to show me.

MARTHY: Yuh kept right on writing him yuh was a nurse girl still, even after yuh was in the house, didn't yuh?

ANNA: Sure (*cynically*) Not that I think he'd care a darn.

MARTHY; Yuh're all wrong about him, kid (*earnestly*)

I know Old Chris well for a long time. He's talked to me 'bout you lots o' times. He thinks the world o' you, honest he does.

ANNA: Aw, quit the kiddin'!

MARTHY: Honest! Only, he's a simple old guy, see? He's got nutty notions. But he means well, honest. Listen to me, kid— (*She is interrupted by the opening and shutting of the street door in the bar and by hearing Chris's voice.*) Ssshh!

ANNA: What's up?

CHRIS (*who has entered the bar. He seems considerably sobered up.*): Py golly, Larry, dat grub taste good. Marthy in back?

LARRY: Sure—and another tramp with her. (*Chris starts for the entrance to the back room.*)

MARTHY (*to Anna in a hurried, nervous whisper*): That's him now. He's comin' in here. Brace up!

ANNA: Who? (*Chris opens the door.*)

MARTHY (*as if she were greeting him for the first time*): Why hello, Old Chris. (*Then before he can speak, she shuffles hurriedly past him into the bar, beckoning him to follow her.*) Come here. I wanta tell yuh somethin'. (*He goes out to her. She speaks hurriedly in a low voice.*) Listen! I'm goin' to beat it down to the barge—pack up me duds and blow. That's her in there—your Anna—just come—waitin' for yuh. Treat her right, see? She's been sick. Well, s'long! (*She goes into the back room—to Anna*) S'long, kid. I gotta beat it now. See yuh later.

ANNA (*nervously*): So long. (*Marthy goes quickly out of the family entrance.*)

LARRY (*looking at the stupefied Chris curiously*): Well, what's up now?

CHRIS (*vaguely*): Nutting—nutting. (*He stands before the door to the back room in an agony of embarrassed emotion—then he forces himself to a bold de-*

178   *Eugene O'Neill*

cision, pushes open the door and walks in. He stands there, casts a shy glance at Anna, whose brilliant clothes, and, to him, high-toned appearance, awe him terribly. He looks about him with pitiful nervousness as if to avoid the appraising look with which she takes in his face, his clothes, etc—his voice seeming to plead for her forbearance.) Anna!

ANNA *(acutely embarrassed in her turn)*: Hello—father. She told me it was you. I yust got here a little while ago.

CHRIS *(goes slowly over to her chair)*: It's good—for see you—after all dem years, Anna. *(He bends down over her. After an embarrassed struggle they manage to kiss each other.)*

ANNA *(a trace of genuine feeling in her voice)*: It's good to see you, too.

CHRIS *(grasps her arms and looks into her face—then overcome by a wave of fierce tenderness)*: Anna Lilla! Anna Lilla! *(takes her in his arms)*

ANNA *(shrinks away from him, half-frightened)*: What's that—Swedish? I don't know it. *(then as if seeking relief from the tension in a voluble chatter)* Gee, I had an awful trip coming here. I'm all in. I had to sit up in the dirty coach all night—couldn't get no sleep, hardly—and then I had a hard job finding this place. I never been in New York before, you know, and—

CHRIS *(who has been staring down at her face admiringly, not hearing what she says—impulsively)*: You know you vas awful pooty gel, Anna? Ay bet all men see you fall in love with you, py yiminy!

ANNA *(repelled—harshly)*: Cut it! You talk same as they all do.

CHRIS *(hurt—humbly):* Ain't no harm for your fader talk dat vay, Anna.

ANNA *(forcing a short laugh)*: No—course not. Only—

it's funny to see you and not remember nothing. You're like—a stranger.

CHRIS (*sadly*): Ay s'pose. Ay never come here only few times ven you vas kit in Sveden. You don't remember dat?

ANNA: No. (*resentfully*) But why didn't you never come home them days? Why didn't you never come out West to see me?

CHRIS (*slowly*): Ay tank, after your mo'der die, ven Ay vas avay on voyage, it's better for you you don't never see me! (*He sinks down in the chair opposite her dejectedly—then turns to her—sadly*) Ay don't know, Anna, vhy Ay never come home Sveden in ole year. Ay vant come home end of every voyage. Ay vant see your mo'der, your two bro'der before dey vas drowned, you ven you vas born—but—Ay—don't go. Ay sign on oder ships—go South America, go Australia, go China, go every port all over world many times—but Ay never go aboard ship sail for Sveden. Ven Ay gat money for pay passage home as passenger den— (*he bows his head guiltily*) Ay forgat and Ay spend all money. Ven Ay tank again, it's too late. (*He sighs.*) Ay don't know vhy but dat's vay with most sailor fallar, Anna. Dat ole davil sea make dem crazy fools with her dirty tricks. It's so.

ANNA (*who has watched him keenly while he has been speaking—with a trace of scorn in her voice*): Then you think the sea's to blame for everything, eh? Well, you're still workin' on it, ain't you, spite of all you used to write me about hating it. That dame was here told me you was captain of a coal barge—and you wrote me you was yanitor of a building!

CHRIS (*embarrassed but lying glibly*): Oh, Ay work on land long time as yanitor. Yust short time ago Ay got dis yob cause Ay vas sick, need open air.

ANNA (*sceptically*): Sick? You? You'd never think it.

CHRIS: And, Anna, dis ain't real sailor yob. Dis ain't real boat on sea. She's yust ole tub—like piece of land with house on it dat float. Yob on her ain't sea yob. No. Ay don't gat yob on sea, Anna, if Ay die first. Ay swear dat, ven your mo'der die. Ay keep my word, py yingo!

ANNA (*perplexed*): Well, I can't see no difference. (*dismissing the subject*) Speaking of being sick, I been there myself—yust out of the hospital two weeks ago.

CHRIS (*immediately all concern*): You, Anna? Py golly! (*anxiously*) You feel better now, dough, don't you? You look little tired, dat's all!

ANNE (*wearily*): I am. Tired to death. I need a long rest and I don't see much chance of getting it.

CHRIS: What you mean, Anna?

ANNA: Well, when I made up my mind to come to see you, I thought you was a yanitor—that you'd have a place where, maybe, if you didn't mind having me, I could visit a while and rest up—till I felt able to get back on the job again.

CHRIS (*eagerly*): But Ay gat place, Anna—nice place. You rest all you want, py yiminy! You don't never have to work as nurse gel no more. You stay with me, py golly!

ANNA (*surprised and pleased by his eagerness—with a smile*): Then you're really glad to see me—honest?

CHRIS (*pressing one of her hands in both of his*): Anna, Ay like see you like hell, Ay tal you! And don't you talk no more about gatting yob. You stay with me. Ay don't see you for long time, you don't forgat dat. (*His voice trembles.*) Ay'm gatting ole. Ay gat no one in vorld but you.

ANNA (*touched—embarrassed by this unfamiliar emotion*): Thanks. It sounds good to hear someone— talk to me that way. Say, though—if you're so lonely—it's funny—why ain't you ever married again?

CHRIS (*shaking his head emphatically—after a pause*): Ay love your mo'der too much to ever do dat, Anna.

ANNA (*impressed—slowly*): I don't remember nothing about her. What was she like? Tell me.

CHRIS: Ay tal you all about everytang—and you tal me all tangs happen to you. But not here now. Dis ain't good place for young gel, anyway. Only no good sailor fallar come here for gat drunk. (*He gets to his feet quickly and picks up her bag.*) You come with me, Anna. You need lie down, gat rest.

ANNA (*half rises to her feet, then sits down again*): Where're you going?

CHRIS: Come, Ve gat on board.

ANNA (*disappointedly*): On board your barge, you mean? (*dryly*) Nix for mine! (*then seeing his crest-fallen look—forcing a smile*) Do you think that's a good place for a young girl like me—a coal barge?

CHRIS (*dully*): Yes, Ay tank. (*He hesitates—then continues more and more pleadingly.*) You don't know how nice it's on barge, Anna. Tug come and ve gat towed out on voyage—yust water all round, and sun, and fresh air, and good grub for make you strong, healthy gel. You see many tangs you don't see before. You gat moonlight at night, maybe; see steamer pass; see schooner make sail—see everytang dat's pooty. You need take rest like dat. You work too hard for young gel already. You need vacation, yes!

ANNA (*who has listened to him with a growing interest—with an uncertain laugh*): It sounds good to hear you tell it. I'd sure like a trip on the water, all right. It's the barge idea has me stopped. Well, I'll go down with you and have a look—and maybe I'll take a chance. Gee, I'd do anything once.

CHRIS (*picks up her bag again*): Ve go, eh?

ANNA: What's the rush? Wait a second. (*Forgetting the situation for a moment, she relapses into the familiar form and flashes one of her winning trade smiles at him.*) Gee, I'm thirsty.

CHRIS (*sets down her bag immediately—hastily*): Ay'm sorry, Anna. What you tank you like for drink, eh?

ANNA (*promptly*): I'll take a—(*then suddenly reminded—confusedly*) I don't know. What'a they got here?

CHRIS (*with a grin*): Ay don't tank dey got much fancy drink for young gel in dis place, Anna. Yinger ale—sas'prilla, maybe.

ANNE (*forcing a laugh herself*): Make it sas, then.

CHRIS (*coming up to her—with a wink): Ay tal you, Anna, ve calabrate, yes—dis one time because ve meet after many year. (*in a half whisper, embarrassedly*) Dey gat good port wine, Anna. It's good for you, Ay tank—little bit—for give you appetite. It ain't strong, neider. One glass don't go to your head, Ay promise.

ANNA (*with a half hysterical laugh*): All right. I'll take port.

CHRIS: Ay go gat him. (*He goes out to the bar. As soon as the door closes, Anna starts to her feet.*)

ANNA (*picking up her bag—half-aloud—stammeringly*): Gawd, I can't stand this! I better beat it. (*Then she lets her bag drop, stumbles over to her chair again, and covering her face with her hands, begins to sob.*)

LARRY (*putting down his paper as Chris comes up—with a grin*): Well, who's the blond?

CHRIS (*proudly*): Dat vas Anna, Larry.

LARRY (*in amazement*): Your daughter, Anna? (*Chris

nods. Larry lets a long, low whistle escape him and turns away embarrassedly.)

CHRIS: Don't you tank she vas pooty gel, Larry?

LARRY (*rising to the occasion*): Sure! A peach!

CHRIS: You bet you! Give me drink for take back— one port vine for Anna—she calabrate dis one time with me—and small beer for me.

LARRY (*as he gets the drinks*): Small beer for you, eh? She's reformin' you already.

CHRIS (*pleased*): You bet! (*He takes the drinks. As she hears him coming, Anna hastily dries her eyes, tries to smile. Chris comes in and sets the drinks down on the table—stares at her for a second anxiously— patting her hand*) You look tired, Anna. Vell, Ay make you take good long rest now. (*picking up his beer*) Come, you drink vine. It put new life in you. (*She lifts her glass—he grins.*) Skoal, Anna! You know dat Svedish word?

ANNA: Skoal! (*downing her port at a gulp like a drink of whiskey—her lips trembling*) Skoal? Guess I know that word, all right, all right!

(*The Curtain Falls*)

ACT TWO

SCENE—*Ten days later. The stern of the deeply-laden barge, "Simeon Winthrop," at anchor in the outer harbor of Provincetown, Mass. It is ten o'clock at night. Dense fog shrouds the barge on all sides, and she floats motionless on a calm. A lantern set up on an immense coil of thick hawser sheds a dull, filtering light on objects near it—the heavy steel bits for making fast the tow lines, etc. In the rear is the cabin, its misty windows glowing wanly with the light of a lamp inside. The chimney of the cabin stove rises a few feet above the roof. The doleful tolling of bells, on Long Point, on ships at anchor, breaks the silence at regular intervals.*

As the curtain rises, ANNA is discovered standing near the coil of rope on which the lantern is placed. She looks healthy, transformed, the natural color has come back to her face. She has on a black, oilskin coat, but wears no hat. She is staring out into the fog astern with an expression of awed wonder. The cabin door is pushed open and CHRIS appears. He is dressed in yellow oilskins—coat, pants, sou'wester—and wears high sea-boots.

CHRIS (*the glare from the cabin still in his eyes, peers blinkingly astern*): Anna! (*Receiving no reply, he calls again, this time with apparent apprehension*) Anna!

ANNA (*with a start—making a gesture with her hand*

184

as if to impose silence—in a hushed whisper): Yes, here I am. What d'you want?

CHRIS (*walks over to her—solicitously*): Don't you come turn in, Anna? It's late—after four bells. It ain't good for you stay out here in fog, Ay tank.

ANNA: Why not? (*with a trace of strange exultation*) I love this fog! Honest! It's so— (*she hesitates, groping for a word*)—funny and still, I feel as if I was— out of things altogether.

CHRIS (*spitting disgustedly*): Fog's vorst one of her dirty tricks, py yingo!

ANNA (*with a short laugh*): Beefing about the sea again? I'm getting so's I love it, the little I've seen.

CHRIS (*glancing at her moodily*): Dat's foolish talk, Anna. You see her more, you don't talk dat vay. (*Then seeing her irritation, he hastily adopts a more cheerful tone.*) But Ay'm glad you like it on barge. Ay'm glad it makes you feel good again. (*with a placating grin*) You like live like dis alone with ole fa'der, eh?

ANNA: Sure I do. Everything's been so different from anything I ever come across before. And now—this fog—Gee, I wouldn't have missed it for nothing. I never thought living on ships was so different from land. Gee, I'd yust love to work on it, honest I would, if I was a man. I don't wonder you always been a sailor.

CHRIS (*vehemently*): Ay ain't sailor, Anna. And dis ain't real sea. You only see nice part. (*Then as she doesn't answer, he continues hopefully.*) Vell, fog lift in morning, Ay tank.

ANNA (*the exultation again in her voice*): I love it! I don't give a rap if it never lifts! (*CHRIS fidgets from one foot to the other worriedly. ANNA continues slowly, after a pause.*) It makes me feel clean—out here—'s if I'd taken a bath.

CHRIS (*after a pause*): You better go in cabin—read book. Dat put you to sleep.

ANNA: I don't want to sleep. I want to stay out here—and think about things.

CHRIS (*walks away from her toward the cabin—then comes back*): You act funny to-night, Anna.

ANNA (*her voice rising angrily*): Say, what're you trying to do—make things rotten? You been kind as kind can be to me and I certainly appreciate it—only don't spoil it all now. (*Then, seeing the hurt expression on her father's face, she forces a smile.*) Let's talk of something else. Come. Sit down here. (*She points to the coil of rope.*)

CHRIS (*sits down beside her with a sigh*): It's gatting pooty late in night, Anna. Must be near five bells.

ANNA (*interestedly*): Five bells? What time is that?

CHRIS: Half past ten.

ANNA: Funny I don't know nothing about sea talk—but those cousins was always talking crops and that stuff. Gee, wasn't I sick of it—and of them!

CHRIS: You don't like live on farm, Anna?

ANNA: I've told you a hundred times I hated it. (*decidedly*) I'd rather have one drop of ocean than all the farms in the world! Honest! And you wouldn't like a farm, neither. Here's where you belong. (*She makes a sweeping gesture seaward.*) But not on a coal barge. You belong on a real ship, sailing all over the world.

CHRIS (*moodily*): Ay've done dat many year, Anna, when Ay vas damn fool.

ANNA (*disgustedly*): Oh, rats! (*After a pause she speaks musingly.*) Was the men in our family always sailors—as far back as you know about?

CHRIS (*shortly*): Yes. Damn fools! All men in our village on coast, Sveden, go to sea. Ain't nutting else for dem to do. My fa'der die on board ship in Indian

Ocean. He's buried at sea. Ay don't never know him only little bit. Den my tree bro'der, older'n me, dey go on ships. Den Ay go, too. Den my mo'der she's left all 'lone. She die pooty quick after dat— all 'lone. Ve vas all avay on voyage when she die. (*He pauses sadly.*) Two my bro'der deyt gat lost on fishing boat same like your bro'ders vas drowned. My oder bro'der, he save money, give up sea, den he die home in bed. He's only one dat ole davil don't kill. (*defiantly*) But me, Ay bet you Ay die ashore in bed, too!

ANNA: Were all of 'em yust plain sailors?

CHRIS: Able body seaman, most of dem. (*with a certain pride*) Dey vas all smart seaman, too—A one. (*then after hesitating a moment—shyly*) Ay vas bo'sun.

ANNA: Bo'sun?

CHRIS: Dat's kind of officer.

ANNA: Gee, that was fine. What does he do?

CHRIS (*after a second's hesitation, plunged into gloom again by his fear of her enthusiasm*) Hard vork all time. It's rotten, Ay tal you, for go to sea. (*determined to disgust her with sea life—volubly*) Dey're all fool fallar, dem fallar in our family. Dey all vork rotten yob on sea for nutting, don't care nutting but yust gat big pay day in pocket, gat drunk, gat robbed, ship avay again on oder voyage. Dey don't come home. Dey don't do anytang like good man do. And at ole davil, sea, sooner, later she svallow dem up.

ANNA (*with an excited laugh*): Good sports, I'd call 'em. (*then hastily*) But say—listen—did all the women of the family marry sailors?

CHRIS (*eagerly—seeing a chance to drive home his point*): Yes—and it's bad on dem like hell vorst of all. Dey don't see deir men only once in long whie.

Dey set and vait all 'lone. And vhen deir boys grows up, go to sea, dey sit and vait some more. (*vehemently*) Any gel marry sailor, she's crazy fool! Your mo'der she tal you same tang if she vas alive. (*He relapses into an attitude of somber brooding.*)

ANNA (*after a pause—dreamily*): Funny! I do feel sort of nutty, to-night. I feel old.

CHRIS (*mystified*): Ole?

ANNA: Sure—like I'd been living a long, long time—out here in the fog. (*frowning perplexedly*) I don't know how to tell you yust what I mean. It's like I'd come home after a long visit away some place. It all seems like I'd been here before lots of times—on boats—in this same fog. (*with a short laugh*) You must think I'm off my base.

CHRIS (*gruffly*): Anybody feel funny dat vay in fog.

ANNA (*persistently*): But why d'you s'pose I feel so—so—like I'd found something I'd missed and been looking for—'s if this was the right place for me to fit in? And I seem to have forgot—everything that's happened—like it didn't matter no more. And I feel clean, somehow—like you feel yust after you've took a bath. And I feel happy for once—yes, honest!—happier than I ever been anywhere before! (*As* CHRIS *makes no comment but a heavy sigh, she continues wonderingly.*) It's nutty for me to feel that way, don't you think?

CHRIS (*a grim foreboding in his voice*): Ay tank Ay'm damn fool for bring you on voyage, Anna.

ANNA (*impressed by his tone*): You talk—nutty to-night yourself. You act 's if you was scared something was going to happen.

CHRIS: Only God know dat, Anna.

ANNA (*half-mockingly*): Then it'll be Gawd's will, like the preachers say—what does happen.

CHRIS (*starts to his feet with fierce protest*) No! Dat ole

davil, sea, she ain't God! (*In the pause of silence
that comes after his defiance a hail in a man's husky,
exhausted voice comes faintly out of the fog to port.*
"*Ahoy!*" CHRIS *gives a startled exclamation.*)

ANNA (*jumping to her feet*): What's that?

CHRIS (*who has regained his composure—sheepishly*):
Py golly, dat scare me for minute. It's only some
fallar hail, Anna—loose his course in fog. Must be
fisherman's power boat. His engine break down, Ay
guess. (*The* "ahoy" *comes again through the wall of
fog, sounding much nearer this time.* CHRIS *goes over
to the port bulwark.*) Sound from dis side. She come
in from open sea. (*He holds his hands to his mouth,
megaphone-fashion, and shouts back*) Ahoy, dere!
Vhat's trouble?

THE VOICE (*this time sounding nearer but up forward
toward the bow*) Heave a rope when we come along-
side. (*then irritably*) Where are ye, ye scut?

CHRIS: Ay hear dem rowing. Dey come up by bow,
Ay tank. (*then shouting out again*) Dis vay!

THE VOICE: Right ye are! (*There is a muffled sound
of oars in oar-locks.*)

ANNA (*half to herself—resentfully*): Why don't that guy
stay where he belongs?

CHRIS (*hurriedly*): Ay go up bow. All hands asleep
'cepting fallar on vatch. Ay gat heave line to dat
faller. (*He picks up a coil of rope and hurries off
toward the bow.* ANNA *walks back toward the extreme stern as if she wanted to remain as much iso-
lated as possible. She turns her back on the
proceedings and stares out into the fog. The voice is
heard again shouting,* "Ahoy" *and* CHRIS *answering*
"Dis vay." *Then there is a pause—the murmur of
excited voices—then the scuffling of feet.* CHRIS *appears from around the cabin to port. He is supporting the limp form of a man dressed in dungarees,*

holding one of the man's arms around his neck. The deckhand, JOHNSON, *a young, blond Swede, follows him, helping along another exhausted man similar fashion. Anna turns to look at them.* CHRIS *stops for a second—volubly)* Anna! You come help, vill you? You find vhiskey in cabin. Dese fallars need drink for fix dem. Dey vas near dead.

ANNA (*hurrying to him*): Sure—but who are they? What's the trouble?

CHRIS: Sailor fallars. Deir steamer gat wrecked. Dey been five days in open boat—four fallars—only one left able stand up. Come, Anna. (*She precedes him into the cabin, holding the door open while he and* JOHNSON *carry in their burdens. The door is shut, then opened again as* JOHNSON *comes out.* CHRIS'S *voice shouts after him*) Go gat oder fallar, Yohnson.

JOHNSON: Yes, sir. (*He goes. The door is closed again.* MAT BURKE *stumbles in around the port side of the cabin. He moves slowly, feeling his way uncertainly, keeping hold of the port bulwark with his right hand to steady himself. He is stripped to the waist, has on nothing but a pair of dirty dungaree pants. He is a powerful, broad-chested six-footer, his face handsome in a hard, rough, bold, defiant way. He is about thirty, in the full power of his heavy-muscled, immense strength. His dark eyes are bloodshot and wild from sleeplessness. The muscles of his arms and shoulders are lumped in knots and bunches, the veins of his forearms stand out like blue cords. He finds his way to the coil of hawser and sits down on it facing the cabin, his back bowed, head in his hands, in an attitude of spent weariness.*)

BURKE (*talking aloud to himself*): Row, ye divil! Row! (*then lifting his head and looking about him*) What's this tub? Well, we're safe anyway—with the help of God. (*He makes the sign of the cross mechanically.*

JOHNSON *comes along the deck to port, supporting the fourth man, who is babbling to himself incoherently.* BURKE *glances at him disdainfully.*) Is it losing the small wits ye iver had, ye are? Deck-scrubbing scut! (*They pass him and go into the cabin, leaving the door open.* BURKE *sags forward wearily.*) I'm bate out—bate out entirely.

ANNA (*comes out of the cabin with a tumbler quarter-full of whiskey in her hand. She gives a start when she sees* BURKE *so near her, the light from the open door falling full on him. Then, overcoming what is evidently a feeling of repulsion, she comes up beside him.*) Here you are. Here's a drink for you. You need it, I guess.

BURKE (*lifting his head slowly—confusedly*): Is it dreaming I am?

ANNA (*half smiling*): Drink it and you'll find it ain't no dream.

BURKE: To hell with the drink—but I'll take it just the same. (*He tosses it down.*) Aah! I'm needin' that—and 'tis fine stuff. (*looking up at her with frank, grinning admiration*) But 'twasnt' the booze I meant when I said, was I dreaming. I thought you was some mermaid out of the sea come to torment me. (*He reaches out to feel of her arm.*) Aye, rale flesh and blood, divil a less.

ANNA (*coldly—stepping back from him*): Cut that.

BURKE: But tell me, isn't this a barge I'm on—or isn't it?

ANNA: Sure.

BURKE: And what is a fine handsome woman the like of you doing on this scow?

ANNA (*coldly*): Never you mind. (*then half-amused in spite of herself*) Say, you're a great one, honest—starting right in kidding after what you been through.

BURKE (*delighted—proudly*): Ah, it was nothing—aisy for a rale an with guts to him, the like of me. (*He laughs.*) All in the day's work, darlin'. (*then, more seriously but still in a boastful tone, confidentially*) But I won't be denying 'twas a damn narrow squeak. We'd all ought to be with Davy Jones at the bottom of the sea, be rights. And only for me, I'm telling you, and the great strength and guts is in me, we'd be being scoffed by the fishes this minute!

ANNA (*contemptuously*): Gee, you hate yourself, don't you? (*then turning away from him indifferently*) Well, you'd better come in and lie down. You must want to sleep.

BURKE (*stung—rising unsteadily to his feet with chest out and head thrown back—resentfully*): Lie down and sleep, is it? Divil a wink I'm after having for two days and nights and divil a bit I'm needing now. Let you not be thinking I'm the like of them three weak scuts come in the boat with me. I could lick the three of them sitting down with one hand tied behind me. They may be bate out, but I'm not— and I've been rowing the boat with them lying in the bottom not able to raise a hand of the last two days we was in it. (*Furiously, as he sees this is making no impression on her*) And I can lick all hands on this tub, wan be wan, tired as I am!

ANNA (*sarcastically*): Gee, ain't you a hard guy! (*then, with a trace of sympathy, as she notices him swaying from weakness*) But never mind that fight talk. I'll take your word for all you've said. Go on and sit down out here, anyway, if I can't get you to come inside. (*He sits down weakly.*) You're all in, you might as well own up to it.

BURKE (*fiercely*): The hell I am!

ANNA (*coldly*): Well, be stubborn then for all I care. And I must say I don't care for your language. The

men I know don't pull that rough stud when ladies
are around.

BURKE (*getting unsteadily to his feet again—in a rage*):
Ladies! Ho-ho! Divil mend you! Let you not be
making game of me. What would ladies be doing
on this bloody hulk? (*As* ANNA *attempts to go to
the cabin, he lurches into her path.*) Aisy, now!
You're not the old Square-head's woman, I suppose
you'll be telling me next—living in his cabin with
him, no less! (*Seeing the cold, hostile expression on*
ANNA'S *face, he suddenly changes his tone to one of
boisterous joviality.*) But I do be thinking, iver since
the first look my eyes took at you, that it's a fool
you are to be wasting yourself—a fine, handsome
girl—on a stumpy runt of a man like that old Swede.
There's too many strapping great lads on the sea
would give their heart's blood for one kiss of you!

ANNA (*scornfully*): Lads like you, eh?

BURKE (*grinning*): Ye take the words out o' my
mouth. I'm the proper lad for you, if it's meself do
be saying it. (*With a quick movement he puts his
arms about her waist.*) Whisht, now, me daisy! Himself's in the cabin. It's wan of your kisses I'm needing to take the tiredness from me bones. Wan kiss,
now! (*He presses her to him and attempts to kiss
her.*)

ANNA (*struggling fiercely*): Leggo of me, you big mut!
(*She pushes him away with all her might.* BURKE,
*weak and tottering, is caught off his guard. He is
thrown down backward and, in falling, hits his head
a hard thump against the bulwark. He lies there still,
knocked out for the moment.* ANNA *stands for a second, looking down at him frightenedly. Then she
kneels down beside him and raises his head to her
knee, staring into his face anxiously for some sign
of life.*)

BURKE (*stirring a bit—mutteringly*): God stiffen it! (*He opens his eyes and blinks up at her with vague wonder.*)

ANNA (*letting his head sink back on the deck, rising to her feet with a sigh of relief*): You're coming to all right, eh? Gee, I was scared for a moment I'd killed you.

BURKE (*with difficulty rising to a sitting position—scornfully*): Killed, is it? It'd take more than a bit of a blow to crack my thick skull. (*then looking at her with the most intense admiration*) But, glory be, it's a power of strength is in them two fine arms of yours. There's not a man in the world can say the same as you, that he seen Mat Burke lying at his feet and him dead to the world.

ANNA (*Rather remorsefully*): Forget it. I'm sorry it happened, see (BURKE *rises and sits on bench. Then severely*) Only you had no right to be getting fresh with me. Listen, now, and don't go getting any more wrong notions. I'm on this barge because I'm making a trip with my father. The captain's my father. Now you know.

BURKE: The old square—the old Swede, I mean?

ANNA: Yes.

BURKE (*rising—peering at her face*): Sure I might have known it, if I wasn't a bloody fool from birth. Where else'd you get that fine yellow hair like a golden crown on your head.

ANNA (*with an amused laugh*): Say, nothing stops you, does it? (*Then attempting a severe tone again*) But don't you think you ought to be apologizing for what you said and done yust a minute ago, instead of trying to kid me with that mush?

BURKE (*indignantly*): Mush! (*then bending forward toward her with very intense earnestness*) Indade and I will ask your pardon a thousand times—and on my knees, if ye like. I didn't mean a word of what I said or did. (*resentful again for a second*) But divil a woman in all the ports of the world has iver made a great fool of me that way before!

ANNA (*with amused sarcasm*): I see. You mean you're a lady-killer and they all fall for you.

BURKE (*offended—passionately*): Leave off your fooling! 'Tis that is after getting my back up at you. (*earnestly*) 'Tis no lie I'm telling you about the women. (*ruefully*) Though it's a great jackass I am to be mistaking you, even in anger, for the like of them cows on the waterfront is the only women I've met up with since I was growed to a man. (*As* ANNA *shrinks away from him at this, he hurries on pleadingly.*) I'm a hard, rough man and I'm not fit, I'm thinking, to be kissing the shoe-soles of a fine, dacent girl the like of yourself. 'Tis only the ignorance of your kind made me see you wrong. So you'll forgive me, for the love of God, and let us be friends from this out. (*passionately*) I'm thinking I'd rather be friends with you than have my wish for anything else in the world. (*He holds out his hand to her shyly.*)

ANNA (*looking queerly at him, perplexed and worried, but moved and pleased in spite of herself—takes his hand uncertainly*): Sure.

BURKE (*with boyish delight*): God bless you! (*in his excitement he squeezes her hand tight.*)

ANNA: Ouch!

BURKE (*hastily dropping her hand—ruefully*): Your pardon, Miss. 'Tis a clumsy ape I am. (*then simply— glancing down his arms proudly*) It's great power I have in my hand and arm, and I do be forgetting it at times.

ANNA (*nursing her crushed hand and glancing at his*

arm, not without a trace of his own admiration) Gee, you're some strong, all right.

BURKE (*delighted*): It's no lie, and why shouldn't I be, with me shoveling a million tons of coal in the stokeholes of ships since I was a lad only. (*He pats the coil of hawser invitingly.*) Let you sit down, now, Miss, and I'll be telling you a bit of myself, and you'll be telling me a bit of yourself, and in an hour we'll be as old friends as if we was born in the same house. (*He pulls at her sleeve shyly.*) Sit down now, if you plaze.

ANNA (*with a half laugh*): Well— (*She sits down.*) But we won't talk about me, see? You tell me about yourself and about the wreck.

BURKE (*flattered*): I'll tell you, surely. But can I be asking you one question, Miss, has my head in a puzzle?

ANNA (*guardedly*): Well—I dunno—what is it?

BURKE: What is it you do when you're not taking a trip with the Old Man? For I'm thinking a fine girl like of you ain't living always on this tub.

ANNA (*wearily*): No—of course I ain't. (*She searches his face suspiciously, afraid there may be some hidden insinuation in his words. Seeing his simple frankness, she goes on confidently.*) Well, I'll tell you. I'm a governess, see? I take care of kids for people and learn them things.

BURKE (*impressed*): A governess, is it? You must be smart, surely.

ANNA: But let's not talk about me. Tell me about the wreck, like you promised me you would.

BURKE (*importantly*): 'Twas this way, Miss. Two weeks out we ran into the divil's own storm, and she sprang wan hell of a leak up for'ard. The skipper was hoping to make Boston before another blow would finish her, but ten days back we met up with another storm the like of the first, only worse. Four days we was in it with green seas raking over her from bow to stern. That was a terrible time, God help us. (*proudly*) And it 'twasn't for me and my great strength, I'm telling you—and it's God's truth—there'd been mutiny itself in the stokehole. 'Twas me held them to it, with a kick to wan and a clout to another, and they not caring a damn for the engineers any more, but fearing a clout of my right arm more than they'd feared the sea itself. (*He glances at her anxiously, eager for her approval.*)

ANNA (*concealing a smile—amused by this boyish boasting of his*): You did some hard work, didn't you?

BUKRE (*promptly*): I did that! I'm a divil for sticking it out when them that's weak give up. But much good it did anyone! 'Twas a mad, fightin' scramble in the last seconds with each man for himself. I disremember how it come about, but there was the four of us in wan boat and when we was raised high on a great wave I took a look about and divil a sight there was of ship or men on top of the sea.

ANNA (*in a hushed voice*): Then all the others was drowned?

BURKE: They was, surely.

ANNA (*with a shudder*): What a terrible end!

BURKE (*turns to her*): A terrible end for the like of them swabs does live on land, maybe. But for the like of us does be roaming the seas, a good end, I'm telling you—quick and clane.

ANNA (*struck by the word*): Yes, clean. That's yust the word for—all of it—the way it makes me feel.

BURKE: The sea, you mean? (*interestedly*) I'm thinking you have a bit of it in your blood, too. Your Old Man wasn't only a barge rat—begging your pardon—all his life, by the cut of him.

ANNA: No, he was bo'sun on sailing ships for years. And all the men on both sides of the family have gone to sea as far back as he remembers, he says. All the women have married sailors, too.

BURKE (*with intense satisfaction*): Did they, now? They had spirit in them. It's only on the sea you'd find rale men with guts is fit to wed with fine, high-tempered girls (*then he adds half-boldly*) the like of yourself.

ANNA (*with a laugh*): There you go kiddin' again. (*then seeing his hurt expression—quickly*) But you was going to tell me about yourself. You're Irish, of course I can tell that.

BURKE (*stoutly*): Yes, thank God, though I've not seen a sight of it in fifteen years or more.

ANNA (*thoughtfully*): Sailors never do go home hardly, do they? That's what my father was saying.

BURKE; He wasn't telling no lie. (*with sudden melan-choly*) It's a hard and lonesome life, the sea is. The only women you'd meet in the ports of the world who'd be willing to speak you a kind word isn't woman at all. You know the kind I mane, and they're a poor, wicked lot. God forgive them. They're looking to steal the money from you only.

ANNA (*her face averted—rising to her feet—agitatedly*): I think—I guess I'd better see what's doing inside.

BURKE (*afraid he has offended her—beseechingly*): Don't go, I'm saying! Is it I've given you offence with my talk of the like of them? Don't heed it at all! I'm clumsy in my wits when it comes to talking proper with a girl the like of you. And why wouldn't I be? Since the day I left home for to go to sea punching coal, this is the first time I've had a word with a rale, dacent woman. So don't turn your back on me now, and we beginning to be friends.

ANNA (*turning to him again—forcing a smile*): I'm not sore at you, honest.

BURKE (*gratefully*): God bless you!

ANNA (*changing the subject abruptly*): But if you honestly think the sea's such a rotten life, why don't you get out of it?

BURKE (*surprised*): Work on land, is it? (*She nods. He spits scornfully*): Digging spuds in the muck from dawn to dark, I suppose? (*vehemently*) I wasn't made for it, Miss.

ANNA (*with a laugh*): I thought you'd say that.

BURKE (*argumentatively*): But there's good jobs and bad jobs at sea, like there'd be on land. I'm thinking if it's in the stokehole of a proper liner I was, I'd be able to have a little house and be home to it wan week out of four. And I'm thinking that maybe then I'd have the luck to find a fine dacent girl— the like of yourself, now—would be willing to wed with me.

ANNA (*turning away from him with a short laugh— uneasily*): Why sure. Why not?

BURKE (*edging up close to her—exultantly*): Then you think a girl the like of yourself might maybe not mind the past at all but only be seeing the good herself put in me?

ANNA (*in the same tone*): Why, sure.

BURKE (*passionately*): She'd not be sorry for it, I'd take my oath! 'Tis no more drinking and roving about I'd be doing then, but giving my pay day into her hand and staying at home with her as meek as a lamb each night of the week I'd be in port.

ANNA (*moved in spite of herself and troubled by this half-concealed proposal—with a forced laugh*): All you got to do is find the girl.

BURKE: I have found her!

ANNA (*half-frightenedly—trying to laugh it off*): You have? When? I thought you was saying—

BUKRE (*boldly and forcefully*): This night. (*hanging his head— humbly*) If she'll be having me. (*then raising his eyes to hers—simply*) 'Tis you I mean.

ANNA (*is held by his eyes for a moment—then shrinks back from him with a strange, broken laugh*): Say— are you—going crazy? Are you trying to kid me? Proposing—to me!—for Gawd's sake!—on such short acquaintance? (*CHRIS comes out of the cabin and stands staring blinkingly astern. When he makes out ANNA in such intimate proximity to this strange sailor, an angry expression comes over his face.*)

BURKE (*following her—with fierce, pleading insistence*): I'm telling you there's the will of God in it that brought me safe through the storm and fog to the wan spot in the world where you was! Think of that now, and isn't it queer—

CHRIS: Anna! (*He comes toward them, raging, his fists clenched.*) Anna, you gat in cabin, you hear!

ANNA (*all her emotions immediately transformed into resentment at his bullying tone*): Who d'you think you're talking to—a slave?

CHRIS (*hurt—his voice breaking—pleadingly*): You need gat rest, Anna. You gat sleep. (*She does not move. He turns on BURKE furiously.*) What you doing here, you sailor fallar? You ain't sick like oders. You gat in fo'c's'tle. Dey give you bunk. (*threateningly*) You hurry, Ay tal you!

ANNA (*impulsively*): But he is sick. Look at him. He can hardly stand up.

BURKE (*straightening and throwing out his chest—with a bold laugh*): Is it giving me orders ye are, me bucko? Let you look out, then! With wan hand, weak as I am, I can break ye in two and fling the pieces over the side—and your crew after you.

(*stopping abruptly*) I was forgetting. You're her Old Man and I'd not raise a fist to you for the world. (*His knees sag, he wavers and seems about to fall. ANNA utters an exclamation of alarm and hurries to his side.*)

ANNA (*taking one of his arms over her shoulder*): Come on in the cabin. You can have my bed if there ain't no other place.

BURKE (*with jubilant happiness—as they proceed toward the cabin*): Glory be to God, is it holding my arm about your neck you are! Anna! Anna! Sure it's a sweet name is suited to you.

ANNA (*guiding him carefully*): Sssh! Sssh!

BURKE: Whilsht, is it? Indade, and I'll not. I'll be roaring it out like a fog horn over the sea! You're the girl of the world and we'll be marrying soon, and I don't care who knows it!

ANNA (*as she guides him through the cabin door*): Ssshh! Never mind that talk. You go to sleep. (*They go out of sight in the cabin. CHRIS, who has been listening to BURKE's last words with open-mouthed amazement stands looking after them helplessly.*)

CHRIS (*turns suddenly and shakes his fist out at the sea—with bitter hatred*): Dat's your dirty trick, damn ole davil, you! (*then in a frenzy of rage*) But, py God, you don't do dat! Not while Ay'm living! No, py God, you don't!

(*The Curtain Falls*)

ACT THREE

SCENE—*The interior of the cabin on the barge, "Simeon Winthrop" (at dock in Boston)—a narrow, low-ceilinged compartment the walls of which are painted a light brown with white trimmings. In the rear on the left, a door leading to the sleeping quarters. In the far left corner, a large locker-closet, painted white, on the door of which a mirror hangs on a nail. In the rear wall, two small square windows and a door opening out on the deck toward the stern. In the right wall, two more windows looking out on the port deck. White curtains, clean and stiff, are at the windows. A table with cane-bottomed chairs stands in the center of the cabin. A dilapidated, wicker rocker, painted brown, is also by the table.*

It is afternoon of a sunny day about a week later. From the harbor and docks outside, muffled by the closed door and windows, comes the sound of steamers' whistles and the puffing snort of the donkey engines of some ship unloading nearby.

As the curtain rises, CHRIS *and* ANNA *are discovered. Anna is seated in the rocking-chair by the table, with a newspaper in her hands. She is not reading but staring straight in front of her. She looks unhappy, troubled, frowningly concentrated on her thoughts.* CHRIS *wanders about the room, casting quick, uneasy side glances at her face, then stopping to peer absentmindedly out of the window. His attitude betrays an overwhelming, gloomy anxiety which has him on tenter hooks. He pretends to be engaged in setting things ship-shape, but this occupation is confined to picking up some object, staring at it stupidly for a second, then aimlessly putting it down again. He clears his throat and starts to sing to himself in a low, doleful voice:* "My Yosephine, come aboard de ship. Long time Ay vait for you."

ANNA (*turning on him, sarcastically*): I'm glad someone's feeling good. (*wearily*) Gee, I sure wish we was out of this dump and back in New York.

CHRIS (*with a sigh*): Ay'm glad vhen ve sail again, too. (*Then, as she makes no comment, he goes on with a ponderous attempt at sarcasm.*) Ay don't see vhy you don't like Boston, dough. You have good time here, Ay tank. You go ashore all time, every day and night veek ve've been here. You go to movies, see show, gat all kinds fun— (*his eyes hard with hatred*) All with that damn Irish fallar!

ANNA (*with weary scorn*): Oh, for heaven's sake, are you off on that again? Where's the harm in his taking me around? D'you want me to sit all day and night in this cabin with you—and knit? Ain't I got a right to have as good a time as I can?

CHRIS: It ain't right kind of fun—not with that fallar, no.

ANNA: I been back on board every night by eleven, ain't I? (*then struck by some thought—looks at him with keen suspicion—with rising anger*) Say, look here, what d'you mean by what you yust said?

CHRIS (*hastily*): Nutting but what Ay say, Anna.

ANNA: You said "ain't right" and you said it funny. Say, listen here, you ain't trying to insinuate that there's something wrong between us, are you?

CHRIS (*horrified*): No, Anna! No, Ay svear to God, Ay never tank dat!

ANNA (*mollified by his very evident sincerity—sitting down again*): Well, don't you never think it neither if you want me ever to speak to you again. (*angrily again*) If I ever dreamt you thought that, I'd get the hell out of this barge so quick you couldn't see me for dust.

CHRIS (*soothingly*): Ay wouldn't ever dream— (*then, after a second's pause, reprovingly*) You vas gatting learn to svear. Dat ain't nice for young gel, you tank?

ANNA (*with a faint trace of a smile*): Excuse me. You ain't used to such language, I know. (*mockingly*) That's what your taking me to sea has done for me.

CHRIS (*indignantly*): No, it ain't me. It's dat damn sailor fallar learn you bad tangs.

ANNA: He ain't a sailor. He's a stoker.

CHRIS (*forcibly*): Dat vas million times vorse, Ay tal you! Dem fallars dat vork below shoveling coal vas de dirtiest, rough gang of no-good fallars in vorld!

ANNA: I'd hate to hear you say that to Mat.

CHRIS: Oh, Ay tal him same tang. You don't gat it in head Ay'm scared of him yust 'cause he vas stronger'n Ay vas. (*menacingly*) You don't gat for fight with fists with dem fallars. Dere's oder vay for fix him.

ANNA (*glancing at him with sudden alarm*): What d'you mean?

CHRIS (*sullenly*): Nutting.

ANNA: You'd better not. I wouldn't start no trouble with him if I was you. He might forget some time that you was old and my father—and then you'd be out of luck.

CHRIS (*with smouldering hatred*): Vell, yust let him! Ay'm ole bird maybe, but Ay bet Ay show him trick or two.

ANNA (*suddenly changing her tone—persuasively*): Aw

come on, be good. What's eating you, anyway? Don't you want no one to be nice to me except yourself?

CHRIS (*placated—coming to her—eagerly*): Yes, Ay do, Anna—only not fallar on sea. But Ay like for you marry steady fallar got good yob on land. You have little home in country all your own—

ANNA (*rising to her feet—brusquely*): Oh, cut it out! (*scornfully*) Little home in the country! I wish you could have seen the little home in the country where you had me in jail till I was sixteen! (*with rising irritation*) Some day you're going to get me so mad with that talk, I'm going to turn loose on you and tell you—a lot of things that'll open your eyes.

CHRIS (*alarmed*): Ay don't vant—

ANNA: I know you don't; but you keep on talking yust the same.

CHRIS: Ay don't talk no more den, Anna.

ANNA: Then promise me you'll cut out saying nasty things about Mat Burke every chance you get.

CHRIS (*evasive and suspicious*): Why? You like dat fallar—very much, Anna?

ANNA; Yes, I certainly do! He's a regular man, no matter what faults he's got. One of his fingers is worth all the hundreds of men I met out there—inland.

CHRIS (*his face darkening*): Maybe you tank you love him, den?

ANNA (*defiantly*): What of it if I do?

CHRIS (*scowling and forcing out the words*): Maybe—you tank you—marry him?

ANNA (*shaking her head*): No! (CHRIS's *face lights up with relief.* ANNA *continues slowly, a trace of sadness in her voice.*) If I'd met him four years ago—or even two years ago—I'd have jumped at the chance, I tell you that straight. And I would now—only he's such a simple guy—a big kid—and I ain't got the heart to fool him. (*She breaks off suddenly.*) But don't never say again he ain't good enough for me. It's me ain't good enough for him.

CHRIS (*snorts scornfully*): Py yiminy, you go crazy, Ay tank

ANNA (*with a mournful laugh*): Well, I been thinking I was myself the last few days. (*She goes and takes a shawl from a hook near the door and throws it over her shoulders.*) Guess I'll take a walk down to the end of the dock for a minute and see what's doing. I love to watch the ships passing. Mat'll be along before long, I guess. Tell him where I am, will you?

CHRIS (*despondently*): Al right, Ay tal him. (ANNA *goes out the doorway on rear.* CHRIS *follows her out and stands on the deck outside for a moment looking after her. Then he comes back inside and shuts the door. He stands looking out of the window—mutters—"Dirty ole davil, you." Then he goes to the table, sets the cloth straight mechanically, picks up the newspaper* ANNA *has let fall to the floor and sits down in the rocking-chair. He stares at the paper for a while, then puts it on table, holds his head in his hands and sighs drearily. The noise of a man's heavy footsteps comes from the deck outside and there is a loud knock on the door.* CHRIS *starts, makes a move as if to get up and go to the door, then thinks better of it and sits still. The knock is repeated—then as no answer comes, the door is flung open and* MAT BURKE *appears.* CHRIS *scowls at the intruder and his hand instinctively goes back to the sheath knife on his hip.* BURKE *is dressed up—wears a cheap blue suit, a striped cotton shirt with a black tie, and black shoes newly shined. His face is beaming with good humor.*)

BURKE (*as he sees* CHRIS—*in a jovial tone of mockery*):

Well, God bless who's here! (*He bends down and squeezes his huge form through the narrow doorway.*) And how is the world treating you this afternoon, Anna's father?

CHRIS (*sullenly*): Pooty goot—if it ain't for some fallars.

BURKE (*with a grin*): Meaning me, do you? (*He laughs.*) Well, if you ain't the funny old crank of a man! (*Then soberly*) Where's herself? (CHRIS *sits dumb, scowling, his eyes averted.* BURKE *is irritated by this silence.*) Where's Anna, I'm after asking you?

CHRIS (*hesitating—then grouchily*): She go down end of dock.

BURKE: I'll be going down to her, then. But first I'm thinking I'll take this chance when we're alone to have a word with you. (*He sits down opposite* CHRIS *at the table and leans over toward him.*) And that word is soon said. I'm marrying your Anna before this day is out, and you might as well make up your mind to it whether you like it or not.

CHRIS (*glaring at him with hatred and forcing a scornful laugh*): Ho-ho! Dat's easy for say!

BURKE: You mean I won't? (*scornfully*) Is it the like of yourself will stop me, are you thinking?

CHRIS: Yes, Ay stop it, if it come to vorst.

BURKE (*with scornful pity*): God help you!

CHRIS: But ain't no need for me to do dat. Anna—

BURKE (*smiling confidently*): Is it Anna you think will prevent me?

CHRIS: Yes.

BURKE: And I'm telling you she'll not. She knows I'm loving her, and she loves me the same and I knows it.

CHRIS: Ho-ho! She only have fun. She make big fool of you, dat's all!

BURKE (*unshaken—pleasantly*): That's a lie in your throat, divil mend you!

CHRIS: No, it ain't lie. She tal me yust before she go out she never marry fallar like you.

BURKE: I'll not believe it. 'Tis a great old liar you are, and a divil to be making a power of trouble if you had your way. But 'tis not trouble I'm looking for, and me sitting down here. (*earnestly*) Let us be talking it out now as a man to man. You're her father, and wouldn't it be a shame for us to be at each other's throats like a pair of dogs, and I married with Anna. So out with the truth man alive What is it you're holding against me at all?

CHRIS (*a bit placated, in spite of himself, by* BURKE's *evident sincerity—but puzzled and suspicious*): Vell—Ay don't vant for Anna gat married. Listen, you fallar. Ay'm a ole man. Ay don't see Anna for fifteen years. She vas all Ay gat in vorld. And now ven she come on first trip—you tank Ay vant her leave me 'lone again?

BURKE (*heartily*): Let you not be thinking I have no heart at all for the way you'd be feeling.

CHRIS (*astonished and encouraged—trying to plead persuasively*): Den you do right tang, eh? You ship avay again, leave Anna alone. (*cajolingly*) Big fallar like you dat's on sea, he don't need vife. He gat new gel in every port, you know dat.

BURKE (*angry for a second*): God stiffen you! (*then controlling himself—calmly*) I'll not be giving you the lie on that. But divil take you, there's a time comes to every man, on sea or land, that isn't a born fool, when he's sick of the lot of them cows, and wearing his heart out to meet up with a fine dacent girl, and have a home to call his own and he rearing up children in it. 'Tis small use you're asking me to leave Anna. She's the wan woman of the world for me, and I can't live without her now, I'm thinking.

CHRIS: You forgat all about her in one veek out of port, Ay bet you!

BURKE: You don't know the like I am. Death itself wouldn't make me forget her. So let you not be making talk to me about leaving her. I'll not, and be damned to you! It won't be so bad for you as you'd make out at all. She'll be living here I the States, and her married to me. And you'd be seeing her often so—a sight more often than ever you saw her the fifteen years she was growing up in the West. It's quare you'd be the one to be making great trouble about her leaving you when you never laid eyes on her once in all them years.

CHRIS (*guiltily*): Ay taught it vas better Anna stay avay, grow up inland where she don't ever know ole davil, sea.

BURKE (*scornfully*): Is it blaming the sea for your troubles ye are again, God help you? Well, Anna knows it now. 'Twas in her blood, anyway.

CHRIS: And Ay don't vant she ever know no-good fallar on sea—

BURKE: She knows one now.

CHRIS (*banging the table with his fist—furiously*): Dat's yust it! Dat's yust what you are—no-good, sailor fallar! You tank Ay lat her life be made sorry by you like her mo'der's vas by me! No, Ay svear! She don't marry you if Ay gat kill you first!

BURKE (*looks at him a moment, in astonishment—then laughing uproariously*): Ho-ho! Glory to be God, it's bold talk you have for a stumpy runt of a man!

CHRIS (*threateningly*): Vell—you see!

BURKE (*with grinning defiance*): I'll see, surely! I'll see myself and Anna married this day, I'm telling you! (*then with contemptuous exasperation*) It's quare fool's blather you have about the sea done this and the sea done that. You'd ought to be shamed to be

saying the like, and you an old sailor yourself. I'm
after hearing a lot of it from you and a lot more
that Anna's told me you do be saying to her, and
I'm thinking it's a poor weak thing you are, and not
a man at all!

CHRIS (*darkly*): You see if Ay'm man—maybe quicker'n you tank.

BURKE (*contemptuously*): Yerra, don't be boasting.
I'm thinking 'tis one of your wits you've got with
fright of the sea. You'd be wishing Anna married
to a farmer, she told me. That'd be a sweat match
surely! Would you have a fine girl the like of Anna
lying down at nights with a muddy scut stinking of
pigs and dung? Or would you have her tied for life
to the like of them skinny, shrivelled swabs does be
working in cities?

CHRIS: Dat's lie, you fool!

BURKE: 'Tis not. 'Tis your own mad notions I'm after
telling. But you know the truth in your heart, if
great fear of the sea has made you a liar and coward
itself. (*pounding the table*) The sea's the only life
for a man with guts in him isn't afraid of his own
shadow! 'Tis only on the sea he's free, and him
roving the face of the world, seeing all things, and
not giving a damn for saving up money, or stealing
from his friends, or any of the black tricks that a
landlubber'd waste his life on. 'Twas yourself knew
it once, and you a bo'sun for years.

CHRIS (*sputtering with rage*): You vas crazy fool, Ay
tal you!

BURKE: You've swallowed the anchor. The sea give
you a clout once knocked you down, and you're not
man enough to get up for another, but lie there for
the rest of your life howling bloody murder.
(*proudly*) Isn't it myself the sea has nearly drowned,
and me battered and bate till I was that close to

hell I could hear the flames roaring, and never a groan out of me till the sea gave up and it seeing the great strength and guts of a man was in me?

CHRIS (*scornfully*): Yes, you vas hell of fallar, hear you tal it!

BURKE (*angrily*): You'll be calling me a liar once too often, me old bucko! Wasn't the whole story of it and my picture itself in the newspapers of Boston a week back? (*looking* CHRIS *up and down belittlingly*) Sure I'd like to see you in the best of your youth do the like of what I done in the storm and after. 'Tis a mad lunatic, screeching with fear, you'd be this minute!

CHRIS: Ho-ho! You vas young fool! In ole years when Ay was on windyammer, Ay vas through hundred storms vorse'n dat! Ships vas ships den—and men dat sail on dem vas real men. And now what you gat on steamers? You gat fallars on deck don't know ship from mudscow. (*with a meaning glance at* BURKE) And below deck you gat fallars yust know how for shovel coal—might yust as vell vork on coal vagon ashore!

BURKE (*stung—angrily*): Is it casting insults at the men in the stokehole ye are, ye old ape! God stiffen you! Wan of them is worth any ten stock-fish-swilling Square-heads ever shipped on a windbag!

CHRIS (*his face working with rage, his hand going back to the sheath-knife on his hip*): Irish svine, you!

BURKE (*tauntingly*): Don't ye like the Irish, ye old baboon? 'Tis that you're needing in your family, I'm telling you—an Irishman and a man of the stokehole—to put guts in it so that you'll be not having grandchildren would be fearful cowards and jackasses the like of yourself!

CHRIS (*half rising from his chair—in a voice choked with rage*): You look out!

BURKE (*watching him intently—a mocking smile on his lips*): And it's that you'll be having, no matter what you'll do to prevent; for Anna and me'll be married this day, and no old fool the like of you will stop us when I've made up my mind.

CHRIS (*with a hoarse cry*): You don't! (*He throws himself at* BURKE, *knife in hand, knocking his chair over backwards.* BURKE *springs to his feet quickly in time to meet the attack. He laughs with the pure love of battle. The old Swede is like a child in his hands.* BURKE *does not strike or mistreat him in any way, but simply twists his right hand behind his back and forces the knife from his fingers. He throws the knife into a far corner of the room—tauntingly*)

BURKE: Old men is getting childish shouldn't play with knives. (*holding the struggling* CHRIS *at arm's length—with a sudden rush of anger, drawing back his fist*) I've half a mind to hit you a great clout will put sense in your square head. Kape off me now, I'm warning you! (*He gives* CHRIS *a push with the flat of his hand which sends the old Swede staggering back against the cabin wall, where he remains standing, panting heavily, his eyes fixed on* BURKE *with hatred, as if he were only collecting his strength to rush at him again.*)

BURKE (*warningly*): Now don't be coming at me again, I'm saying, or I'll flatten you on the floor with a blow, if 'tis Anna's father you are itself! I've no patience left for you. (*then with an amused laugh*) Well, 'tis a bold old man you are just the same, and I'd never think it was in you to come tackling me alone. (*A shadow crosses the cabin windows. Both men start.* ANNA *appears in the doorway.*)

ANNA (*with pleased surprise as she sees* BURKE): Hello, Mat. Are you here already? I was down— (*She stops, looking from one to the other, sensing immedi-*

ately that something has happened.) What's up? (*then noticing the overturned chair—in alarm*) How'd that chair get knocked over? (*turning on* BURKE *reproachfully*) You ain't been fighting with him, Mat—after you promised?

BUKRE (*his old self again*): I've not laid a hand on him, Anna. (*He goes and picks up the chair, then turning on the still questioning* ANNA—*with a reassuring smile*) Let you not be worried at all. 'Twas only a bit of an argument we was having to pass the time till you'd come.

ANNA: It must have been some argument when you got to throwing chairs. (*She turns to* CHRIS.) Why don't you say something? What was it about?

CHRIS (*relaxing at last—avoiding her eyes—sheepishly*): Ve vas talking about ships and fallars on sea.

ANNA (*with a relieved smile*): Oh—the old stuff, eh?

BURKE (*suddenly seeming to come to a bold decision—with a defiant grin at* CHRIS): He's not after telling you the whole of it. We was arguing about you mostly.

ANNA (*with a frown*): About me?

BUKRE: And we'll be finishing it out right here and now in your presence if you're willing. (*He sits down at the left of table.*)

ANNA (*uncertainly—looking from him to her father*): Sure. Tell me what it's all about.

CHRIS (*advancing toward the table—protesting to* BURKE): No! You don't do dat, you! You tal him you don't vant for hear him talk, Anna.

ANNA: But I do. I want this cleared up.

CHRIS (*miserably afraid now*): Vell, not now, anyvay. You vas going ashore, yes? You ain't got time—

ANNA (*firmly*): Yes, right here and now. (*She turns to* BURKE.) You tell me, Mat, since he don't want to.

BURKE (*draws a deep breath—then plunges in boldly*):

The whole of it's in a few words only. So's he'd make no mistake, and him hating the sight of me, I told him in his teeth I loved you. (*passionately*) And that's God truth, Anna, and well you know it!

CHRIS (*scornfully—forcing a laugh*): Ho-ho! He tal same tang to gel every port he go!

ANNA (*shrinking from her father with repulsion—resentfully*): Shut up, can't you? (*then to* BURKE—*feelingly*) I know it's true, Mat. I don't mind what he says.

BURKE (*humbly grateful*): God bless you!

ANNA: And then what?

BURKE: And then— (*hesitantly*) And then I said—(*he looks at her pleadingly*) I said I was sure—I told him I thought you have a bit of love for me, too. (*passionately*) Say you do, Anna! Let you not destroy me entirely, for the love of God! (*He grasps both her hands in his two.*)

ANNA (*deeply moved and troubled—forcing a trembling laugh*): So you told him that, Mat? No wonder he was mad. (*Forcing out the words*) Well, maybe it's true, Mat. Maybe I do. I been thinking and thinking—I didn't want to, Mat. I'll own up to that—I tried to cut it out—but—(*she laughs helplessly*) I guess I can't help it anyhow. So I guess I do, Mat. (*then with a sudden joyous defiance*) Sure I do! What's the use of kidding myself different? Sure I love you, Mat!

CHRIS (*with a cry of pain*): Anna! (*He sits crushed.*)

BURKE (*with a great depth of sincerity in his humble gratitude*): God be praised!

ANNA (*assertively*): And I ain't never loved a man in my life before, you can always believe that—no matter what happens.

BURKE (*goes over to her and puts his arms around her*): Sure I do be believing ivery word you iver said or iver will say. And 'tis you and me will be having a grand, beautiful life together to the end of our days! (*He tries to kiss her. At first she turns away her head—then, overcome by a fierce impulse of passionate love, she takes his head in both her hands and holds his face close to hers, staring into his eyes. Then she kisses him full on the lips.*)

ANNA (*pushing him away from her—forcing a broken laugh*): Good-by. (*She walks to the doorway in rear—stands with her back toward them, looking out. Her shoulders quiver once or twice as if she were fighting back her sobs.*)

BURKE (*too in the seventh heaven of bliss to get any correct interpretation of her word—with a laugh*): Good-by, is it? The divil you say! I'll be coming back at you in a second for more of the same! (*to* CHRIS, *who has quickened to instant attention at his daughter's good-by, and has looked back at her with a stirring of foolish hope in his eyes*) Now, me old bucko, what'll you be saying? You heard the words from her own lips. Confess I've bate you. Own up like a man when you're bate fair and square. And here's my hand to you— (*holds out his hand*) And let you take it and we'll shake and forget what's over and done, and be friends from this out.

CHRIS (*with implacable hatred*): Ay don't shake hands with you fallar—not vhile Ay live!

BURKE (*offended*): The back of my hand to you then, if that suits you better. (*growling*) 'Tis a rotten bad loser you are, divil mend you!

CHRIS: Ay don't lose— (*trying to be scornful and self-convincing*) Anna say she like you little bit and you don't hear her say she marry you, Ay bet. (*At the sound of her name* ANNA *has turned round to them. Her face is composed and calm again, but it is the dead calm of despair.*)

BURKE (*scornfully*): No, and I wasn't hearing her say the sun is shining either.

CHRIS (*doggedly*): Dat's all right. She don't say it, yust same.

ANNA (*quietly—coming forward to them*): No, I didn't say it, Mat.

CHRIS (*eagerly*): Dere! You hear!

BURKE (*misunderstanding her—with a grin*): You're waiting till you do be asked, you mane? Well, I'm asking you now. And we'll be married this day, with the help of God!

ANNA (*gently*): You heard what I said, Mat—after I kissed you?

BURKE (*alarmed by something in her manner*): No— I disremember.

ANNA: I said good-bye. (*her voice trembling*) That kiss was for good-bye, Mat.

BURKE (*terrified*): What d'you mane?

ANNA: I can't marry you, Mat—and we've said good-by. That's all.

CHRIS (*unable to hold back his exultation*): Ay know it! Ay know dat vas so!

BURKE (*jumping to his feet—unable to believe his ears*): Anna! Is it making game of me you'd be? 'Tis a quare time to joke with me and don't be doing it, for the love of God.

ANNA (*looking him in the eyes—steadily*): D'you think I'd kid you now? No, I'm not joking, Mat. I mean what I said.

BURKE: Ye don't! Ye can't! 'Tis mad you are, I'm telling you!

ANNA (*fixedly*): No I'm not.

BURKE (*desperately*): But what's come over you so sudden? You was saying you loved me—

ANNA: I'll say that as often as you want me to. It's true.

BURKE (*bewilderedly*): Then why—what, in the divil's name—Oh, God help me, I can't make head or tail to it at all!

ANNA: Because it's the best way out I can figure, Mat. (*her voice catching*) I been thinking it over and thinking it over day and night all week. Don't think it ain't hard on me, too, Mat.

BURKE: For the love of God, tell me then, what is it that's preventing you wedding me when the two of us has love? (*suddenly getting an idea and pointing at* CHRIS—*exasperatedly*) Is it giving heed to the like of that old fool ye are, and him hating me and filling your ears full of bloody lies against me?

CHRIS (*getting to his feet—raging triumphantly before* ANNA *has a chance to get in a word*): Yes, Anna believe me, not you! She know her old fa'der don't lie like you.

ANNA (*turning on her father angrily*): You sit down, d'you hear? Where do you come in butting in and making things worse? You're like a devil, you are! (*harshly*) Good Lord, and I was beginning to like you, beginning to forget all I've got held up against you!

CHRIS (*crushed—feebly*): You ain't got nutting for hold against me, Anna.

ANNA: Ain't I yust! Well, lemme tell you— (*she glances at* BURKE *and stops abruptly.*) Say, Mat, I'm s'prised at you. You didn't think anything he'd said—

BURKE (*glumly*): Sure, what else would it be?

ANNA: Think I've ever paid any attention to all his crazy bull? Gee, you must take me for a five-year-old kid.

BURKE (*puzzled and beginning to be irritated at her too*): I don't know how to take you, with your saying this one minute and that the next.

ANNA: Well, he has nothing to do with it.

BURKE: Then what is it has? Tell me, and don't keep me waiting and sweating blood.

ANNA (*resolutely*): I can't tell you—I won't. I got a good reason—and that's all you need to know. I can't marry you, that's all there is to it. (*distractedly*) So, for Gawd's sake, let's talk of something else.

BURKE: I'll not! (*then fearfully*) Is it married to someone else you are—in the West maybe?

ANNA (*vehemently*): I should say not.

BURKE (*regaining his courage*): To the divil with all other reasons then. They don't matter with me at all. (*He gets to his feet confidently, assuming a masterful tone.*) I'm thinking you're the like of them women can't make up with mind till they're drove to it. Well, then, I'll make up your mind for you bloody quick. (*He takes her by the arms, grinning to soften his serious bullying.*) We've had enough of talk! Let you be going into your room now and be dressing in your best and we'll be going ashore.

CHRIS (*aroused—angrily*): No, py God, she don't do that (*takes hold of her arm*)

ANNA (*who has listened to* BURKE *in astonishment. She draws away from him, instinctively repelled by his tone, but not exactly sure if he is serious or not—a trace of resentment in her voice*) Say, where do you get that stuff?

BURKE (*imperiously*): Never mind, now! Let you go get dressed, I'm saying (*then turning to* CHRIS) We'll be seeing who'll win in the end—me or you.

CHRIS (*to* ANNA—*also in an authoritative tone*) You stay right here, Anna, you hear! (ANNA *stands looking from one to the other of them as if she thought they had both gone crazy. Then the expression of her face freezes into the hardened sneer of her experience.*)

BURKE (*violently*): She'll not! She'll do what I say! You've had your hold on her long enough. It's my turn now.

ANNA (*with a hard laugh*): Your turn? Say, what am I, anyway?

BURKE: 'Tis not what you are, 'tis what you're going to be this day—and that's wedded to me before night comes. Hurry up now with your dressing.

CHRIS (*commandingly*): You don't do one tang he say, Anna! (ANNA *laughs mocking*.)

BURKE: She will, so!

CHRIS: Ay tal you she don't! Ay'm her fa'der.

BURKE: She will in spite of you. She's taking my orders from this out, not yours.

ANNA (*laughing again*): Orders is good!

BURKE (*turning to her impatiently*): Hurry up now, and shake a leg. We've no time to be wasting. (*irritated as she doesn't move*) Do you hear what I'm telling you?

CHRIS: You stay dere, Anna!

ANNA (*at the end of her patience—blazing out at them passionately*): You can go to hell, both of you! (*There is something in her tone that makes them forget their quarrel and turn to her in a stunned amazement.* ANNA *laughs wildly*.) You're just like the rest of them—you two! Gawd, you'd think I was a piece of furniture! I'll show you! Sit down now! (*as they hesitate—furiously*) Sit down and let me talk for a minute. You're all wrong, see? Listen to me! I'm going to tell you something—and then I'm going to beat it. (*to* BURKE—*with a harsh laugh*) I'm going to tell you a funny story, so pay attention. (*pointing to* CHRIS) I've been meaning to turn it loose on him every time he'd get my goat with his bull about keeping me safe inland. I wasn't going to tell you, but you've forced me into it. What's the dig? It's all wrong anyway, and you might as well get cured that way as any other. (*with hard mocking*) Only don't forget what you aid a minute ago about it not mattering to you what other reason I got so long as I wasn't married to no one else.

BURKE (*manfully*): That's my word, and I'll stick to it!

ANNA (*laughing bitterly*): What a chance! You make me laugh, honest! Want to bet you will? Wait 'n see! (*She stands at the table rear, looking from one to the other of the two men with her hard, mocking smile. Then she begins, fighting to control her emotion and speak calmly.*) First thing is, I want to tell you two guys something. You was going on 's if one of you had got to own me. But nobody owns me, see?—'cepting myself. I'll do what I please and no man, I don't give a hoot who he is, can tell me what to do! I ain't asking either of you for a living. I can make it myself—one way or other. I'm my own boss. So put that in our pipe and smoke it! You and your orders!

BURKE (*protestingly*): I wasn't meaning it that way at all and well you know it. You've no call to be raising this rumpus with me. (*pointing to* CHRIS) 'Tis him you've a right—

ANNA: I'm coming to him. But you—you did mean it that way, too. You sounded—just like all the rest. (*hysterically*) But, damn it, shut up! Let me talk for a change!

BURKE: 'Tis quare, rough talk, that—for a dacent girl the like of you!

ANNA (*with a hard laugh*): Decent? Who told you I was? (CHRIS *sitting with bowed shoulders, his head in his hands. She leans over in exasperation and shakes him violently by the shoulder.*) Don't go to sleep, Old Man! Listen here, I'm talking to you now!

CHRIS (*straightening up and looking about as if he were seeking a way to escape—with frightened foreboding in his voice*): Ay don't vant for hear it. You vas going out of head, Ay tank, Anna.

ANNA (*violently*): Well, living with you is enough to drive anyone off their nut. Your bunk abut the farm being so fine! Didn't I write you year after year how rotten it was and what a dirty slave them cousins made of me? What'd you care? Nothing! Not even enough to come out and see me! That crazy bull about wanting to keep me away from the sea don't go down with me! You yust didn't want to be bothered with me! You're like all the rest of 'em!

CHRIS (*feebly*): Anna! It ain't so—

ANNA (*not heeding his interruption—revengefully*): But one thing I never wrote you. It was one of them cousins that you think is such nice people—the youngest son—Paul—that started me wrong. (*loudly*) It wasn't none of my fault. I hated him worse'n hell and he knew it. But he was big and strong— (*pointing to* BURKE)—like you!

BURKE (*half springing to his feet—his fists clenched*): God blarst it! (*He sinks slowly back in his chair again, the knuckles showing white on his clenched hands, his face tense with the effort to suppress his grief and rage.*)

CHRIS (*in a cry of horrified pain*): Anna!

ANNA (*to him—seeming not to have heard their interruptions*): That was why I run away from the farm. That was what made me get a yob as nurse girl in St. Paul. (*with a hard, mocking laugh*) And you think that was a nice yob for a girl, too, don't you? (*sarcastically*) With all them nice inland fellers yust looking for a chance to marry me, I s'pose. Marry me? What a chance! They wasn't looking for marrying. (*as* BURKE *lets a groan of fury escape him—*

desperately) I'm owning up to everything fair and
square. I was caged in, I tell you—yust like in yail—
taking care of other people's kids—listening to 'em
bawling and crying day and night—when I wanted
to be out—and I was lonesome—lonesome as hell!
(*with a sudden weariness in her voice*) So I give up
finally. What was the use? (*She stops and looks at
the two men. Both are motionless and silent.* CHRIS
*seems in a stupor of despair, his house of cards fallen
about him.* BURKE'S *face is livid with the rage that
is eating him up, but he is too stunned and bewildered yet to find a vent for it. The condemnation she
feels in their silence goads* ANNA *into a harsh, strident defiance.*) You don't say nothing—either of
you—but I know what you're thinking. You're like
all the rest! (*to* CHRIS—*furiously*) And who's to
blame for it, me or you? If you'd even acted like a
man—if you'd even been a regular father and had
me with you—maybe things would be different!

CHRIS (*in agony*): Don't talk dat vay, Anna! Ay go
crazy! Ay von't listen! (*puts his hands over his ears*)

ANNA (*infuriated by his action—stridently*): You will
too listen! (*She leans over and pulls his hands from
his ears—with hysterical rage*) You—keeping me
safe inland—I wasn't no nurse girl the last two
years—I lied when I wrote you—I was in a house,
that's what!—yes, that kind of a house—the kind
sailors like you and Mat goes to in port—and your
nice inland men, too—and all men, God damn 'em!
I hate 'em! Hate 'em! (*She breaks into hysterical
sobbing, throwing herself into the chair and hiding
her face in her hands on the table. The two men have
sprung to their feet.*)

CHRIS (*whimpering like a child*): Anna! Anna! It's lie!
It's lie! (*he stands wringing his hands together and
begins to weep.*)

BURKE (*his whole great body tense like a spring—dully and gropingly*): So that's what's in it!

ANNA (*raising her head at the sound of his voice—with extreme mocking bitterness*): I s'pose you remember your promise, Mat? No other reason was to count with you so long as I wasn't married already. So I s'pose you want me to get dressed and go ashore, don't you? (*She laughs.*) Yes, you do!

BURKE (*on the verge of his outbreak—stammeringly*): God stiffen you!

ANNA (*trying to keep up her hard, bitter tone, but gradually letting a note of pitiful pleading creep in*): I s'pose if I tried to tell you I wasn't—that—no more you'd believe me, wouldn't you? Yes, you would! And if I told you that yust getting out in this barge, and being on the sea had changed me and made me feel different about things, 's if all I'd been through wasn't me and didn't count and was yust like it never happened—you'd laugh, wouldn't you? And you'd die laughing sure if I said that meeting you that funny way that night in the fog, and afterwards seeing that you was straight goods stuck on me, had got me to thinking for the first time, and I sized you up as a different kind of man—a sea man as different from the ones on land as water is from mud—and that was why I got stuck on you, too. I wanted to marry you and fool you, but I couldn't. Don't you see how I'd changed? I couldn't marry you with you believing a lie—and I was shamed to tell you the truth—till the both of you forced my hand, and I seen you was the same as all the rest. And now, give me a bawling out and beat it, like I can tell you're going to. (*She stops, looking at* BURKE. *He is silent, his face averted, his features beginning to work with fury. She pleads passionately.*) Will you believe it if I tell you that loving you has made me—clean? It's the straight goods, honest! (*then as he doesn't reply—bitterly*) Like hell you will! You're like all the rest!

BURKE (*blazing out—turning on her in a perfect frenzy of rage—his voice trembling with passion*): The rest, is it? God's curse on you! Clane, is it? You slut, you, I'll be killing you now! (*He picks up the chair on which he has been sitting and, swinging it high over his shoulder, springs toward her.* CHRIS *rushes forward with a cry of alarm, trying to ward off the blow from his daughter.* ANNA *looks up into* BURKE'S *eyes with the fearlessness of despair.* BURKE *checks himself, the chair held in the air.*)

CHRIS (*wildly*): Stop, you crazy fool! You vant for murder her!

ANNA (*pushing her father away brusquely, her eyes still holding* BURKE'S): Keep out of this, you! (*to* BURKE— *dully*) Well, ain't you got the nerve to do it? Go ahead! I'll be thankful to you, honest! I'm sick of the whole game.

BURKE (*throwing the chair away into a corner of the room—helplessly*): I can't do it, God help me, and your two eyes looking at me. (*furiously*) Though I do be thinking I've have a good right to smash your skull like a rotten egg. Was there iver a woman in the world had the rottenness in her that you have, and was there iver a man the like of me was made the fool of the world, and me thinking thoughts about you, and having great love for you, and dreaming dreams of the fine life we'd have when we'd be wedded! (*his voice high pitched in a lamentation that is like a keen*) Yerra, God help me! I'm destroyed entirely and my heart is broken in bits! I'm asking God Himself, was it for this He'd have me roaming the earth since I was a lad only, to come to black shame in the end, where I'd be giving a power of love to a woman is the same as others you'd meet in any hooker-shanty in port, with red gowns on them and paint on their grinning mugs, would be sleeping with any man for a dollar or two!

ANNA (*in a scream*): Don't, Mat! For Gawd's sake! (*then raging and pounding on the table with her hands*) Get out of here! Leave me alone! Get out of here!

BURKE (*his anger rushing back on him*): I'll be going, surely! And I'll be drinking sloos of whiskey will wash that black kiss of yours off my lips; and I'll be getting dead rotten drunk so I'll not remember if 'twas iver born you was at all; and I'll be shipping away on some boat will take me to the other end of the world where I'll never see your face again! (*He turns toward the door.*)

CHRIS (*who has been standing in a stupor—suddenly grasping BURKE by the arm—stupidly*): No, you don't go. Ay tank maybe it's better Anna marry you now.

BURKE (*shaking CHRIS off—furiously*): Lave go of me, ye old ape! Marry her, is it? I'd see her roasting in hell first! I'm shipping away out of this, I'm telling you! (*pointing to ANNA—passionately*) And my curse on you and the curse of Almighty God and all the Saints! You've destroyed me this day and may you lie awake in the long nights, tormented with thoughts of Mat Burke and the great wrong you've done him!

ANNA (*in anguish*): Mat! (*But he turns without another word and strides out of the doorway. ANNA looks after him wildly, starts to run after him, then hides her face in her outstretched arms, sobbing. CHRIS stands in a stupor, staring at the floor.*)

CHRIS (*after a pause, dully*): Ay tank Ay go ashore, too.

ANNA (*looking up, wildly*): Not after him! Let him go! Don't you dare—

CHRIS (*somberly*): Ay go for gat drink.

ANNA (*with a harsh laugh*): So I'm driving you to drink, too, eh? I s'pose you want to get drunk so's you can forget—like him?

CHRIS (*bursting out angrily*): Yes, Ay vant! You tank Ay like hear dem tangs. (*breaking down—weeping*) Ay tank you vasn't dat kind of gel, Anna.

ANNA (*mockingly*): And I s'pose you want me to beat it, don't you? You don't want me here disgracing you, I s'pose?

CHRIS: No, you stay here! (*goes over and pats her on the shoulder, the ears running down his face*) Ain't your fault, Anna, Ay know dat. (*She looks up at him, softened. He bursts into rage.*) It's dat ole davil, as, do this to me! (*He shakes his fist at the door.*) It's her dirty tricks! It vas all right on barge with yust you and me. Den she bring dat Irish fallar in fog, she make you like him, she make you fight with me all time! If dat Irish fallar don't never come, you don't never tal me dem tangs, Ay don't never know, and everytang's all right. (*He shakes his fist again.*) Dirty ole davil!

ANNA (*with spent weariness*): Oh, what's the use? Go on ashore and get drunk.

CHRIS (*goes into room on left and gets his cap. He goes to the door, silent and stupid—then turns.*) You vait here, Anna?

ANNA (*dully*): Maybe—and maybe not. Maybe I'll get drunk, too. Maybe I'll— But what the hell do you care what I do? Go on and beat it. (*CHRIS turns stupidly and goes out. ANNA sits at the table, staring straight in front of her.*)

(*The Curtain Falls*)

ACT FOUR

SCENE—*Same as Act Three, about nine o'clock of a foggy night two days later. The whistles of steamers in the harbor can be heard. The cabin is lighted by a small lamp on the table. A suit case stands in the middle of the floor.* ANNA *is sitting in the rocking-chair. She wears a hat, is all dressed up as in Act One. Her face is pale, looks terribly tired and worn, as if the two days just past had been ones of suffering and sleepless nights. She stares before her despondently, her chin in her hands. There is a timid knock on the door in rear.* ANNA *jumps to her feet with a startled exclamation and looks toward the door with an expression of mingled hope and fear.*

ANNA (*faintly*): Come in. (*then summoning her courage—more resolutely*) Come in. (*The door is opened and* CHRIS *appears in the doorway. He is in a very bleary, bedraggled condition, suffering from the after effects of his drunk. A tin pail full of foaming beer is in his hand. He comes forward, his eyes avoiding* ANNA'S. *He mutters stupidly*) It's foggy.

ANNA (*looking him over with contempt*): So you come back at last, did you? You're a fine looking sight! (*then jeeringly*) I thought you'd beaten it for good on account of the disgrace I'd brought on you.

CHRIS (*wincing—faintly*): Don't say dat, Anna, please!

227

(*He sits in a chair by the table, setting down the can of beer, holding his head in his hands.*)

ANNA (*looks at him with a certain sympathy*): What's the trouble? Feeling sick?

CHRIS (*dully*): Inside my head feel sick.

ANNA: Well, what d'you expect after being soused for two days? (*resentfully*) It serves you right. A fine thing—you leaving me alone on this barge all that time!

CHRIS (*humbly*): Ay'm sorry, Anna.

ANNA (*scornfully*): Sorry!

CHRIS: But Ay'm not sick inside head vay you mean. Ay'm sick from tank too much about you, about me.

ANNA: And how about me? D'you suppose I ain't been thinking, too?

CHRIS: Ay'm sorry, Anna. (*He sees her bag and gives a start.*) You pack your bag, Anna? You vas going—?

ANNA (*forcibly*): Yes, I was going right back to what you think.

CHRIS: Anna!

ANNA: I went ashore to get a train for New York. I'd been waiting and waiting 'till I was sick of it. Then I changed my mind and decided not to go to-day. But I'm going first thing to-morrow, so it'll all be the same in the end.

CHRIS (*raising his head—pleadingly*): No, you never do dat, Anna!

ANNA (*with a sneer*): Why not, I'd like to know?

CHRIS: You don't never gat to do—dat vay—no more, Ay tal you. Ay fix dat up all right.

ANNA (*suspiciously*): Fix what up?

CHRIS (*not seeming to have heard her question—sadly*): You vas vaiting, you say? You vasn't vaiting for me, Ay bet.

ANNA (*callously*): You'd win.

CHRIS: For dat Irish fallar?

ANNA (*defiantly*): Yes—if you want to know! (*then with a forlorn laugh*) If he did come back it'd only be 'cause he wanted to beat me up or kill me, I suppose. But even if he did, I'd rather have him come than not show up at all. I wouldn't care what he did.

CHRIS: Ay guess it's true you vas in love with him all right.

ANNA: You guess!

CHRIS (*turning to her earnestly*): And Ay'm sorry for you like hell he don't come, Anna!

ANNA (*softened*): Seems to me you've changed your tune a lot.

CHRIS: Ay've been tanking, and Ay guess it vas all my fault—all bad tangs dat happen to you. (*pleadingly*) You try for not hate me, Anna. Ay'm crazy ole fool, dat's all.

ANNA: Who said I hated you?

CHRIS: Ay'm sorry for everytang Ay do wrong for you, Anna. Ay vant for you be happy all rest of your life for make up! It make you happy marry dat Irish fallar, Ay vant it, too.

ANNA (*dully*): Well, there ain't no chance. But I'm glad you think different about it, anyway.

CHRIS (*supplicating*): And you tank—maybe—you forgive me sometime?

ANNA (*with a wan smile*): I'll forgive you right now.

CHRIS (*seizing her hand and kissing it—brokenly*): Anna lilla! Anna lilla!

ANNA (*touched but a bit embarrassed*): Don't bawl about it. There ain't nothing to forgive, anyway. It ain't your fault, and it ain't mine, and it ain't his neither. We're all poor nuts, and things happen, and we yust get mixed in wrong, that's all.

CHRIS (*eagerly*): You say right tang, Anna, py golly!

It ain't nobody's fault! (*shaking his fist*) It's dat ole davil, sea!

ANNA (*with an exasperated laugh*): Gee, won't you ever can that stuff? (CHRIS *relapses into injured silence. After a pause* ANNA *continues curiously.*) You said a minute ago you'd fixed something up—about me. What was it?

CHRIS (*after a hesitating pause*): Ay'm shipping avay on sea again, Anna.

ANNA (*astounded*): You're—what?

CHRIS: Ay sign on steamer sail to-morrow. Ay gat my ole yob—bo'sun. (ANNA *stares at him. As he goes on, a bitter smile comes over her face.*) Ay tank dat's best tang for you. Ay only bring you bad luck, Ay tank. Ay make your mo'der's life sorry. Ay don't vant make your dat way, but Ay do yust same. Dat ole davil, sea, she make me Yonah man ain't no good for nobody. And Ay tank now it ain't no use fight with sea. No man dat live going to beat her, py yingo!

ANNA (*with a laugh of helpless bitterness*): So that's how you've fixed me, is it?

CHRIS: Yes, Ay tank if dat ole davil gat me back she leave you alone den.

ANNA (*bitterly*): But, for Gawd's sake, don't you see, you're doing the same thing you've always done? Don't you see—? (*But she sees the look of obsessed stubbornness on her father's face and gives it up helplessly.*) But what's the use of talking. You ain't right, that's what. I'll never blame you for nothing no more. But how you could figure out that was fixing me—!

CHRIS: Dat ain't all. Ay gat dem fallars in steamship office to pay you all money coming to me every month vhile Ay'm avay.

ANNA (*with a hard laugh*): Thanks. But I guess I won't be hard up for no small change.

CHRIS (*hurt—humbly*): It ain't much, Ay know, but it's plenty to keep you so you never gat go back—

ANNA (*shortly*): Shut up, will you? We'll talk about it later, see?

CHRIS (*after a pause—irritatingly*): You like Ay go ashore look for dat Irish fallar, Anna?

ANNA (*angrily*): Not much! Think I want to drag him back?

CHRIS (*after a pause—uncomfortably*): Py golly, dat booze don't go vell. Give me fever, Ay tank. Ay feel hot like hell. (*He takes off his coat and lets it drop on the floor. There is a loud thud.*)

ANNA (*with a start*): What you got in your pocket, for Pete's sake—a ton of lead? (*She reaches down, takes the coat and pulls out a revolver—looks from it to him in amazement.*) A gun? What were you doing with this?

CHRIS (*sheepishly*): Ay forgat. Ain't nutting. Ain't loaded, anyway.

ANNA (*breaking it open to make sure—then closing it again—looking at him suspiciously*): That ain't telling me why you got it?

CHRIS (*sheepishly*): Ay'm ole fool. Ay gat it vhen Ay go ashore first. Ay tank den it's all fault of dat Irish fallar.

ANNA (*with a shudder*): Say, you're crazier than I thought. I never dreamt you'd go that far.

CHRIS (*quickly*): Ay don't. Ay gat better sense right avay. Ay don't never buy bullets even. It ain't his fault, Ay know.

ANNA (*still suspicious of him*): Well, I'll take care of this for a while, loaded or not. (*She puts it in the drawer of table and closes the drawer.*)

CHRIS (*placatingly*): Throw it overboard if you vant.

Ay don't care. (*then after a pause*) Py golly, Ay tank Ay go lie down. Ay feel sick. (ANNA *takes a magazine from the table.* CHRIS *hesitates by her chair.*) Ve talk again before Ay go, yes?

ANNA (*dully*): Where's this ship going to?

CHRIS: Cape Town. Dat's in South Africa. She's British steamer called Londonderry. (*He stands hesitatingly—finally blurts out*) Anna—you forgive me sure?

ANNA (*wearily*): Sure I do. You ain't to blame. You're yust—what you are—like me.

CHRIS (*pleadingly*): Den—you lat me kiss you again once?

ANNA (*raising her face—forcing a wan smile*): Sure. No hard feelings.

CHRIS (*kisses her—brokenly*): Anna lilla! Ay— (*He fights for words to express himself, but finds none—miserably—with a sob*) Ay can't say it. Goodnight, Anna.

ANNA: Good-night. (*He picks up the can of beer and goes slowly into the room on left, his shoulders bowed, his head sunk forward dejectedly. He closes the door after him.* ANNA *turns over the pages of the magazine, trying desperately to banish her thoughts by looking at the pictures. This fails to distract her, and flinging the magazine back on the table, she springs to her feet and walks about the cabin distractedly, clenching and unclenching her hands. She speaks aloud to herself in a tense, trembling voice.*) Gawd, I can't stand this much longer! What am I waiting for anyway?—like a damn fool! (*She laughs helplessly, then checks herself abruptly, as she hears the sound of heavy footsteps on the deck outside. She appears to recognize these and her face lights up with joy. She gasps*) Mat! (*A strange terror seems suddenly to seize her. She rushes to the table, takes*

*the revolver out of drawer and crouches down in the
corner, left, behind the cupboard. A moment later
the door is flung open and* MAT BURKE *appears in
the doorway. He is in bad shape—his clothes torn
and dirty, covered with sawdust as if he had been
groveling or sleeping on barroom floors. There is a
red bruise on his forehead over one of his eyes, another over one cheekbone, his knuckles are skinned
and raw—plain evidence of the fighting he has been
through on his "bat." His eyes are bloodshot and
heavy-lidded, his face has a bloated look. But beyond
these appearances—the results of heavy drinking—
there is an expression in his eyes of wild mental tur-
moil, of important animal rage baffled by its own
abject misery.)*

BURKE (*peers blinkingly about the cabin—hoarsely*):
Let you not be hiding from me, whoever's here—
though 'tis well you know I'd have a right to come
back and murder you. (*He stops to listen. Hearing
no sound, he closes the door behind him and comes
forward to the table. He throws himself into the
rocking-chair—despondently*) There's no one here,
I'm thinking, and 'tis a great fool I am to be coming.
(*with a sort of dumb, uncomprehending anguish*)
Yerra, Mat Burke, 'tis a great jackass you've become and what's got into you at all, at all. She's
gone out of this long ago, I'm telling you, and you'll
never see her face again. (ANNA *stands up, hesitating, struggling between joy and fear.* BURKE'S *eyes
fall on* ANNA'S *bag. He leans over to examine it.*)
What's this? (*joyfully*) It's hers. She's not gone! But
where is she? Ashore? (*darkly*) What would she be
doing ashore on this rotten night? (*his face suddenly
convulsed with grief and rage*) 'Tis that, is it? Oh,
God's curse on her! (*raging*) I'll wait 'till she comes
and choke her dirty life out. (ANNA *starts, her face*

grows hard. She steps into the room, the revolver in her right hand by her side.)

ANNA (*in a cold, hard tone*): What are you doing here?

BURKE (*wheeling about with a terrified gasp*): Glory be to God! (*They remain motionless and silent for a moment, holding each other's eyes.*)

ANNA (*in the same hard voice*): Well, can't you talk?

BURKE (*trying to fall into an easy, careless tone*): You've a year's growth scared out of me, coming at me so sudden and me thinking I was alone.

ANNA: You've got your nerve butting in here without knocking or nothing. What d'you want?

BURKE (*airily*): Oh, nothing much. I was wanting to have a last word with you, that's all. (*He moves a step toward her.*)

ANNA (*sharply—raising the revolver in her hand*): Careful now! Don't try getting too close. I heard what you said you'd do to me.

BURKE (*noticing the revolver for the first time*): Is it murdering me you'd be now, God forgive you? (*then with a contemptuous laugh*) Or is it thinking I'd be frightened by that old tin whistle? (*He walks straight for her.*)

ANNA (*wildly*): Look out, I tell you!

BURKE (*who has come so close that the revolver is almost touching his chest*): Let you shoot, then! (*then with sudden wild grief*) Let you shoot, I'm saying, and be done with it! Let you end me with a shot and I'll be thanking you, for it's a rotten dog's life I've lived the past two days since I've known what you are, 'til I'm after wishing I was never born at all!

ANNA (*overcome—letting the revolver drop to the floor, as if her fingers had no strength to hold it—hysterically*): What d'you want coming here? Why don't you beat it? Go on! (*She passes him and sinks down in the rocking-chair.*)

BURKE (*following her—mournfully*): 'Tis right you'd be asking why did I come. (*then angrily*) 'Tis because 'tis a great weak fool of the world I am, and me tormented with the wickedness you'd told of yourself, and drinking oceans of booze that'd make me forget. Forget? Divil a word I'd forget, and your face grinning always in front of my eyes, awake or asleep, 'til I do be thinking a madhouse is the proper place for me.

ANNA (*glancing at his hands and face—scornfully*): You look like you ought to be put away some place. Wonder you wasn't pulled in. You been scraping, too, ain't you?

BURKE: I have—with every scut would take off his coat to me! (*fiercely*) And each time I'd be hitting one a clout in the mug, it wasn't his face I'd be seeing at all, but yours, and me wanting to drive you a blow would knock you out of this world where I wouldn't be seeing or thinking more of you.

ANNA (*her lips trembling pitifully*): Thanks!

BURKE (*walking up and down—distractedly*): That's right, make game of me! Oh, I'm a great coward surely, to be coming back to speak with you at all. You've a right to laugh at me.

ANNA: I ain't laughing at you, Mat.

BURKE (*unheeding*): You to be what you are, and me to be Mat Burke, and me to be drove back to look at you again! 'Tis black shame is on me!

ANNA (*resentfully*): Then get out. No one's holding you!

BURKE (*bewilderedly*): And me to listen to that talk from a woman like you and be frightened to close her mouth with a slap! Oh, God help me, I'm a yellow coward for all men to spit at! (*then furiously*)

But I'll not be getting out of this 'till I've had me word. (*raising his fist threateningly*) And let you look out how you'd drive me! (*letting his fist fall helplessly*) Don't be angry now! I'm raving like a real lunatic, I'm thinking, and the sorrow you put on me has my brains drownded in grief. (*suddenly bending down to her and grasping her arm intensely*) Tell me it's a lie, I'm saying! That's what I'm after coming to hear you say.

ANNA (*dully*): A lie? What?

BURKE (*with passionate entreaty*): All the badness you told me two days back. Sure it must be a lie! You was only making game of me, wasn't you? Tell me 'twas a lie, Anna, and I'll be saying prayers of thanks on my two knees to the Almighty God!

ANNA (*terribly shaken—faintly*): I can't, Mat. (*as he turns away—imploring*) Oh, Mat, won't you see that no matter what I was I ain't that any more? Why listen! I packed up my bag this afternoon and went ashore. I'd been waiting here all alone for two days, thinking maybe you'd come back—thinking maybe you'd think over all I'd said—and maybe—oh, I don't know what I was hoping! But I was afraid to even go out of the cabin for a second, honest— afraid you might come and not find me here. Then I gave up hope when you didn't show up and I went to the railroad station. I was going to New York. I was going back—

BURKE (*hoarsely*): God's curse on you!

ANNA: Listen, Mat! You hadn't come, and I'd gave up hope. But—in the station—I couldn't go. I'd bought my ticket and everything. (*She takes the ticket from her dress and tries to hold it before his eyes.*) But I got to thinking about you—and I couldn't take the train—I couldn't! So I come back here—to wait some more. Oh, Mat, don't you see

I've changed? Can't you forgive what's dead and gone—and forget it?

BURKE (*turning on her—overcome by rage again*): Forget, is it? I'll not forget 'til my dying day, I'm telling you, and me tormented with thoughts. (*in a frenzy*) Oh, I'm wishing I had wan of them fornenst me this minute and I'd beat him with my fists 'till he'd be a bloody corpse! I'm wishing the whole lot of them will roast in hell 'til the Judgment Day—and yourself along with them, for you're as bad as they are.

ANNA (*shuddering*): Mat! (*then after a pause—in a voice of dead, stony calm*) Well, you've had your say. Now you better beat it.

BURKE (*starts slowly for the door—hesitates—then after a pause*): And what'll you be doing?

ANNA: What difference does it make to you?

BURKE: I'm asking you!

ANNA (*in the same tone*): My bag's packed and I got my ticket. I'll go to New York to-morrow.

BURKE (*helplessly*): You mean—you'll be doing the same again?

ANNA (*stonily*): Yes.

BURKE (*in anguish*): You'll not! Don't torment me with that talk! 'Tis a she-divil you are sent to drive me mad entirely!

ANNA (*her voice breaking*): Oh, for Gawd's sake, Mat, leave me alone! Go away! Don't you see I'm licked? Why d'you want to keep on kicking me?

BURKE (*indignantly*): And don't you deserve the worst I'd say, God forgive you?

ANNA: All right. Maybe I do. But don't rub it in. Why ain't you done what you said you was going to? Why ain't you got that ship was going to take you to the other side of the earth where you'd never see me again?

BURKE: I have.

ANNA (*startled*): What—then you're going—honest?

BURKE: I signed on to-day at noon, drunk as I was—and she's sailing to-morrow.

ANNA: And where's she going to?

BURKE: Cape Town.

ANNA (*the memory of having heard that name a little while before coming to her—with a start, confusedly*): Cape Town? Where's that. Far away?

BURKE: 'Tis the end of Africa. That's far for you.

ANNA (*forcing a laugh*): You're keeping your word all right, ain't you? (*after a slight pause—curiously*) What's the boat's name?

BURKE: The Londonderry.

ANNA (*It suddenly comes to her that this is the same ship her father is sailing on.*): The Londonderry! It's the same— Oh, this is too much! (*with wild, ironical laughter*) Ha-ha-ha!

BURKE: What's up with you now?

ANNA: Ha-ha-ha! It's funny, funny! I'll die laughing!

BURKE (*irritated*): Laughing at what?

ANNA: It's a secret. You'll know soon enough. It's funny. (*controlling herself—after a pause—cynically*) What kind of a place is this Cape Town? Plenty of dames there, I suppose?

BURKE: To hell with them! That I may never see another woman to my dying hour!

ANNA: That's what you say now, but I'll bet by the time you get there you'll have forgot all about me and start in talking the same old bull you talked to me to the first one you meet.

BURKE (*offended*): I'll not, then! God mend you, is it making me out to be the like of yourself you are, and you taking up with this one and that all the years of your life?

ANNA (*angrily assertive*): Yes, that's yust what I do mean! You been doing the same thing all your life,

picking up a new girl in every port. How're you any
better than I was?

BURKE (*thoroughly exasperated*): Is it no shame you
have at all? I'm a fool to be wasting talk on you
and you hardened in badness. I'll go out of this and
lave you alone forever. (*He starts for the door—then
stops to turn on her furiously.*) And I suppose 'tis
the same lies you told them all before that you told
to me?

ANNA (*indignantly*): That's a lie! I never did!

BURKE (*miserably*): You'd be saying that, anyway.

ANNA (*forcibly, with growing intensity*): Are you trying to accuse me—of being in love—really in love—
with them?

BURKE: I'm thinking you were, surely.

ANNA (*furiously, as if this were the last insult—advancing on him threateningly*): You mutt, you! I've stood
enough from you. Don't you dare. (*with scornful
bitterness*) Love 'em! Oh, my Gawd! You damn
thick-head! Love 'em? (*savagely*) I hated 'em, I tell
you! Hated 'em, hated 'em, hated 'em! And may
Gawd strike me dead this minute and my mother,
too, if she was alive, if I ain't telling you the honest truth!

BURKE (*immensely pleased by her vehemence—a light
beginning to break over his face—but still uncertain,
torn between doubt and the desire to believe—helplessly*): If I could only be believing you now!

ANNA (*distractedly*): Oh what's the use? What's the
use of me talking? What's the use of anything?
(*pleadingly*) Oh, Mat, you mustn't think that for a
second! You mustn't! Think all the other bad about
me you want to, and I won't kick, 'cause you've a
right to. But don't think that! (*on the point of tears*)
I couldn't bear it! It'd be yust too much to know

you was going away where I'd never see you
again—thinking that about me!

BURKE (*after an inward struggle—tensely—forcing out
the words with difficulty*): If I was believing—that
you'd never had love for any other man in the world
but me—I could be forgetting the rest, maybe.

ANNA (*with a cry of joy*): Mat!   .

BURKE (*slowly*): If 'tis truth you're after telling, I'd
have a right, maybe, to believe you'd changed—and
that I'd changed you myself 'til the thing you'd been
all your life wouldn't be you any more at all.

ANNA (*hanging on his words—breathlessly*): Oh, Mat!
That's what I been trying to tell you all along!

BURKE (*simply*): For I've a power of strength in me
to lead me the way I want, and women, too, maybe,
and I'm thinking I'd change you to a new woman
entirely, so I'd never know, or you either, what kind
of woman you'd been in the past at all.

ANNA: Yes, you could, Mat! I know you could!

BURKE: And I'm thinking 'twasn't your fault, maybe,
but having that old ape for a father that left you to
grow up alone, made you what you was. And if I
could be believing 'tis only me you—

ANNA (*distractedly*): You got to believe it, Mat! What
can I do? I'll do anything, anything you want to
prove I'm not lying!

BURKE (*suddenly seems to have a solution. He feels
in the pocket of his coat and grasps something—
solemnly*): Would you be willing to swear an oath,
now—a terrible, fearful oath would send your soul
to the divils in hell if you was lying?

ANNA (*eagerly*): Sure, I'll swear, Mat—on anything!

BURKE (*takes a small, cheap old crucifix from his
pocket and holds it up for her to see*): Will you swear
on this?

ANNA (*reaching out for it*): Yes. Sure I will. Give it to me.

BURKE (*holding it away*): 'Tis a cross was given me by my mother, God rest her soul. (*He makes the sign of the cross mechanically.*) I was a lad only, and she told me to keep it by me if I'd be waking or sleeping and never lose it, and it'd bring me luck. She died soon after. But I'm after keeping it with me from that day to this, and I'm telling you there's great power in it, and 'tis great bad luck it's saved me from and me roaming the seas, and I having it tied round my neck when my last ship sunk, and it bringing me safe to land when the others went to their death. (*very earnestly*) And I'm warning you, now, if you'd swear an oath on this, 'tis my old woman herself will be looking down from Hivin above, and praying Almighty God and the Saints to put a great curse on you if she'd hear you swearing a lie!

ANNA (*awed by his manner—superstitiously*): I wouldn't have the nerve—honest—if it was a lie. But it's the truth and I ain't scared to swear. Give it to me.

BURKE (*handing it to her—almost frightenedly, as if he feared for her safety*): Be careful what you'd swear, I'm saying.

ANNA (*holding the cross gingerly*): Well—what do you want me to swear? You say it.

BURKE: Swear I'm the only man in the world ivir you felt love for.

ANNA (*looking into his eyes steadily*): I swear it.

BURKE: And that you'll be forgetting from this day all the badness you've done and never do the like of it again.

ANNA (*forcibly*): I swear it! I swear it by God!

BURKE: And may the blackest curse of God strike you if you're lying. Say it now!

ANNA: And may the blackest curse of God strike me if I'm lying!

BURKE (*with a stupendous sigh*): Oh, glory be to God, I'm after believing you now! (*He takes the cross from her hand, his face beaming with joy, and puts it back in his pocket. He puts his arms about her waist and is about to kiss her when he stops, appalled by some terrible doubt.*)

ANNA (*alarmed*): What's the matter with you?

BURKE (*with sudden fierce questioning*): Is it Catholic ye are?

ANNA (*confused*): No. Why?

BURKE (*filled with a sort of bewildered foreboding*): Oh, God, help me! (*with a dark glance of suspicion at her*) There's some divil's trickery in it, to be swearing an oath on a Catholic cross and you wan of the others.

ANNA (*distractedly*): Oh, Mat, don't you believe me?

BURKE (*miserably*): If it isn't a Catholic you are—

ANNA: I ain't nothing. What's the difference? Didn't you hear me swear?

BURKE (*passionately*): Oh, I'd a right to stay away from you—but I couldn't! I was loving you in spite of it all and wanting to be with you, God forgive me, no matter what you are. I'd go mad if I'd not have you! I'd be killing the world— (*He seizes her in his arms and kisses her fiercely.*)

ANNA (*with a gasp of joy*): Mat!

BURKE (*suddenly holding her away from him and staring into her eyes as if to probe into her soul—slowly*): If your oath is no proper oath at all, I'll have to be taking your naked word for it and have you anyway, I'm thinking—I'm needing you that bad!

ANNA (*hurt—reproachfully*): Mat! I swore, didn't I?

BURKE (*defiantly, as if challenging fate*): Oath or no oath, 'tis no matter. We'll be wedded in the morning, with the help of God. (*still more defiantly*) We'll be happy now, the two of us, in spite of the divil! (*He crushes her to him and kisses her again. The door on the left is pushed open and* CHRIS *appears in the doorway. He stands blinking at them. At first the old expression of hatred of* BURKE *comes into his eyes instinctively. Then a look of resignation and relief takes its place. His face lights up with a sudden happy thought. He turns back into the bedroom—reappears immediately with the tin can of beer in his hand—grinning.*)

CHRIS: Ve have drink on this, py golly! (*They break away from each other with startled exclamations.*)

BURKE (*explosively*): God stiffen it! (*He takes a step toward* CHRIS *threateningly.*)

ANNA (*happily—to her father*): That's the way to talk! (*with a laugh*) And say, it's abut time for you and Mat to kiss and make up. You're going to be shipmates on the Londonderry, did you know it?

BURKE (*astounded*): Shipmates— Has himself—

CHRIS (*equally astounded*): Ay vas bo'sun on her.

BURKE: The divil! (*then angrily*) You'd be going back to sea and leaving her alone, would you?

ANNA (*quickly*): It's all right, Mat. That's where he belongs, and I want him to go. You got to go, too; we'll need the money. (*with a laugh, as she gets the glasses*) And as for me being alone, that runs in the family, and I'll get used to it. (*pouring out their glasses*) I'll get a little house somewhere and I'll make a regular place for you two to come back to,—wait and see And now you drink up and be friends.

BURKE (*happily—but still a bit resentful against the old man*): Sure! (*clinking his glass against* CHRIS') Here's luck to you! (*He drinks.*)

CHRIS (*subdued—his face melancholy*): Skoal. (*He drinks.*)

BURKE (*to* ANNA, *with a wink*): You'll not be lonesome long. I'll see to that with the help of God. 'Tis himself here will be having a grandchild to ride on his foot, I'm telling you!

ANNA (*turning away in embarrassment*): Quit the kidding, now. (*She picks up her bag and goes into the room on left. As soon as she is gone* BURKE *relapses into an attitude of gloomy thought.* CHRIS *stares at his beer absent-mindedly. Finally* BURKE *turns on him.*)

BURKE: Is it any religion at all you have, you and your Anna?

CHRIS (*surprised*): Why yes. Ve vas Lutheran in ole country.

BURKE (*horrified*): Luthers, is it? (*then with a grim resignation, slowly, aloud to himself*) Well, I'm damned then surely. Yerra, what's the difference? 'Tis the will of God, anyway.

CHRIS (*moodily preoccupied with his own thoughts— speaks with somber premonition as* ANNA *re-enters from the left*): It's funny. It's queer, yes—you and me shipping on same boat dat vay. It ain't right. Ay don't know—it's dat funny vay ole davil sea do her vorst dirty tricks, yes. It's so. (*He gets up and goes back and, opening the door, stares out into the darkness.*)

BURKE (*nodding his head in gloomy acquiescence— with a great sigh*): I'm fearing you have the right of it for once, divil take you.

ANNA (*forcing a laugh*): Gee, Mat, you ain't agreeing with him, are you? (*She comes forward and puts her arm about his shoulder—with a determined gaiety*) Aw say, what's the matter? Cut out the gloom. We're all fixed now, ain't we, me and you? (*pours*

*out more beer into his glass and fills one for herself—
slaps him on the back*) Come on! Here's to the sea,
no matter what! Be a game sport and drink to that!
Come on! (*She gulps down her glass.* BURKE *ban-
ishes his superstitious premonitions with a defiant
jerk of his head, grins up at her, and drinks to her
toast.*)

CHRIS (*looking out into the night—lost in his somber
preoccupation—shakes his head and mutters*) Fog,
fog, fog, all bloody time. You can't see vhere you
vas going, no. Only dat ole davil, sea—she knows!
(*The two stare at him. From the harbor comes the
muffled mournful wail of steamers' whistles.*)

(*The Curtain Falls*)

THE HAIRY APE

*A Comedy of Ancient and
Modern Life in Eight Scenes*

CHARACTERS

ROBERT SMITH, "YANK"
PADDY
LONG
MILDRED DOUGLAS
HER AUNT
SECOND ENGINEER
A GUARD
A SECRETARY OF AN ORGANIZATION
STOKERS, LADIES, GENTLEMEN, ETC.

SCENES

SCENE ONE

The firemen's forecastle of a transatlantic liner an hour after sailing from New York for the voyage across. Tiers of narrow, steel bunks, three deep, on all sides. An entrance in rear. Benches on the floor before the banks. The room is crowded with men, shouting, cursing, laughing, singing—a confused, inchoate uproar swelling into a sort of unity, a meaning—the bewildered, furious, baffled defiance of a beast in a cage. Nearly all the men are drunk. Many bottles are passed from hand to hand. All are dressed in dungaree pants, heavy ugly shoes. Some wear singlets, but the majority are stripped to the waist.

The treatment of this scene, or of any other scene in the play, should by no means be naturalistic. The effect sought after is a cramped space in the bowels of a ship, imprisoned by white steel. The lines of bunks, the uprights supporting them, cross each other like the steel framework of a cage. The ceiling crushes down upon the men's heads. They cannot stand upright. This accentuates the natural stooping posture which shoveling coal and the resultant over-development of back and shoulder muscles have given them. The men themselves should resemble those pictures in which the appearance of Neanderthal Man is guessed at. All are hairy-chested, with long arms of tremendous power, and low, receding brows above their small, fierce, resentful eyes. All the civilized white races are represented, but except for the slight differentiation in color of hair, skin, eyes, all these men are alike.

The curtain rises on a tumult of sound. Yank is seated in the foreground. He seems broader, fiercer, more truculent, more powerful, more sure of himself than the rest. They respect his superior strength—the grudging respect of fear. Then, too, he represents to them a self-expression, the very last word in what they are, their most highly developed individual.

VOICES: Gif me trink dere, you!
'Ave a wet!
Salute!
Gesundheit!
Skoal!
Drink as a lord, God stiffen you!
Here's how!
Luck!
Pass back that bottle, damn you!
Pourin' it down his neck!
Ho, Froggy! Where the devil have you been?
La Touraine.
I hit him smash in yaw, py Gott!
Jenkins—the First—he's a rotten swine—
And the coppers nabbed him—and I run—
I like peer better. It don't pig head gif you.
A slut, I'm sayin'! She robbed me aslape—
To hell with 'em all!
You're a bloody liar!
Say dot again! (*Commotion. Two men about to fight are pulled apart.*)
No scrappin' now!
Tonight—
See who's the best man!
Bloody Dutchman!
Tonight on the for'ard square.

I'll bet on Dutchy.

He packa da wallop, I tell you!

Shut up, Wop!

No fightin', maties. We're all chums, ain't we?

(*A voice starts bawling a song.*)

"Beer, beer, glorious beer!

Fill yourselves right up to here."

YANK (*for the first time seeming to take notice of the uproar about him, turns around threateningly—in a tone of contemptuous authority*): Choke off dat noise! Where d'yuh get dat beer stuff? Beer, hell! Beer's for goils—an Dutchmen. Me for somep'n wit a kick to it! Gimme a drink, one of youse guys. (*Several bottles are eagerly offered. He takes a tremendous gulp at one of them; then, keeping the bottle in his hand, glares belligerently at the owner, who hastens to acquiesce in this robbery by saying* All righto, Yank. Keep it and have another. *Yank contemptuously turns his back on the crowd again. For a second there is an embarrassed silence. Then—*)

VOICES: We must be passing the Hook.

She's beginning to roll to it.

Six days in hell—and then Southampton.

Py Yesus, I vish somepody take my first vatch for me!

Gittin' seasick, Square-head?

Drink up and forget it!

What's in your bottle?

Gin.

Dot's nigger trink.

Absinthe? It's doped. You'll go off your chump, Froggy!

Cochon!

Whisky, that's the ticket!

Where's Paddy?

Going asleep.

Sing us that whisky song, Paddy.

(*They all turn to an old, wizened Irishman who is dozing, very drunk, on the benches forward. His face is extremely monkey-like with all the sad, patient pathos of that animal in his small eyes.*)

Singa da song, Caruso Pat!

He's gettin' old. The drink is too much for him.

He's too drunk.

PADDY (*blinking about him, starts to his feet resentfully, swaying, holding on to the edge of a bunk*): I'm never too drunk to sing. 'Tis only when I'm dead to the world I'd be wishful to sing at all. (*with a sort of sad contempt*) "Whisky Johnny," ye want? A chanty, ye want? Now that's a queer wish from the ugly like of you. God help you. But no matter. (*He starts to sing in a thin, nasal, doleful tone*)

Oh, whisky is the life of man!

Whisky! O Johnny! (*they all join in on this.*)

Oh, whisky is the life of man!

Whisky for my Johnny! (*again chorus*)

Oh, whisky drove my old man mad!

Whisky! O Johnny!

Oh, whisky drove my old man mad!

Whisky for my Johnny!

YANK (*again turning around scornfully*): Aw hell! Nix on dat old sailing ship stuff! All dat bull's dead, see? And you're dead, too, yuh damned old Harp, on'y yuh don't know it. Take it easy, see. Give us a rest. Nix on de loud noise. (*with a cynical grin*) Can't youse see I'm tryin' to t'ink?

ALL (*repeating the word after him as one with the same cynical amused mockery*): Think! (*The chorused word has a brazen metallic quality as if their throats were phonograph horns. It is followed by a general uproar of hard, barking laughter.*)

VOICES: Don't be cracking your head wit ut, Yank.

You gat headache, py yingo!

One thing about it—it rhymes with drink!

Ha, ha, ha!

Drink, don't think!

Drink, don't think!

Drink, don't think!

(*A whole chorus of voices has taken up this refrain, stamping on the floor, pounding on the benches with fists.*)

YANK (*taking a gulp from his bottle—good-naturedly*): Aw right. Can de noise. I got yuh de foist time. (*The uproar subsides. A very drunken sentimental tenor begins to sing*)

"Far away in Canada,

  Far across the sea,

There's a lass who fondly waits

  Making a home for me—"

YANK (*fiercely contemptuous*): Shut up, yuh lousy boob! Where d'yuh get dat tripe? Home? Home, hell! I'll make a home for yuh! I'll knock yuh dead. Home! T'hell wit home! Where d'yuh get dat tripe! Dis is home, see? What d'yuh want wit home? (*proudly*) I runned away from mine when I was a kid. On'y to glad to beat it, dat was me. Home was lickings for me, dat's all. But yuh can bet your shoit no one ain't never licked me since! Wanter try it, any of youse? Huh! I guess not. (*in a more placated but still contemptuous tone*) Goils waitin' for yuh, huh? Aw, hell! Dat's all tripe. Dey don't wait for no one. Dey'd double-cross yuh for a nickel. Dey're all tarts, get me? Treat 'em rough, dat's me. To hell wit 'em. Tarts, dat's what, de whole bunch of 'em.

LONG (*very drunk, jumps on a bench excitedly, gesticulating with a bottle in his hand*): Listen 'ere, Comrades! Yank 'ere is right. 'E says this 'ere stinkin' ship is our 'ome. And 'e says as 'ome is 'ell. And

'e's right! This is 'ell. We lives in 'ell,—Comrades—
and right enough we'll die in it. (*raging*) And who's
ter blame, I arsks yer? We ain't. We wasn't born
this rotten way. All men is born free and ekal.
That's in the bleedin' Bible, maties. But what d'they
care for the Bible—them lazy, bloated swine what
travels first cabin? Them's the ones. They dragged
us down 'til we're on'y wage slaves in the bowels
of a bloody ship, sweatin', burnin' up, eatin' coal
dust! Hit's them's ter blame—the damned Capitalist
clarss! (*There had been a gradual murmur of contemptuous resentment rising among the men until
now he is interrupted by a storm of catcalls, hisses,
boos, hard laughter.*)

VOICES: Turn it off!

Shut up!

Sit down!

Clossa da face!

Tamn fool! (*etc.*)

YANK (*standing up and glaring at Long*): Sit down before I knock yuh down! (*Long makes haste to efface
himself. Yank goes on contemptuously.*) De Bible,
huh? De Cap'tlist class, huh? Aw nix on dat Salvation Army—Socialist bull. Git a soapbox! Hire a
hall! Come and be saved, huh? Jerk us to Jesus,
huh? Aw g'wan! I've listened to lots of guys like
you, see. Yuh're all wrong. Wanter know what I
t'ink? Yuh ain't no good for no one. Yuh're de
bunk. Yuh ain't got no noive, get me? Yuh're yellow, dat's what. Yellow, dat's you. Say! What's dem
slobs in de foist cabin got to do wit us? We're better
men dan dey are, ain't we? Sure! One of us guys
could clean up de whole mob wit one mit. Put one
of 'em down here for one watch in the stokehole,
what'd happen? Dey'd carry him off on a stretcher.
Dem boids don't amount to nothin'. Dey're just

baggage. Who makes dis old tub run? Ain't it us guys? Well den, we belong, don't we? We belong and dey don't. Dat's all. (*A loud chorus of approval. Yank goes on.*) As for dis bein' hell—aw, nuts! Yuh lost your noive, dat's what. Dis is a man's job, get me? It belongs. It runs dis tub. No stiffs need apply. But yuh're a stiff, see Yuh're yellow, dat's you.

VOICES (*with a great hard pride in them*):
Righto!
A man's job!
Talk is cheap, Long.
He never could hold up his end.
Divil take him!
Yank's right. We make it go.
Py Gott, Yank say right ting!
We don't need no one cryin' over us.
Makin' speeches.
Throw him out!
Yellow!
Chuck him overboard!
I'll break his jaw for him!

(*They crowd around Long threateningly.*)

YANK (*half good-natured again—contemptuously*): Aw, take it easy. Leave him alone. He ain't woith a punch. Drink up. Here's how, whoever owns dis. (*He takes a long swallow from his bottle. All drink with him. In a flash all is hilarious amiability again, back-slapping, loud talk, etc.*)

PADDY (*who has been sitting in a blinking, melancholy daze—suddenly cries out in a voice full of old sorrow*): We belong to this, you're saying? We make the ship to go, you're saying? Yerra then, that Almighty God have pity on us! (*His voice runs into the wail of a keen, he rocks back and forth on his bench. The men stare at him, startled and impressed in spite of themselves.*) Oh, to be back in the fine

days of my youth, ochone! Oh, there was fine beautiful ships them days—clippers wid tall masts touching the sky—fine strong men in them—men that was
sons of the sea as if 'twas the mother that bore
them. Oh, the clean skins of them, and the clear
eyes, the straight backs and full chests of them!
Brave men they was, and bold men surely! We'd be
sailing out, bound down round the Horn maybe.
We'd be making sail in the dawn, with a fair breeze,
singing a chanty song wid no care to it. And astern
the land would be sinking low and dying out, but
we'd give it no heed but a laugh, and never a look
behind. For the day that was, was enough, for we
was free men—and I'm thinking 'tis only slaves do
be giving heed to the day that's gone or the day to
come—until they're old like me. (*with a sort of religious exultation*) Oh, to be scudding south again wid
the power of the Trade Wind driving her on steady
through the nights and the days! Full sail on her!
Nights and days! Nights when the foam of the wake
would be flaming wid fire, when the sky'd be blazing
and winking wid stars. Or the full of the moon
maybe. Then you'd see her driving through the gray
night, her sails stretching aloft all silver and white,
not a sound on the deck, the lot of us dreaming
dreams, till you'd believe 'twas no real ship at all
you was on but a ghost ship like the *Flying
Dutchman* they say does be roaming the seas forev-
ermore widout touching a port. And there was the
days, too. A warm sun on the clean decks. Sun
warming the blood of you, and wind over the miles
of shiny green ocean like strong drink to your lungs.
Work—aye, hard work—but who'd mind that at all?
Sure you worked under the sky and 'twas work wid
skill and daring to it. And wid the day done, in the

dog watch, smoking me pipe at ease, the lookout would be raising land maybe, and we'd see the mountains of South Americy wid the red fire of the setting sun painting their white tops and the clouds floating by them! (*His tone of exaltation ceases. He goes on mournfully.*) Yerra, what's the use of talking? 'Tis a dead man's whisper. (*to* YANK *resentfully*) 'Twas them days men belonged to ships not now. 'Twas them days a ship was part of the sea, and a man was part of a ship, and the sea joined all together and made it one. (*scornfully*) Is it one wid this you'd be, Yank—black smoke from the funnels smudging the sea, smudging the decks—the bloody engines pounding and throbbing and shaking—wid divil a sight of sun or a breath of clean air—choking our lungs wid coal dust—breaking our backs and hearts in the hell of the stokehole—feeding the bloody furnace—feeding our lives along wid the coal, I'm thinking—caged in by steel from a sight of the sky like bloody apes in the Zoo! (*with a harsh laugh*) Ho-ho, divil mend you! Is it to belong to that you're wishing? Is it a flesh and blood wheel of the engines you'd be?

YANK (*who has been listening with a contemptuous sneer, barks out the answer*): Sure ting! Dat's me. What about it?

PADDY (*as if to himself—with great sorrow*): Me time is past due. That a great wave wid sun in the heart of it may sweep me over the side sometime I'd be dreaming of the days that's gone!

YANK: Aw, yuh crazy Mick! (*He springs to his feet and advances on Paddy threateningly—then stops, fighting some queer struggle within himself—lets his hands fall to his sides—contemptuously*) Aw, take it easy. Yuh're aw right, at dat. Yuh're bugs, dat's

all—nutty as a cuckoo. All dat tripe yuh been pullin'—Aw, dat's all right. On'y it's dead, get me?
Yuh don't belong no more, see. Yuh don't get de
stuff. Yuh're too old. (*disgustedly*) But aw say, come
up for air onct in a while, can't yuh? See what's
happened since yuh croaked. (*He suddenly bursts
forth vehemently, growing more and more excited*)
Say! Sure! Sure I meant it! What de hell— Say,
lemme talk! Hey! Hey, you old Harp! Hey, youse
guys! Say, listen to me—wait a moment—I gotter
talk, see. I belong and he don't. He's dead but I'm
livin'. Listen to me! Sure I'm part of de engines!
Why de hell not! Dey move, don't dey? Dey're
speed, ain't dey! Dey smash trou, don't dey?
Twenty-five knots an hour! Dat's goin' some! Dat's
new stuff! Dat belongs! But him, he's too old. He
gets dizzy. Say, listen. All dat crazy tripe about
nights and days; all dat crazy tripe about stars and
moons; all dat crazy tripe about suns and winds,
fresh air and de rest of it—Aw hell, dat's all a dope
dream! Hittin' de pipe of de past, dat's what he's
doin'. He's old and don't belong no more. But me,
I'm young! I'm in de pink! I move wit it! It, get
me! I mean de ting dat's de guts of all dis. It ploughs
trou all de tripe he's been sayin'. It blows dat up!
It knocks dat dead! It slams dat offen de face of do
oith! It, get me! De engines and de coal and de
smoke and all de rest of it! He can't breathe and
swallow coal dust, but I kin, see? Dat's fresh air for
me! Dat's food for me! I'm new, get me? Hell in
de stokehole? Sure! It takes a man to work in hell.
Hell, sure, dat's my fav'rite climate. I eat it up! I
git fat on it! It's me makes it hot! It's me makes it
roar! It's me makes it move! Sure, on'y for me
everything stops. It all goes dead, get me? De noise
and smoke and all de engines movin' de woild, dey

stop. Dere ain't nothin' no more! Dat's what I'm sayin'. Everyting else dat makes de woild move, somep'n makes it move. It can't move without somep'n else, see? Den yuh get down to me. I'm at de bottom, get me! Dere ain't nothin' foither. I'm de end! I'm de start! I start somep'n and de woild moves! It—dat's me!—de new dat's moiderin' de old! I'm de ting in coal dat makes it boin; I'm steam and oil for de engines; I'm de ting in noise dat makes yuh hear it; I'm smoke and express trains and steamers and factory whistles; I'm de ting in gold dat makes it money! And I'm what makes iron into steel! Steel, dat stands for de whole ting! And I'm steel—steel—steel! I'm de muscles in steel, de punch behind it! (*As he says this he pounds with his fist against the steel bunks. All the men, roused to a pitch of frenzied self-glorification by his speech, do likewise. There is a deafening metallic roar, through which* YANK's *voice can be heard bellowing*) Slaves, hell! We run de whole woiks. All de rich guys dat tink dey're somep'n, dey ain't nothin'! Dey don't belong. But us guys, we're in de move, we're at de bottom, de whole ting is us! (PADDY *from the start of* YANK's *speech has been taking one gulp after another from his bottle, at first frightenedly, as if he were afraid to listen, then desperately, as if to drown his senses, but finally has achieved complete indifferent, even amused, drunkenness.* YANK *sees his lips moving. He quells the uproar with a shout.*) Hey, youse guys, take it easy! Wait a moment! De nutty Harp is sayin' somep'n.

PADDY (*is heard now—throws his head back with a mocking burst of laughter*): Ho-ho-ho-ho-ho—

YANK (*drawing back his fist, with a snarl*): Aw! Look out who yuh're givin' the bark!

PADDY (*begins to sing the "Miller of Dee" with enormous good nature*):
"I care for nobody, no, not I,
And nobody cares for me."

YANK (*good-natured himself in a flash, interrupts* PADDY *with a slap on the bare back like a report*): Dat's de stuff! Now yuh're gettin' wise to somep'm. Care for nobody, dat's de dope! To hell wit 'em all! And nix on nobody else carin'. I kin care for myself, get me! (*Eight bells sound, muffled, vibrating through the steel walls as if some enormous brazen gong were imbedded in the heart of the ship. All the men jump up mechanically, file through the door silently close upon each other's heels in what is very like a prisoner's lockstep.* YANK *slaps* PADDY *on the back.*) Our watch, yuh old Harp! (*mockingly*) Come on down in hell. Eat up de coal dust. Drink in de heat. It's it, see! Act like yuh liked it, yuh better— or croak yuhself.

PADDY (*with jovial defiance*): To the divil wid it! I'll not report this watch. Let thim log me and be damned. I'm not slave the like of you. I'll be sittin' here at me ease, and drinking, and thinking, and dreaming dreams.

YANK (*contemptuously*): Tinkin' and dreamin', what'll that get yuh? What's tinkin' got to do wit it? We move, don't we? Speed, ain't it? Fog, dat's all you stand for. But we drive trou dat, don't we? We split dat up and smash trou—twenty-five knots a hour! (*turns his back on* PADDY *scornfully*) Aw, yuh make me sick! Yuh don't belong! (*He strides out the door in rear.* PADDY *hums to himself, blinking drowsily.*)

(*Curtain*)

SCENE TWO

Two days out. A section of the promenade deck. MIL-
DRED DOUGLAS *and her aunt are discovered reclining
in deck chairs. The former is a girl of twenty, slender,
delicate, with a pale, pretty face marred by a self-
conscious expression of disdainful superiority. She
looks fretful, nervous and discontented, bored by her
own anemia. Her aunt is a pompous and proud—and
fat—old lady. She is a type even to the point of a double chin and lorgnettes. She is dressed pretentiously, as
if afraid her face alone would never indicate her position in life.* MILDRED *is dressed all in white.*

*The impression to be conveyed by this scene is one
of the beautiful, vivid life of the sea all about—sunshine
on the deck in a great flood, the fresh sea wind blowing
across it. In the midst of this, these two incongruous,
artificial figures, inert and disharmonious, the elder like
a gray lump of dough touched up with rouge, the
younger looking as if the vitality of her stock had been
sapped before she was conceived, so that she is the
expression not of its life energy but merely of the artifi-
cialities that energy had won for itself in the spending.*

MILDRED (*looking up with affected dreaminess*): How
the black smoke swirls back against the sky! Is it
not beautiful?
AUNT (*without looking up*): I dislike smoke of any
kind.

MILDRED: My great-grandmother smoked a pipe—a clay pipe.

AUNT (*ruffling*): Vulgar!

MILDRED: She was too distant a relative to be vulgar. Time mellows pipes.

AUNT (*pretending boredom but irritated*): Did the sociology you took up at college teach you that—to play the ghoul on every possible occasion, excavating old bones? Why not let your great-grandmother rest in her grave?

MILDRED (*dreamily*): With her pipe beside her—puffing in Paradise.

AUNT (*with spite*): Yes, you are a natural born ghoul. You are even getting to look like one, my dear.

MILDRED (*in a passionless tone*): I detest you, Aunt. (*looking at her critically*) Do you know what you remind me of? Of a cold pork pudding against a background of linoleum tablecloth in the kitchen of a—but the possibilities are wearisome. (*She closes her eyes.*)

AUNT (*with a bitter laugh*): Merci for your candor. But since I am and must be your chaperon—in appearance, at least—let us patch up some sort of armed truce. For my part you are quite free to indulge any pose of eccentricity that beguiles you—as long as you observe the amenities—

MILDRED (*drawling*): The inanities?

AUNT (*going on as if she hadn't heard*): After exhausting the morbid thrills of social service work on New York's East Side—how they must have hated you, by the way, the poor that you made so much poorer in their own eyes!—you are now bent on making your slumming international. Well, I hope Whitechapel will provide the needed nerve tonic. Do not ask me to chaperon you there, however. I told your father I would not. I loathe deformity.

We will hire an army of detectives and you may investigate everything—they allow you to see.

MILDRED (*protesting with a trace of genuine earnestness*): Please do not mock at my attempts to discover how the other half lives. Give me credit for some sort of groping sincerity in that at least. I would like to help them. I would like to be some use in the world. Is it my fault I don't know how? I would like to be sincere, to touch life somewhere. (*with weary bitterness*) But I'm afraid I have neither the vitality nor integrity. All that was burnt out in our stock before I was born. Grandfather's blast furnaces, flaming to the sky, melting steel, making millions—then father keeping those home fires burning, making more millions—and little me at the tail-end of it all. I'm a waste product in the Bessemer process—like the millions. Or rather, I inherit the acquired trait of the by-product, wealth, but none of the energy, none of the strength of the steel that made it. I am sired by gold and damned by it, as they sat at the race track—damned in more ways than one. (*She laughs mirthlessly.*)

AUNT (*unimpressed—superciliously*): You seem to be going in for sincerity today. It isn't becoming to you, really—except as an obvious pose. Be as artificial as you are, I advise. There's a sort of sincerity in that, you know. And, after all, you must confess you like that better.

MILDRED (*again affected and bored*): Yes, I suppose I do. Pardon me for my outburst. When a leopard complains of its spots, it must sound rather grotesque. (*in a mocking tone*) Purr, little leopard. Purr, scratch, tear, kill, gorge yourself and be happy—only stay in the jungle where your spots are camouflage. In a cage they make you conspicuous.

AUNT: I don't know what you are talking about.

MILDRED: It would be rude to talk about anything to you. Let's just talk. (*She looks at her wrist watch.*) Well, thank goodness, it's about time for them to come for me. That ought to give me a new thrill, Aunt.

AUNT (*affectedly troubled*): You don't mean to say you're really going? The dirt—the heat must be frightful—

MILDRED: Grandfather started as a puddler. I should have inherited an immunity to heat that would make a salamander shiver. It will be fun to put it to the test.

AUNT: But don't you have to have the captain's—or someone's—permission to visit the stokehole?

MILDRED (*with a triumphant smile*): I have it—both his and the chief engineer's. Oh, they didn't want to at first, in spite of my social service credentials. They didn't seem a bit anxious that I should investigate how the other half lives and works on a ship. So I had to tell them that my father, the president of Nazareth Steel, chairman of the board of directors of this line, had told me it would be all right.

AUNT: He didn't.

MILDRED: How naïve age makes one! But I said he did, Aunt. I even said he had given me a letter to them—which I had lost. And they were afraid to take the chance that I might be lying. (*excitedly*) So it's ho! for the stokehole. The second engineer is to escort me. (*looking at her watch again*) It's time. And here he comes, I think. (*The second engineer enters. He is a husky, fine-looking man of thirty-five or so. He stops before the two and tips his cap, visibly embarrassed and ill-at-ease.*)

SECOND ENGINEER: Miss Douglas?

MILDRED: Yes. (*throwing off her rugs and getting to her feet*) Are we all ready to start?

SECOND ENGINEER: In just a second, ma'am. I'm waiting for the Fourth. He's coming along.

MILDRED (*with a scornful smile*): You don't care to shoulder this responsibility alone, is that it?

SECOND ENGINEER (*forcing a smile*): Two are better than one. (*disturbed by her eyes, glances out to sea—blurts out*) A fine day we're having.

MILDRED: Is it?

SECOND ENGINEER: A nice warm breeze—

MILDRED: It feels cold to me.

SECOND ENGINEER: But it's hot enough in the sun—

MILDRED: Not hot enough for me. I don't like Nature. I was never athletic.

SECOND ENGINEER (*forcing a smile*): Well, you'll find it hot enough where you're going.

MILDRED: Do you mean hell?

SECOND ENGINEER (*flabbergasted, decides to laugh*): Ho-ho! No, I mean the stokehole.

MILDRED: My grandfather was a puddler. He played with boiling steel.

SECOND ENGINEER (*all at sea—uneasily*): Is that so? Hum, you'll excuse me, ma'am, but are you intending to wear that dress?

MILDRED: Why not?

SECOND ENGINEER: You'll likely rub against oil and dirt. It can't be helped.

MILDRED: It doesn't matter. I have lots of white dresses.

SECOND ENGINEER: I have an old coat you might throw over—

MILDRED: I have fifty dresses like this. I will throw this one into the sea when I come back. That ought to wash it clean, don't you think?

SECOND ENGINEER (*doggedly*): There's ladders to climb down that are none too clean—and dark alleyways—

MILDRED: I will wear this very dress and none other.

SECOND ENGINEER: No offense meant. It's none of my business. I was only warning you—

MILDRED: Warning? That sounds thrilling.

SECOND ENGINEER (*looking down the deck—with a sigh of relief*): There's the Fourth now. He's waiting for us. If you'll come—

MILDRED: Go on. I'll follow you. (*He goes.* MILDRED *turns a mocking smile on her aunt.*) An oaf—but a handsome, virile oaf.

AUNT (*scornfully*): Poser!

MILDRED: Take care. He said there were dark alleyways—

AUNT (*in the same tone*): Poser!

MILDRED (*biting her lips angrily*): You are right. But would that my millions were not so anemically chaste!

AUNT: Yes, for a fresh pose I have no doubt you would drag the name of Douglas in the gutter!

MILDRED: From which it sprang. Good-by, Aunt. Don't pray too hard that I may fall into the fiery furnace.

AUNT: Poser!

MILDRED (*viciously*): Old hag! (*she slaps her aunt insultingly across the face and walks off, laughing gaily.*)

AUNT (*screams after her*): I said poser!

(*Curtain*)

SCENE THREE

The stokehole. In the rear, the dimly-outlined bulks of the furnaces and boilers. High overhead one hanging electric bulb sheds just enough light through the murky air laden with coal dust to pile up masses of shadows everywhere. A line of men, stripped to the waist, is before the furnace doors. They bend over, looking neither to right nor left, handling their shovels as if they were part of their bodies, with a strange, awkward, swinging rhythm. They use the shovels to throw open the furnace doors. Then from these fiery round holes in the black a flood of terrific light and heat pours full upon the men who are outlined in silhouette in the crouching, inhuman attitudes of chained gorillas. The men shovel with a rhythmic motion, swinging as on a pivot from the coal which lies in heaps on the floor behind to hurl it into the flaming mouths before them. There is a tumult of noise—the brazen clang of the furnace doors as they are flung open or slammed shut, the grating, teeth-gritting grind of steel against steel, of crunching coal. This clash of sounds stuns one's ears with its rending dissonance. But there is order in it, rhythm, a mechanical regulated recurrence, a tempo. And rising above all, making the air hum with the quiver of liberated energy, the roar of leaping flames in the furnaces, the monotonous throbbing beat of the engines.

As the curtain rises, the furnace doors are shut. The

men are taking a breathing spell. One or two are ar-
ranging the coal behind them, pulling it into more ac-
cessible heaps. The others can be dimly made out
leaning on their shovels in relaxed attitudes of
exhaustion.

PADDY (*from somewhere in the line—plaintively*):
Yerra, will this divil's own watch nivir end? Me back
is broke. I'm destroyed entirely.

YANK (*from the center of the line—with exuberant
scorn*): Aw, yuh make me sick! Lie down and croak,
why don't yuh? Always beefin', dat's you! Say, dis
is a cinch! Dis was made for me! It's my meat, get
me! (*A whistle is blown—a thin, shrill note from
somewhere overhead in the darkness.* YANK *curses
without resentment.*) Dere's de damn engineer
crackin' de whip. He tinks we're loafin'.

PADDY (*vindictively*): God stiffen him!

YANK (*in an exultant tone of command*): Come on,
youse guys! Git into de game! She's gittin' hungry!
Pile some grub in her. Trow it into her belly! Come
on now, all of youse! Open her up! (*At this last all
the man, who have followed his movements of getting
into position, throw open their furnace doors with
a deafening clang. The fiery light floods over their
shoulders as they bend round for the coal. Rivulets
of sooty sweat have traced maps on their backs. The
enlarged muscles form bunches of high light and
shadow.*)

YANK (*chanting a count as he shovels without seeming
effort*): One—two—tree— (*his voice rising exultantly
in the joy of battle*) Dat's de stuff! Let her have it!
All togedder now! Sling it into her! Let her ride!
Shoot de piece now! Call de toin on her! Drive her
into it! Feel her move! Watch her smoke! Speed,
dat's her middle name! Give her coal, youse guys!

Coal, dat's her booze! Drink it up, baby! Let's see
yuh sprint! Dig in and gain a lap! Dere she go-o-
es. (*This last in the chanting formula of the gallery
gods at the six-day bike race. He slams his furnace
door shut. The others do likewise with as much unison as their wearied bodies will permit. The effect is
of one fiery eye after another being blotted out with
a series of accompanying bangs.*)

PADDY (*groaning*): Me back is broke. I'm bate out—
bate— (*There is a pause. Then the inexorable whistle
sounds again from the dim regions above the electric
light. There is a growl of cursing rage from all sides.*)

YANK (*shaking his fist upward—contemptuously*):
Take it easy dere, you! Who d'yuh tinks runnin' dis
game, me or you? When I git ready, we move. Not
before! When I git ready, get me!

VOICES (*approvingly*): That's the stuff!
Yank tal him, py golly!
Yank ain't affeerd.
Goot poy, Yank!
Give him hell!
Tell 'im 'e's a bloody swine!
Bloody slave-driver!

YANK (*contemptuously*): He ain't got no noive. He's
yellow, get me? All de engineers is yellow. Dey got
streaks a mile wide. Aw, to hell wit him! Let's move,
youse guys. We had a rest. Come on, she needs it!
Give her pep! It ain't for him. Him and his whistle,
dey don't belong. But we belong, see! We gotter
feed de baby! Come on! (*He turns and flings his
furnace door open. They all follow his lead. At this
instant the Second and Fourth Engineers enter from
the darkness on the left with* MILDRED *between them.
She starts, turns paler, her pose is crumbling, she
shivers with fright in spite of the blazing heat, but
forces herself to leave the engineers and take a few*

steps nearer the men. She is right behind Yank. All this happens quickly while the men have their backs turned.)

YANK: Come on, youse guys! (*He is turning to get coal when the whistle sounds again in a peremptory, irritating note. This drives YANK into a sudden fury. While the other men have turned full around and stopped dumbfounded by the spectacle of MILDRED standing there in her white dress, YANK does not turn far enough to see her. Besides, his head is thrown back, he blinks upward through the murk trying to find the owner of the whistle, he brandishes his shovel murderously over his head in one hand, pounding on his chest, gorilla-like, with the other, shouting*) Toin off dat whistle! Come down outa dere, yuh yellow, brass buttoned, Belfast bum, yuh! Come down and I'll knock yer brains out! Yuh lousy, stinkin', yellow mut of a Catholic-moiderin' bastard! Come down and I'll moider yuh! Pullin' dat whistle on me, huh? I'll show yuh! I'll crash yer skull in! I'll drive yer teet' down yer troat! I'll slam yer nose trou de back of yer head! I'll cut yer guts out for a nickel, yuh lousy boob, yuh dirty, crummy, muck-eatin' son of a— (*Suddenly he becomes conscious of all the other men staring at something directly behind his back. He whirls defensively with a snarling, murderous growl, crouching to spring, his lips drawn back over his teeth, his small eyes gleaming ferociously. He sees MILDRED, like a white apparition in the full light from the open furnace doors. He glares into her eyes, turned to stone. As for her, during his speech she has listened, paralyzed with horror, terror, her whole personality crushed, beaten in, collapsed, by the terrific impact of this unknown, abysmal brutality, naked and shameless. As she looks at his gorilla face, as his eyes bore into hers, she*

*utters a low, choking cry and shrinks away from him,
putting both hands up before her eyes to shut out the
sight of his face, to protect her own. This startles*
YANK *to a reaction. His mouth falls open, his eyes
grow bewildered.*)

MILDRED (*about to faint—to the engineers, who now
have her one by each arm—whimperingly*): Take me
away! Oh, the filthy beast! (*She faints. They carry
her quickly back, disappearing in the darkness at the
left, rear. An iron door clangs shut. Rage and bewildered fury rush back on* YANK. *He feels himself in-
sulted in some unknown fashion in the very heart of
his pride. He roars* God damn yuh! *and hurls his
shovel after them at the door which has just closed.
It hits the steel bulkhead with a clang and falls clattering on the steel floor. From overhead the whistle
sounds again in a long, angry, insistent command.*)

(*Curtain*)

SCENE FOUR

The firemen's forecastle. YANK'S *watch has just come of duty and had dinner. Their faces and bodies shine from a soap and water scrubbing but around their eyes, where a hasty dousing does not touch, the coal dust sticks like black make-up, giving them a queer, sinister expression.* YANK *has not washed either face or body. He stands out in contrast to them, a blackened, brooding figure. He is seated forward on a bench in the exact attitude of Rodin's "The Thinker." The others, most of them smoking pipes, are staring at* YANK *half-apprehensively, as if fearing an outburst; half-amusedly, as if they saw a joke somewhere that tickled them.*

VOICES: He ain't ate nothing'.
    Py golly, a fallar gat to gat grub in him.
    Divil a lie.
    Yank feeda da fire, no feeda da face.
    Ha-ha.
    He ain't even washed hisself.
    He's forgot.
    Hey, Yank, you forgot to wash.
YANK (*sullenly*): Forgot nothin'! To hell wit washin'.
VOICES: It'll stick to you.
    It'll get under your skin.
    Give yer the bleedin' itch, that's wot.
    It makes spots on you—like a leopard.
    Like a piebald nigger, you mean.

274

Better wash up, Yank.
You sleep better.
Wash up, Yank.
Wash up! Wash up!

YANK (*resentfully*): Aw say, youse guys. Lemme alone. Can't youse see I'm tryin' to tink?

ALL (*repeating the word after him as one with cynical mockery*): Think! (*The word has a brazen, metallic quality as if their throats were phonograph horns. It is followed by a chorus of hard, barking laughter.*)

YANK (*springing to his feet and glaring at them belligerently*): Yes, tink! Tink, dat's what I said! What about it? (*They are silent, puzzled by his sudden resentment at what used to be one of his jokes.* YANK *sits down again in the same attitude of "The Thinker."*)

VOICES: Leave him alone.
He's got a grouch on.
Why wouldn't he?

PADDY (*with a wink at the others*): Sure I know what's the matter. 'Tis aisy to see. He's fallen in love, I'm telling you.

ALL (*repeating the word after him as one with cynical mockery*): Love! (*The word has a brazen, metallic quality as if their throats were phonograph horns. It is followed by a chorus of hard, barking laughter.*)

YANK (*with a contemptuous snort*): Love, hell! Hate, dat's what. I've fallen in hate, get me?

PADDY (*philosophically*): 'Twould take a wise man to tell one from the other. (*with a bitter, ironical scorn, increasing as he goes on*) But I'm telling you it's love that's in it. Sure what else but love for us poor bastes in the stokehole would be bringing a fine lady, dressed like a white quane, down a mile of ladders and steps to be havin' a look at us? (*A growl of anger goes up from all sides.*)

LONG (*jumping on a bench—hectically*): Hinsultin' us!

Hinsultin us, the bloody cow! And them bloody engineers! What right 'as they got to be exhibitin' us's
as if we was bleedin' monkeys in a menagerie? Did
we sign for hinsults to our dignity as 'onest workers?
Is that in the ship's articles? You kin bloody well
bet it ain't! But I knows why they done it. I arsked
a deck steward 'o she was and 'e told me. 'Er old
man's a bleedin' millionaire, a bloody Capitalist!
'E's got enuf bloody gold to sink this bleedin' ship!
'E makes arf the bloody steel in the world! 'E owns
this bloody boat! And you and me, Comrades, we're
'is slaves! And the skipper and mates and engineers,
they're 'is slaves! And she 'is bloody daughter and
we're all 'er slaves, too! And she gives 'er orders as
'ow she wants to see the bloody animals below
decks and down they takes 'er! (*There is a roar of
rage from all sides.*)

YANK (*blinking at him bewilderedly*): Say! Wait a moment! Is all dat straight goods?

LONG: Straight as string! The bleedin' steward as waits
on 'em, 'e told me about 'er. And what're we goin'
ter do, I arsks yer? 'Ave we got ter swaller 'er hinsults like dogs? It ain't in the ship's articles. I tell
yer we got a case. We kin go to law—

YANK (*with abysmal contempt*): Hell! Law!

ALL (*repeating the word after him as one with cynical
mockery*): Law! (*The word has a brazen metallic
quality as if their throats were phonograph horns. It
is followed by a chorus of hard, barking laughter.*)

LONG (*feeling the ground slipping from under his
feet—desperately*): As voters and citizens we kin
force the bloody governments—

YANK (*with abysmal contempt*) Hell! Governments!

ALL (*repeating the word after him as one with cynical
mockery*): Governments! (*The word has a brazen
metallic quality as if their throats were phonograph*

horns. It is followed by a chorus of hard, barking laughter.)

LONG (*hysterically*): We're free and equal in the sight of God—

YANK (*with abysmal contempt*): Hell! God!

ALL (*repeating the word after him as one with cynical mockery*): God! (*The word has a brazen metallic quality as if their throats were phonograph horns. It is followed by a chorus of hard, barking laughter.*)

YANK (*witheringly*): Aw, join de Salvation Army!

ALL: Sit down! Shut up! Damn fool! Sea-lawyer! (LONG *slinks back out of sight.*)

PADDY (*continuing the trend of his thoughts as if he had never been interrupted—bitterly*): And there she was standing behind us, and the Second pointing at us like a man you'd hear in a circus would be saying: In this cage is a queerer kind of baboon than ever you'd find in darkest Africy. We roast them in their own sweat—and be damned if you won't hear some of thim saying they like it! (*he glances scornfully at* YANK.)

YANK (*with a bewildered uncertain growl*): Aw!

PADDY: And there was Yank roarin' curses and turning round wid his shovel to brain her—and she looked at him, and him at her—

YANK (*slowly*): She was all white. I tought she was a ghost. Sure.

PADDY (*with heavy, biting sarcasm*): 'Twas love at first sight, divil a doubt of it! If you'd seen the endearin' look on her pale mug when she shriveled away with her hands over her eyes to shut out the sight of him! Sure, 'twas as if she'd seen a great hairy ape escaped from the Zoo!

YANK (*stung—with a growl of rage*): Aw!

PADDY: And the loving way Yank heaved his shovel at the skull of her, only she was out the door! (*a*

grin breaking over his face) 'Twas touching, I'm telling you! It put the touch of home, swate home in
the stokehole. (*There is a roar of laughter from all.*)

YANK (*glaring at* PADDY *menacingly*): Aw, choke dat
off, see!

PADDY (*not heeding him—to the others*): And her
grabbin' at the Second's arm for protection. (*with a
grotesque imitation of a woman's voice*) Kiss me,
Engineer dear, for it's dark down here and me old
man's in Wall Street making money! Hug me tight,
darlin', for I'm afeerd in the dark and me mother's
on deck makin' eyes at the skipper! (*another roar
of laughter*)

YANK (*threateningly*): Say! What you tryin' to do, kid
me, yuh old Harp?

PADDY: Divil a bit! Ain't I wishin' myself you'd
brained her?

YANK (*fiercely*): I'll brain her! I'll brain her yet, wait
'n' see! (*coming over to* PADDY—*slowly*) Say, is dat
what she called me—a hairy ape?

PADDY: She looked it at you if she didn't say the
word itself.

YANK (*grinning horribly*): Hairy ape, huh? Sure! Dat's
de way she looked at me, aw right. Hairy ape! So
dat's me, huh? (*bursting into rage—as if she were
still in front of him*) Yuh skinny tart! Yuh white-
faced bum, yuh! I'll show yuh who's a ape! (*turning
to the others, bewilderment seizing him again*) Say,
youse guys. I was bawlin' him out for pullin' de
whistle on us. You heard me. And den I seen youse
lookin' at somep'n and I tought he'd sneaked down
to come up in back of me, and I hopped round to
knock him dead wit de shovel. And dere she was
wit de light on her! Christ, yuh coulda pushed me
over with a finger! I was scared, get me? Sure! I
tought she was a ghost, see? She was all in white

like dey wrap around stiffs. You seen her. Kin yuh
blame me? She didn't belong, dat's what. And den
when I come to and seen it was a real skoit and
seen de way she was lookin' at me—like Paddy
said—Christ, I was sore, get me? I don't stand for
dat stuff from nobody. And I flung de shovel—on'y
she'd beat it. (*furiously*) I wished it'd banged her! I
wished it'd knocked her block off!

LONG: And be 'anged for murder or 'lectrocuted? She
ain't bleedin' well worth it.

YANK: I don't give a damn what! I'd be square wit
her, wouldn't I? Tink I wanter let her put somep'n
over on me? Tink I'm goin' to let her git away wit
dat stuff? Yuh don't know me! No one ain't never
put nothin' over on me and got away wit it, see!—
not dat kind of stuff—no guy and no skoit neither!
I'll fix her! Maybe she'll come down again—

VOICE: No chance, Yank. You scared her out of a
year's growth.

YANK: I scared her? Why de hell should I scare her?
Who de hell is she? Ain't she de same as me? Hairy
ape, huh? (*with his old confident bravado*) I'll show
her I'm better'n her, if she on'y knew it. I belong
and she don't, see! I move and she'd dead! Twenty-
five knots an hour, dat's me! Dat carries her but I
make dat. She's on'y baggage. Sure! (*again bewilderedly*) But, Christ, she was funny lookin'! Did yuh
pipe her hands? White and skinny. Yuh could see
de bones through 'em. And her mush, dat was dead
white, too. And her eyes, dey was like dey'd seen
a ghost. Me, dat was! Sure! Hairy ape! Ghost, huh?
Look at dat arm! (*He extends his right arm, swelling
out the great muscles.*) I coulda took her wit dat,
wit' just my little finger even, and broke her in two.
(*again bewilderedly*) Say, who is dat skoit, huh?
What is she? What's she come from? Who made

her? Who give her de noive to look at me like dat?
Dis ting's got my goat right. I don't get her. She's
new to me. What does a skoit like her mean, huh?
She don't belong, get me! I can't see her. (*with
growing anger*) But one ting I'm wise to, aw right,
aw right! Youse all kin bet your shoits I'll git even
wit her. I'll show her if she tinks she— She grinds
de organ and I'm on de string, huh? I'll fix her! Let
her come down again and I'll fling her in de furnace!
She'll move den! She won't shiver at nothin', den!
Speed, dat'll be her! She'll belong den! (*He grins
horribly.*)

PADDY: She'll never come. She's had her belly-full,
I'm telling you. She'll be in bed now, I'm thinking,
wid ten doctors and nurses feedin' her salts to clean
the fear out of her.

YANK (*enraged*): Yuh tink I made her sick, too, do
yuh? Just lookin' at me, huh? Hairy ape, huh? (*in
a frenzy of rage*) I'll fix her! I'll tell her where to
git off! She'll git down on her knees and take it
back or I'll bust de face offen her! (*shaking one fist
upward and beating on his chest with the other*) I'll
find yuh! I'm comin', d'yuh hear? I'll fix yuh, God
damn yuh! (*He makes a rush for the door.*)

VOICES: Stop him!
   He'll get shot!
   He'll murder her!
   Trip him up!
   Hold him!
   He's gone crazy!
   Gott, he's strong!
   Hold him down!
   Look out for a kick!
   Pin his arms!

(*They have all piled on him and, after a fierce struggle,*

by sheer weight of numbers have borne him to the floor just inside the door.)

PADDY (*who has remained detached*): Kape him down till he's cooled off. (*scornfully*) Yerra, Yank, you're a great fool. Is it payin' attention at all you are to the like of that skinny sow widout one drop of rale blood in her?

YANK (*frenziedly, from the bottom of the heap*): She done me doit! She done me doit, didn't she? I'll git square wit her! I'll get her some way! Git offen me, youse guys! Lemme up! I'll show her who's a ape!

(*Curtain*)

SCENE FIVE

Three weeks later. A corner of Fifth Avenue in the Fifties on a fine Sunday morning. A general atmosphere of clean, well-tidied, wide street; a flood of mellow, tempered sunshine; gentle, genteel breezes. In the rear, the show windows of two shops, a jewelry establishment on the corner, a furrier's next to it. Here the adornments of extreme wealth are tantalizingly displayed. The jeweler's window is gaudy with glittering diamonds, emeralds, rubies, pearls, etc., fashioned in ornate tiaras, crowns, necklaces, collars, etc. From each piece hangs an enormous tag from which a dollar sign and numerals in intermittent electric lights wink out the incredible prices. The same in the furrier's. Rich furs of all varieties hang there bathed in a down pour of artificial light. The general effect is of a background of magnificence cheapened and made grotesque by commercialism, a background in tawdry disharmony with the clear light and sunshine on the street itself.

Up the side street YANK *and* LONG *come swaggering.* LONG *is dressed in shore clothes, wears a black Windsor tie, cloth cap.* YANK *is in his dirty dungarees. A fireman's cap with black peak is cocked defiantly on the side of his head. He has not shaved for days and around his fierce, resentful eyes—as around those of* LONG *to a lesser degree—the black smudge of coal dust still sticks like make-up. They hesitate and stand to-*

*gether at the corner, swaggering, looking about them
with a forced, defiant contempt.*

LONG (*indicating it all with an oratorical gesture*): Well,
'ere we are. Fif' Avenoo. This 'ere's their bleedin'
private lane, as yer might say. (*bitterly*) We're tres-
passers 'ere. Proletarians keep orf the grass!

YANK (*dully*): I don't see no grass, yuh boob. (*staring
at the sidewalk*) Clean, ain't it? Yuh could eat a
fried egg offen it. The white wings got some job
sweepin' dis up. (*looking up and down the avenue—
surlily*) Where's all de white-collar stiffs yuh said
was here—and de skoits—*her* kind?

LONG: In church, blarst 'em Arskin' Jesus to give 'em
more money.

YANK: Choich, huh? I useter go to choich onct—
sure—when I was a kid. Me old man and woman,
dey made me. Dey never went demselves, dough.
Always got too big a head on Sunday mornin', dat
was dem. (*with a grin*) Dey was scrappers for fair,
bot' of dem. On Satiday nights when dey bot' got a
skinful dey could put up a bout oughter been staged
at de Garden. When dey got troue dere wasn't a
chair or table wit a leg under it. Or else dey bot'
jumped on me for somep'n. Dat was where I loined
to take punishment. (*with a grin and a swagger*) I'm
a chip offen de old block, get me?

LONG: Did yer old man follow the sea?

YANK: Naw. Worked along shore. I runned away when
me old lady croaked wit de tremens. I helped at
truckin' and in de market. Den I shipped in de
stokehole. Sure. Dat belongs. De rest was nothin'.
(*looking around him*) I ain't never seen dis before.
De Brooklyn waterfront, dat was where I was
dragged up. (*taking a deep breath*) Dis ain't so bad
at dat, huh?

LONG: Not bad? Well, we pays for it wiv our bloody sweat, if yer wants to know!

YANK (*with sudden angry disgust*): Aw, hell! I don't see no one, see—like her. All dis gives me a pain. It don't belong. Say, ain't dere a back room around dis dump? Let's go shoot a ball. All dis is too clean and quiet and dolled-up, get me! It gives me a pain.

LONG: Wait and yer'll bloody well see—

YANK: I don't wait for no one. I keep on de move. Say, what yuh drag me up here for, anyway? Tryin' to kid me, yuh simp, yuh?

LONG: Yer wants to get back at 'er, don't yer? That's what yer been sayin; every bloomin' hour since she hinsulted yer.

YANK (*vehemently*): Sure ting I do! Didn't I try to get even wit her in Southampton? Didn't I sneak on de dock and wait for her by de gangplank? I was goin' to spit in her pale mug, see! Sure, right in her pop-eyes! Dat woulda made me even, see? But no chanct. Dere was a whole army of plain-clothes bulls around. Dey spotted me and gimme de bum's rush. I never seen her. But I'll git square wit her yet, you watch! (*furiously*) De lousy tart! She tinks she kin get away wit moider—but not wit me! I'll fix her! I'll tink of a way!

LONG (*as disgusted as he dares to be*): Ain't that why I brought yer up 'ere—to show yer? Yer been lookin' at this 'ere 'ole affair wrong. Yer been actin' an' talkin' 's if it was all a bleedin' personal matter between yer and that bloody cow. I wants to convince yer she was on'y a representative of 'er clarss. I wants to awaken yer bloody clarss consciousness. The yer'll see it's 'er clarss yer've got to fight, not 'er alone. There's a 'ole mob of 'em like 'er, Gawd blind 'em!

YANK (*spitting on his hands—belligerently*): De more de merrier when I gits started. Bring on de gang!

LONG: Yer'll see 'em in arf a mo', when that church lets out. (*He turns and sees the window display in the two stores for the first time.*) Blimey! Look at that, will yer? (*They both walk back and stand looking in the jeweler's. LONG flies into a fury.*) Just look at this 'ere bloomin' mess! Just look at it! Look at the bleedin' prices on 'em—more'n our 'ole bloody stokehole makes in ten voyages sweatin' in 'ell! And they—'er and 'er bloody clarss—buys 'em for toys to dangle on 'em! One of these 'ere would buy scoff for a starvin' family for a year!

YANK: Aw, cut de sob stuff! T' hell wit de starvin' family! Yuh'll be passin' de hat to me next. (*with naïve admiration*) Say, dem tings is pretty, huh? Bet yuh dey'd hock for a piece of change aw right. (*then turning away, bored*) But, aw hell, what good are dey? Let her have 'em. Dey don't belong no more'n she does. (*with a gesture of sweeping the jewelers into oblivion*) All dat don't count, get me?

LONG (*who has moved to the furrier's—indignantly*): And I s'pose this 'ere don't count neither—skins of poor, 'armless animals slaughtered so as 'er and 'ers can keep their bleedin' noses warm!

YANK (*who has been staring at something inside—with queer excitement*) Take a slant at dat! Give it de once-over! Monkey fur—two t'ousand bucks! (*bewilderedly*) Is dat straight goods—monkey fur? What de hell—?

LONG (*bitterly*): It's straight enuf (*with grim humor*) They wouldn't bloody well pay for a 'airy ape's skin—no, nor for the ole' livin' ape with all 'is 'ead, and body, and soul thrown in!

YANK (*clenching his fists, his face growing pale with*

*rage as if the skin in the window were a personal
insult*): Trowin' it up in my face! Christ! I'll fix her!

LONG (*excitedly*): Church is out. 'Ere they come, the
bleedin' swine. (*after a glance at* YANK's *lowering face—
uneasily*) Easy goes, Comrade. Keep yer bloomin'
temper. Remember force defeats itself. It ain't our
weapon. We must impress our demands through
peaceful means—the votes of the on-marching proletarians of the bloody world!

YANK (*with abysmal contempt*): Votes, hell! Votes is
a joke, see. Votes for women! Let dem do it!

LONG (*still more uneasily*): Calm, now. Treat 'em wiv
the proper contempt. Observe the bleedin' parasites
but 'old yer 'orses.

YANK (*angrily*): Git away from me! Yuh're yellow,
dat's what. Force, dat's me! De punch, dat's me
every time, see! (*The crowd from church enter from
the right, sauntering slowly and affectedly, their
heads held stiffly up, looking nether to right nor left,
talking in toneless, simpering voices. The women are
rouged, calcimined, dyed, overdressed to the nth degree. The men are in Prince Alberts, high hats, spats,
canes, etc. A procession of gaudy marionettes, yet
with something of the relentless horror of Franken-
steins in their detached, mechanical unawareness.*)

VOICES: Dear Doctor Caiaphas! He is so sincere!

What was the sermon? I dozed off.

About the radicals, my dear—and the false doc-
trines that are being preached.

We must organize a hundred per cent American
bazaar.

And let everyone contribute one one-hundredth per
cent of their income tax.

What an original idea!

We can devote the proceeds to rehabilitating the
veil of the temple.

But that has been done so many times.

YANK (*glaring from one to the other of them—with an insulting snort of scorn*): Huh! Huh! (*Without seeming to see him, they make wide detours to avoid the spot where he stands in the middle of the sidewalk.*)

LONG (*frightenedly*): Keep yer bloomin' mouth shut, I tells yer.

YANK (*viciously*): G'wan! Tell it to Sweeney! (*He swaggers away and deliberately lurches into a top-hatted gentleman, then glares at him pugnaciously.*) Say, who d'yuh tink yuh're bumpin'? Tink yuh own de oith?

GENTLEMAN (*coldly and affectedly*): I beg your pardon. (*He has not looked at* YANK *and passes on without a glance, leaving him bewildered.*)

LONG (*rushing up and grabbing* YANK'S *arm*) 'Ere! Come away! This wasn't what I meant. Yer'll 'ave the bloody coppers down on us.

YANK (*savagely—giving him a push that sends him sprawling*): G'wan!

LONG (*picks himself up—hysterically*): I'll pop orf then. This ain't what I meant. And whatever 'appens, yer can't blame me. (*He slinks off left.*)

YANK: T' hell wit youse! (*He approaches a lady—with a vicious grin and a smirking wink*) Hello, Kiddo. How's every little ting? Got anyting on for tonight? I know an old boiler down to de docks we kin crawl into. (*The lady stalks by without a look, without a change of pace.* YANK *turns to others—insultingly*) Holy smokes, what a mug! Go hide yuhself before de horses shy at yuh. Gee, pipe de heine on dat one! Say, youse, yuh look like de stoin of a ferry-boat. Paint and powder! All dolled up to kill! Yuh look like stiffs laid out for de boneyard! Aw, g'wan, de lot of youse! Yuh give me de eyeache. Yuh don't belong, get me! Look at me, why don't youse dare?

I belong, dat's me! (*pointing to a skyscraper across the street which is in process of construction—with bravado*) See dat buliding goin' up dere? See de steel work? Steel, dat's me! Youse guys live on it and tink yuh're somep'n. But I'm *in* it, see! I'm de hoistin' engine dat makes it go up! I'm it—de inside and bottom of it! Sure! I'm steel and steam and smoke and de rest of it! It moves—speed—twenty-five stories up—and me at de top and bottom—movin'! Youse simps don't move. Yuh're on'y dolls I winds up to see 'm spin. Yuh're de garbage, get me—de leavins—de ashes we dump over de side! Now, what 'a' yuh gotta say? (*But as they seem neither to see nor hear him, he flies into a fury.*) Bums! Pigs! Tarts! Bitches! (*He turns in a rage on the men, bumping viciously into them but not jarring them the least bit. Rather it is he who recoils after each collision. He keeps growling*) Git off de oith! G'wan, yuh bum! Look where yuh're goin', can't yuh? Git outa here! Fight, why don't yuh? Put up yer mits! Don't be a dog! Fight or I'll knock yuh dead! (*But, without seeming to see him, they all answer with mechanical affected politeness:* I beg your pardon. *Then at a cry from one of the women, they all scurry to the furrier's window.*)

THE WOMAN (*ecstatically, with a gasp of delight*): Monkey fur! (*The whole crowd of men and women chorus after her in the same tone of affected delight:* Monkey fur!)

YANK (*with a jerk of his head back on his shoulders, as if he had received a punch full in the face—raging*): I see yuh, all in white! I see yuh, yuh white-faced tart, yuh! Hairy ape, huh? I'll hairy ape yuh! (*He bends down and grips at the street curbing as if to pluck it out and hurl it. Foiled in this, snarling with passion, he leaps to the lamp-post on the corner and tries to pull it up for a club. Just at that moment a bus is heard, rumbling up. A fat, high-hatted, spatted gentleman runs out from the side street. He calls out plaintively:* Bus! Bus! Stop there! *and runs full tilt into the bending, straining* YANK, *who is bowled off his balance.*)

YANK (*seeing a fight—with a roar of joy as he springs to his feet*): At last! Bus, huh? I'll bust yuh! (*He lets drive a terrific swing, his fist landing full on the fat gentleman's face. But the gentleman stands unmoved as if nothing had happened.*)

GENTLEMAN I beg your pardon. (*then irritably*) You have made me lose my bus. (*He claps his hands and begins to scream*) Officer! Officer! (*Many police whistles shrill out on the instant and a whole platoon of policemen rush in on* YANK *from all sides. He tries to fight but is clubbed to the pavement and fallen upon. The crowd at the window have not moved or noticed this disturbance. The clanging gong of the patrol wagon approaches with a clamoring din.*)

(*Curtain*)

SCENE SIX

*Night of the following day. A row of cells in the prison
on Blackwells Island. The cells extend back diagonally
from right front to left rear. They do not stop, but
disappear in the dark background as if they ran on,
numberless, into infinity. One electric bulb from the low
ceiling of the narrow corridor sheds its light through the
heavy steel bars of the cell at the extreme front and
reveals part of the interior. YANK can be seen within,
crouched on the edge of his cot in the attitude of Rodin's "The Thinker." His face is spotted with black
and blue bruises. A blood-stained bandage is wrapped
around his head.*

YANK (*suddenly starting as if awakening from a dream,
reaches out and shakes the bars—aloud to himself,
wonderingly*): Steel. Dis is de Zoo, huh? (*A burst
of hard, barking laughter comes from the unseen oc-
cupants of the cells, runs back down the tier, and
abruptly ceases.*)

VOICES (*mockingly*): The Zoo? That's a new name for
this coop—a damn good name!

Steel, eh? You said a mouthful. This is the old
iron house.

Who is that boob talkin'?

He's the bloke they brung in out of his head. The
bulls had beat him up fierce.

YANK (*dully*): I musta been dreamin'. I tought I was in a cage at de Zoo—but de apes don't talk, do dey?

VOICES (*with mocking laughter*): You're in a cage awe right.

A coop!

A pen!

A sty!

A kennel! (*hard laughter—a pause*)

Say, guy! Who are you? No, never mind lying. What are you?

Yes, tell us your sad story. What's your game?

What did they jug yuh for?

YANK (*dully*): I was a fireman—stokin' on de liners. (*then with sudden rage, rattling his cell bars*) I'm a hairy ape, get me? And I'll bust youse all in de jaw if yuh don't lay off kiddin' me.

VOICES: Huh! You're a hard boiled duck, ain't you! When you spit, it bounces! (*laughter*)

Aw, can it. He's a regular guy. Ain't you?

What did he say he was—a ape?

YANK (*defiantly*): Sure ting! Ain't dat what youse all are—apes? (*A silence. Then a furious rattling of bars from down the corridor.*)

A VOICE (*thick with rage*): I'll show yuh who's a ape, yuh bum!

VOICES: Ssshh! Nix!

Can de noise!

Piano!

You'll have the guard down on us!

YANK (*scornfully*): De guard? Yuh mean de keeper, don't yuh? (*angry exclamations from all the cells*)

VOICE (*placatingly*): Aw, don't pay no attention to him. He's off his nut from the beatin'-up he got. Say, you guy! We're waitin' to hear what they landed you for—or ain't yuh tellin'?

YANK: Sure, I'll tell youse. Sure! Why de hell not?

On'y—youse won't get me. Nobody gets me but me, see? I started to tell de Judge and all he says was: "Toity days to tink it over." Tink it over! Christ, dat's all I been doin' for weeks! (*after a pause*) I was tryin' to git even wit someone, see?—someone dat done me doit.

VOICES (*cynically*): De old stuff, I bet. Your goil, huh? Give yuh the double-cross, huh?

That's them every time!

Did yuh beat up de odder guy?

YANK (*disgustedly*): Aw, yuh're all wrong! Sure dere was a skoit in it—but not what youse mean, not dat old tripe. Dis was a new kind of skoit. She was dolled up all in white—in de stokehole. I thought she was a ghost. Sure. (*a pause*)

VOICES (*whispering*): Gee, he's still nutty.

Let him rave. It's fun listenin'.

YANK (*unheeding—groping in his thoughts*): Her hands—dey was skinny and white like dey wasn't real but painted on somep'n. Dere was a million miles from me to her—twenty-five knots a hour. She was like some dead ting de cat brung in. Sure, dat's what. She didn't belong. She belonged in de window of a toy store, or on de top of a garbage can, see! Sure! (*He breaks out angrily*) But would yuh believe it, she had de noive to do me doit. She lamped me like she was seein' somep'n broke loose from de menagerie. Christ, yuh'd oughter seen her eyes! (*He rattles the bars of his cell furiously.*) But I'll get back at her yet, you watch! And if I can't find her I'll take it out on de gang she runs wit. I'm wise to where dey hangs out now. I'll show her who belongs! I'll show her who's in de move and who ain't. You watch my smoke!

VOICES (*serious and joking*): Dat's de talkin'!

Take her for all she's got!

What was this dame, anyway? Who was she, eh?

YANK: I dunno. First cabin stiff. Her old man's a millionaire, dey says—name of Douglas.

VOICES: Douglas? That's the president of the Steel Trust, I bet.

Sure, I seen his mug in de papers.

He's filthy with dough.

VOICE: Hey, feller, take a tip from me. If you want to get back at that dame, you better join the Wobblies. You'll get some action then.

YANK: Wobblies? What de hell's dat?

VOICE: Ain't you ever heard of the I. W. W.?

YANK: Naw. What is it?

VOICE: A gang of blokes—a tough gang. I been readin' about 'em today in the paper. The guard give me the *Sunday Times*. There's a long spiel about 'em. It's from a speech made in the Senate by a guy named Senator Queen. (*He is in the cell next to* YANK'S. *There is a rustling of paper.*) Wait'll I see if I got light enough and I'll read you. Listen. (*He reads*) "There is a menace existing in this country today which threatens the vitals of our fair Republic—as foul a menace against the life-blood of the American Eagle as was the foul conspiracy of Cataline against the eagles of ancient Rome!"

VOICE (*disgustedly*): Aw, hell! Tell him to salt de tail of dat eagle!

VOICE (*reading*): "I refer to that devil's brew of rascals, jailbirds, murderers and cutthroats who libel all honest working men by calling themselves the Industrial Workers of the World; but in the light of their nefarious plots, I call them the Industrious *Wreckers* of the World!"

YANK (*with vengeful satisfaction*): Wreckers, dat's de right dope! Dat belongs! Me for dem!

VOICE: Ssshh! (*reading*) "This fiendish organization is a foul ulcer on the fair body of our Democracy—"

VOICE: Democracy, hell! Give him the boid, fellers—the raspberry! (*They do.*)

VOICE: *Ssshh!* (*reading*) "Like Cato I say to this Senate, the I. W. W. must be destroyed! For they represent an ever-present dagger pointed at the heart of the greatest nation the world has ever known, where all men are born free and equal, with equal opportunities to all, where the Founding Fathers have guaranteed to each one happiness, where Truth, Honor, Liberty, Justice, and the Brotherhood of Man are a religion absorbed with one's mother milk, taught at our father's knee, sealed, signed, and stamped upon in the glorious Constitution of these United States!" (*a perfect storm of hisses, catcalls, boos, and hard laughter*)

VOICES (*scornfully*): Hurrah for de Fort' of July!
Pass de hat!
Liberty!
Justice!
Honor!
Opportunity!
Brotherhood!

ALL (*with abysmal scorn*): Aw, hell!

VOICE: Give that Queen Senator guy the bark! All togedder now—one—two—tree— (*a terrific chorus of barking and yapping*)

GUARD (*from a distance*): Quit there, youse—or I'll git the hose. (*The noise subsides.*)

YANK (*with growling rage*): I'd like to catch dat senator guy alone for a second. I'd lion him some trute!

VOICE: Ssshh! Here's where he gits down to cases on the Wobblies. (*reads*) "They plot with fire in one hand and dynamite in the other. They stop not before murder to gain their ends, nor at the outraging of defenseless womanhood. They would tear down society, put the lowest scum in the seats of the mighty, turn Almighty God's revealed plan for the world topsy-turvy, and make of our sweet and lovely civilization a shambles, a desolation where man, God's masterpiece, would soon degenerate back to the ape!"

VOICE (*to* YANK): Hey, you guy. There's your ape stuff again.

YANK (*with a growl of fury*): I got him. So dey blow up tings, do dey? Dey turn tings round, do dey? Hey, lend me dat paper, will yuh?

VOICE: Sure. Give it to him. On'y keep it to yourself, see. We don't wanter listen to no more of that slop.

VOICE: Here you are. Hide it under your mattress.

YANK (*reaching out*): Tanks. I can't read much but I kin manage. (*He sits, the paper in the hand at his side, in the attitude of Rodin's "The Thinker." A pause. Several snores from down the corridor. Suddenly* YANK *jumps to his feet with a furious groan as if some appalling thought had crashed on him— bewilderedly*) Sure—her old man—president of de Steel Trust—makes half de steel in de world— steel—where I tought I belonged—drivin' trou— movin'—in dat—to make *her*—and cage me in for her to spit on! Christ (*He shakes the bars of his cell door till the whole tier trembles. Irritated, protesting exclamations from those awakened or trying to get to sleep.*) He made dis—dis cage! Steel! *It* don't belong, dat's what! Cages, cells, locks, bolts, bars— dat's what it means!—holdin' me down wit him at de top! But I'll drive trou! Fire, dat melts it! I'll be fire—under de heap—fire dat never goes out—hot as hell—breakin' out in de night— (*While he has been saying this last he had shaken his cell door to a clanging accompaniment. As he comes to the "breakin' out" he seizes one bar with both hands and, putting his two feet up against the others so that his position is parallel to the floor like a monkey's, he gives a great wrench backwards. The bar bends like a licorice stick under his tremendous strength. Just at this moment the prison guard rushes in, dragging a hose behind him.)*

GUARD (*angrily*): I'll loin youse bums to wake me up! (*sees* YANK) Hello, it's you, huh? Got the D. Ts., hey? Well, I'll cure 'em. I'll drown your snakes for yuh! (*noticing the bar*) Hell, look at dat bar bended! On'y a bug is strong enough for dat!

YANK (*glaring at him*): Or a hairy ape, yuh big yellow bum! Look out! Here I come! (*He grabs another bar.*)

GUARD (*scared now—yelling off left*): Toin de hose on, Ben!—full pressure! And call de others—and a straitjacket! (*The curtain is falling. As it hides* YANK *from view, there is a splattering smash as the stream of water hits the steel of* YANK'S *cell.*)

(*Curtain*)

SCENE SEVEN

*Nearly a month later. An I. W. W. local near the water-
front, showing the interior of a front room on the
ground floor, and the street outside. Moonlight on
the narrow street, buildings massed in black shadow.
The interior of the room, which is general assembly
room, office, and reading room, resembles some dingy
settlement boys' club. A desk and high stool are in one
corner. A table with papers, stacks of pamphlets, chairs
about it, is at center. The whole is decidedly cheap,
banal, commonplace and unmysterious as a room
could well be. The secretary is perched on the stool
making entries in a large ledger. An eye shade casts his
face into shadows. Eight or ten men, longshoremen,
iron workers, and the like, are grouped about the table.
Two are playing checkers. One is writing a letter. Most
of them are smoking pipes. A big signboard is on the
wall at the rear, "Industrial Workers of the World—
Local No. 57."*

YANK (*comes down the street outside. He is dressed as
in Scene Five. He moves cautiously, mysteriously. He
comes to a point opposite the door; tiptoes softly up
to it, listens, is impressed by the silence within,
knocks carefully, as if he were guessing at the password to some secret rite. Listens. No answer. Knocks
again a bit louder. No answer. Knocks impatiently,
much louder.*)

SECRETARY (*turning around on his stool*): What the hell is that—someone knocking? (*shouts*) Come in, why don't you? (*All the men in the room look up. Yank opens the door slowly, gingerly, as if afraid of an ambush. He looks around for secret doors, mystery, is taken aback by the commonplaceness of the room and the men in it, thinks he may have gotten in the wrong place, then sees the signboard on the wall and is reassured.*)

YANK (*blurts out*): Hello.

MEN (*reservedly*): Hello.

YANK (*more easily*): I tought I'd bumped into de wrong dump.

SECRETARY (*scrutinizing him carefully*): Maybe you have. Are you a member?

YANK: Naw, not yet. Dat's what I come for—to join.

SECRETARY: That's easy. What's your job—longshore?

YANK: Naw. Fireman—stoker on de liners.

SECRETARY (*with satisfaction*): Welcome to our city. Glad to know you people are waking up at last. We haven't got many members in your line.

YANK: Naw. Dey're all dead to de woild.

SECRETARY: Well, you can help to wake 'em. What's your name? I'll make out your card.

YANK (*confused*): Name? Lemme tink.

SECRETARY (*sharply*): Don't you know your name?

YANK: Sure; but I been just Yank for so long—Bob, dat's it—Bob Smith.

SECRETARY (*writing*): Robert Smith. (*fills out the rest of card*) Here you are. Cost you half a dollar.

YANK: Is dat all—four bits? Dat's easy. (*gives the Secretary the money*)

SECRETARY (*throwing it in drawer*): Thanks. Well, make yourself at home. No introductions needed. There's literature on the table. Take some of those pamphlets with you to distribute aboard ship. They

may bring results. Sow the seed, only go about it
right. Don't get caught and fired. We got plenty out
of work. What we need is men who can hold their
jobs—and work for us at the same time.

YANK: Sure. (*But he still stands, embarrassed and
uneasy.*)

SECRETARY (*looking at him—curiously*): What did you
knock for? Think we had a coon in uniform to
open doors?

YANK: Naw. I tought it was locked—and dat yuh'd
wanter give me the once-over trou a peep-hole or
somep'n to see if I was right.

SECRETARY (*alert and suspicious but with an easy
laugh*): Think we were running a crap game? That
door is never locked. What put that in your nut?

YANK (*with a knowing grin, convinced that this is all
camouflage, a part of the secrecy*): Dis burg is full
of bulls, ain't it?

SECRETARY (*sharply*): What have the cops got to do
with us? We're breaking no laws.

YANK (*with a knowing wink*): Sure. Youse wouldn't
for woilds. Sure. I'm wise to dat.

SECRETARY: You seem to be wise to a lot of stuff
none of us knows about.

YANK (*with another wink*): Aw, dat's aw right, see.
(*then made a bit resentfully by the suspicious glances
from all sides*) Aw, can it! Youse needn't put me
trou de toid degree. Can't youse see I belong? Sure!
I'm reg'lar. I'll stick, get me? I'll shoot de woiks for
youse. Dat's why I wanted to join in.

SECRETARY (*breezily, feeling him out*): That's the right
spirit. Only are you sure you understand what
you've joined? It's all plain and above aboard; still,
some guys get a wrong slant on us. (*sharply*) What's
your notion of the purpose of the I. W. W.?

YANK: Aw, I know all about it.

SECRETARY (*sarcastically*): Well, give us some of your valuable information.

YANK (*cunningly*): I know enough not to speak outa my toin. (*then resentfully again*) Aw, say! I'm reg'lar. I'm wise to de game. I know yuh got to watch your step wit a stranger. For all youse know, I might be a plain-clothes dick, or somep'n, dat's what yuh're tinkin', huh? Aw, forget it! I belong, see? Ask any guy down to de docks if I don't.

SECRETARY: Who said you didn't?

YANK: After I'm 'nitited, I'll show yuh.

SECRETARY (*astounded*): Initiated? There's no initiation.

YANK (*disappointed*): Ain't there no password—no grip nor nothin'?

SECRETARY: What'd you think this is—the Elks—or the Black Hand?

YANK: De Elks, hell! De Black Hand, dey're a lot of yellow backstickin' Ginees. Naw. Dis is a man's gang, ain't it?

SECRETARY: You said it! That's why we stand on our two feet in the open. We got no secrets.

YANK (*surprised but admiringly*): Yuh mean to say yuh always run wide open—like dis?

SECRETARY: Exactly.

YANK: Den yuh sure got your noive wit youse!

SECRETARY (*sharply*): Just what was it made you want to join us? Come out with that straight.

YANK: Yuh call me? Well, I got noive, too! Here's my hand. Yuh wanter blow tings up, don't yuh? Well, dat's me! I belong!

SECRETARY (*with pretended carelessness*): You mean change the unequal conditions of society by legitimate direct action—or with dynamite?

YANK: Dynamite! Blow it offen do oith—steel—all de

cages—all de factories, steamers, buildings, jails—
de Steel Trust and all dat makes it go.

SECRETARY: So—that's your idea, eh? And did you
have any special job in that line you wanted to pro-
pose to us? (*He makes a sign to the men, who get
up cautiously one by one and group behind* YANK.)

YANK (*boldly*): Sure, I'll come out wit it. I'll show
youse I'm one of de gang. Dere's dat millionaire
guy, Douglas—

SECRETARY: President of the Steel Trust, you mean?
Do you want to assassinate him?

YANK: Naw, dat don't get yuh nothin'. I mean blow
up de factory, de woiks, where he makes de steel.
Dat's what I'm after—to blow up de steel, knock
all de steel in de woild up to de moon. Dat'll fix
tings! (*eagerly, with a touch of bravado*) I'll do it by
me lonesome! I'll show yuh! Tell me where his
woiks is, how to git there, all de dope. Gimme de
stuff, de old butter—and watch me do de rest!
Watch de smoke and see it move! I don't give a
damn if dey nab me—long as it's done! I'll soive
life for it—and give 'em de laugh! (*half to himself*)
And I'll write her a letter and tell her de hairy ape
done it. Dat'll square tings.

SECRETARY (*stepping away from* YANK): Very interesting. (*He gives a signal. The men, huskies all,
throw themselves on* YANK *and before he knows it
they have his legs and arms pinioned. But he is too
flabbergasted to make a struggle, anyway. They feel
him over for weapons.*)

MAN: No gat, no knife. Shall we give him what's what
and put the boots to him?

SECRETARY: No. He isn't worth the trouble we'd get
into. He's too stupid. (*He comes closer and laughs
mockingly in* YANK's *face.*) Ho-ho! By God, this is
the biggest joke they've put up on us yet. Hey, you

Joke! Who sent you—Burns or Pinkerton? No, by
God, you're such a bonehead I'll bet you're in the
Secret Service! Well, you dirty spy, you rotten agent
provocator, you can go back and tell whatever
skunk is paying you blood-money for betraying your
brothers that he's wasting his coin. You couldn't
catch a cold. And tell him that all he'll ever get on
us, or ever has got, is just his own sneaking plots
that he's framed up to put us in jail. We are what
our manifesto says we are, neither more nor less—
and we'll give him a copy of that any time he calls.
And as for you— (*He glares scornfully at* YANK,
who is sunk in an oblivious stupor.) Oh, hell, what's
the use of talking? You're a brainless ape.

YANK (*aroused by the word to fierce but futile struggles*): What's dat, yuh Sheeny bum, yuh!

SECRETARY: Throw him out, boys. (*In spite of his
struggles, this is done with gusto and éclat. Propelled
by several parting kicks,* YANK *lands sprawling in
the middle of the narrow cobbled street. With a growl
he starts to get up and storm the closed door, but
stops bewildered by the confusion in his brain, pa-
thetically impotent. He sits there, brooding, in as near
to the attitude of Rodin's "Thinker" as he can get in
his position.*)

YANK (*bitterly*): So dem boids don't tink I belong,
neider. Aw, to hell wit 'em! Dey're in de wrong
pew—de same old bull—soapboxes and Salvation
Army—no guts! Cut out an hour offen de job a day
and make me happy! Gimme a dollar more a day
and make me happy! Tree square a day, and cauli-
flowers in de front yard—ekal rights—a woman and
kids—a lousy vote—and I'm all fixed for Jesus, huh?
Aw, hell! What does dat get yuh? Dis ting's in your
inside, but it ain't your belly. Feedin' your face—
sinkers and coffee—dat don't touch it. It's way

down—at de bottom. Yuh can't grab it, and yuh can't stop it. It moves, and everything moves. It stops and de whole woild stops. Dat's me now—I don't tick, see?—I'm a busted Ingersoll, dat's what. Steel was me, and I owned de woild. Now I ain't steel, and de woild owns me. Aw, hell! I can't see— it's all dark, get me? It's all wrong! (*He turns a bitter mocking face up like an ape gibbering at the moon.*) Say, youse up dere, Man in de Moon, yuh look so wise, gimme de answer, huh? Slip me de inside dope, de information right from de stable— where I do get off at, huh?

A POLICEMAN (*who had come up the street in time to hear this last—with grim humor*): You'll get off at the station, you boob, if you don't get up out of that and keep movin'.

YANK (*looking up at him—with a hard, bitter laugh*): Sure! Lock me up! Put me in a cage! Dat's de on'y answer yuh know. G'wan, lock me up!

POLICEMAN: What you been doin'?

YANK: Enuf to gimme life for! I was born, see? Sure, dat's de charge Write it in de blotter. I was born, get me!

POLICEMAN (*jocosely*): God pity your old woman! (*then matter-of-fact*) But I've no time for kidding You're soused. I'd run you in but it's too long a walk to the station. Come on now, get up, or I'll fan your ears with this club. Beat it now! (*He hauls* YANK *to his feet.*)

YANK (*in a vague mocking tone*): Say, where do I go from here?

POLICEMAN (*giving him a push—with a grin, indifferently*): Go to hell.

(*Curtain*)

SCENE EIGHT

Twilight of the next day. The monkey house at the Zoo. One spot of clear gray light falls on the front of one cage so that the interior can be seen. The other cages are vague, shrouded in shadow from which chatterings pitched in a conversational tone can be heard. On the one cage a sign from which the word "gorilla" stands out. The gigantic animal himself is seen squatting on his haunches on a bench in much the same attitude as Rodin's "Thinker." YANK *enters from the left. Immediately a chorus of angry chattering and screeching breaks out. The gorilla turns his eyes but makes no sound or move.*

YANK (*with a hard, bitter laugh*): Welcome to your city, huh? Hail, hail, de gang's all here! (*At the sound of his voice the chattering dies away into an attentive silence.* YANK *walks up to the gorilla's cage and, leaning over the railing, stares in at its occupant, who stares back at him, silent and motionless. There is a pause of dead stillness. Then* YANK *begins to talk in a friendly confidential tone, half-mockingly, but with a deep undercurrent of sympathy.*) Say, yuh're some hard-lookin' guy, ain't yuh? I seen lots of tough nuts dat de gang called gorillas, but yuh're de foist real one I ever seen. Some chest yuh got, and shoulders, and dem arms and mits! I bet yuh got a punch in eider fist dat'd knock 'em all silly!

(*This with genuine admiration. The gorilla, as if he understood, stands upright, swelling out his chest and pounding on it with his fist.* YANK *grins sympathetically.*) Sure, I get yuh. Yuh challenge de whole woild, huh? Yuh got what I was sayin' even if yuh muffled de woids. (*then bitterness creeping in*) And why wouldn't yuh get me? Ain't we both members of de same club—de Hairy Apes? (*They stare at each other—a pause—then* YANK *goes on slowly and bitterly.*) So yuh're what she seen when she looked at me, de white-faced tart! I was you to her, get me? On'y outa de cage—broke out—free to moider her, see? Sure! Dat's what she tought. She wasn't wise dat I was in a cage, too—worser'n yours—sure—a damn sight—'cause you got some chanct to bust loose—but me— (*He grows confused.*) Aw, hell! It's all wrong, ain't it (*a pause*) I s'pose yuh wanter know what I'm doin' here, huh? I been warmin' a bench down to de Battery—ever since last night. Sure. I seen de sun come up. Dat was pretty, too—all red and pink and green. I was lookin' at de skyscrapers—steel—and all de ships comin' in, sailin' out, all over de oith—and dey was steel, too. De sun was warm, dey wasn't no clouds, and dere was a breeze blowin'. Sure, it was great stuff. I got it aw right—what Paddy said about dat bein' de right dope—on'y I couldn't get *in* it, see? I couldn't belong in dat. It was over my head. And I kept tinkin'—and den I beat it up here to see what youse was like. And I waited till dey was all gone to git yuh alone. Say, how d'yuh feel sittin' in dat pen all de time, havin' to stand for 'em comin' and starin' at yuh—de white-faced, skinny tarts and de bobs what marry 'em—makin' fun of yuh, laughin' at yuh, gittin' scared of yuh—damn 'em! (*He pounds on the rail with his fist. The gorilla rattles the bars of his cage and snarls. All the other monkeys set up an angry chattering in the darkness.* YANK *goes on excitedly.*) Sure! Dat's de way it hits me, too. On'y yuh're lucky, see? Yuh don't belong wit 'em and yuh know it. But me, I belong wit 'em—but I don't, see? Dey don't belong wit me, dat's what. Get me? Tinkn' is hard— (*He passes one hand across his forehead with a painful gesture. The gorilla growls impatiently.* YANK *goes on gropingly.*) It's dis way, what I'm drivin' at. Youse can sit and dope dream in de past, green woods, de jungle and de rest of it. Den yuh belong and dey don't. Den yuh kin laugh at 'em, see? Yuh're de champ of de woild. But me— I ain't got no past to tink in, nor nothin' dat's comin', on'y what's now—and dat don't belong. Sure, you're de best off! Yuh can't tink, can yuh? Yuh can't talk neider. But I kin make a bluff at talkin' and tinkin'—a'most git away wit it— a'most!—and dat's where de joker comes in. (*He laughs.*) I ain't on oith and I ain't in heaven, get me? I'm in de middle tryin' to separate 'em, takin' all de woist punches from bot' of 'em. Maybe dat's what dey call hell, huh? But you, yuh're at de bottom. You belong! Sure! Yuh're de on'y one in de woild dat does, yuh lucky stiff! (*The gorilla growls proudly.*) And dat's why dey gotter put yuh in a cage, see? (*The gorilla roars angrily.*) Sure! Yuh get me. It beats in when you try to tink it or talk it— it's way down—deep—behind—you 'n' me we feel it. Sure! Bot' members of dis club! (*He laughs— then in a savage tone*) What de hell! T' hell wit it! A little action, dat's our meat! Dat belongs! Knock 'em down and keep bustin' 'em till dey croaks yuh wit a gat—wit steel! Sure! Are yuh game? Dey've looked at youse, ain't dey—in a cage? Wanter git even? Wanter wind up like a sport 'stead of croakin' slow in dere? (*The gorilla roars an emphatic affirmative.* YANK *goes on with a sort of furious exaltation.*) Sure! Yuh're reg'lar! Yuh'll stick to de finish! Me 'n' you, huh?—bot' members of this club! We'll put up one last star bout dat'll knock 'em offen deir seats! Dey'll have to make de cages stronger after we're trou! (*The gorilla is straining at his bars, growling, hopping from one foot to the other.* YANK *takes a jimmy from under his coat and forces the lock on the cage door. He throws this open.*) Pardon from de governor! Step out and shake hands! I'll take yuh for a walk down Fif' Avenoo. We'll knock 'em offen de oith and croak wit de band playin'. Come on, Brother. (*The gorilla scrambles gingerly out of his cage. Goes to* YANK *and stands looking at him.* YANK *keeps his mocking tone—holds out his hand.*) Shake—de secret grip of our order. (*Something, the tone of mockery, perhaps, suddenly enrages the animal. With a spring he wraps his huge arms around* YANK *in a murderous hug. There is a cracking snap of crushed ribs—a gasping cry, still mocking, from* YANK.) Hey, I didn't say kiss me! (*The gorilla lets the crushed body slip to the floor, stands over it uncertainly, considering; then picks it up, throws it in the cage, shuts the door, and shuffles off menacingly into the darkness at left. A great uproar of frightened chattering and whimpering comes from the other cages. Then* YANK *moves, groaning, opening his eyes, and there is silence. He mutters painfully*) Say—dey oughter match him—wit Zybszko. He got me, aw right. I'm trou. Even him didn't tink I belonged. (*then, with sudden passionate despair*) Christ, where do I get off at? Where do I fit in? (*checking himself as suddenly*) Aw, what de hell! No squawkin', see! No quittin', get me! Croak wit your boots on! (*He grabs hold of the bars of the cage and hauls himself painfully to his feet—looks around him bewilderedly—forces a mocking laugh.*) In de cage, huh? (*in the strident tones of a circus barker*) Ladies and gents, step forward and take a slant at de one and only— (*his voice weakening*)— one and original—Hairy Ape from de wilds of— (*He slips in a heap on the floor and dies. The monkeys set up a chattering, whimpering wail. And, perhaps, the Hairy Ape at last belongs.*)

(*Curtain*)

AFTERWORD
by Arthur and Barbara Gelb

Looking back, it sometimes seems to us that from the very beginning O'Neill was writing drafts for the final masterworks that have stamped him as America's foremost dramatist. Three of the four plays in this volume—*Beyond the Horizon*, *Anna Christie* and *The Hairy Ape*—anticipate situations and characters from his own life that reappear in those final works, twenty-seven plays later. Those last plays, of course, are *The Iceman Cometh*, *Long Day's Journey Into Night*, *A Touch of the Poet* and *A Moon for the Misbegotten*—all written between 1939 and 1944, the year that illness finally silenced him.

O'Neill was always an intensely personal writer and most of his major plays are layered with autobiographical references. Over and over, we meet versions of his father, mother, older brother and himself (along with his lovers and children). The O'Neills were a family more often embattled than at peace—a family O'Neill once described as "very close—perhaps too close."

In *Beyond the Horizon*, we find an early representation of O'Neill's father—the actor James O'Neill—in the form of a hard-bitten farmer, James Mayo. This character, after appearing in numerous other guises, ultimately evolved as the actor James Tyrone in *Long Day's Journey Into Night*, the most transparently autobiographical of O'Neill's plays.

O'Neill depicts his father in *Beyond the Horizon* as the father of two sons, both of whom have disappointed him. The sons, Andrew and Robert, are locked in rivalry—Andrew, the older son, pragmatic and materialistic; Robert, the younger son, a dreamy idealist. And they, in turn, are early imaginings of the two conflicted Tyrone brothers of *Long Day's Journey Into Night*, who are based on the two O'Neill brothers, Jamie and Eugene. (In that play, O'Neill called Jamie by his real name and called the character who represented himself Edmund, the name of a brother who had died in infancy.)

"There is a touch of the poet about [Robert Mayo]," wrote O'Neill in his stage directions for *Beyond the Horizon*—echoed in *Long Day's Journey Into Night* when James Tyrone tells Edmund, "You've the makings of a poet." And then the phrase is used as the actual title of *A Touch of the Poet*—referring to the young, idealistic Simon Harford, the offstage character based, once again, on O'Neill himself. Also in that play O'Neill drew yet another portrait of his father, this time depicting him as Cornelius Melody, a retired early-nineteenth-century Irish cavalry officer forced by hard times into running an inn on the outskirts of Boston.

When O'Neill began writing *Beyond the Horizon* in 1918, he and his actor father had finally overcome much of the personal antagonism that for years had scorched their relationship. Eugene, in his late twenties, had at last found a milieu—far removed from the commercial Broadway theater—where he was appreciated for the daringly tragic outlook of his one-act plays. And James O'Neill was relieved that his self-destructive and destitute son seemed at last to be launched on a career, however antithetical to his own traditional beliefs.

For James insisted that it was "impossible to be resigned to the commonplaces of the modern style of play" (naturalistic themes with unconventional denouements); these plays, as James well knew, included Eugene's innovative one acters, as presented in Greenwich Village by the experimental group of writers and actors calling themselves the Provincetown Players.

Eugene, for his part, was contemptuous of the outmoded, melodramatic theater of the late-nineteenth and early-twentieth centuries, in which his father had made his reputation as a matinee idol. Eugene deplored the fact that his father—forsaking a career as a gifted Shakespearean actor—had chosen to perform endlessly in the moneymaking eponymous role in *The Count of Monte Cristo*, a popular melodrama that earned him a small fortune. Ever the uncompromising idealist himself, Eugene saw his father as materialistic and insensitive.

Even now a subterranean antagonism, both professional and personal, smoldered between father and son. It was the tension between the poetic ideal—as personified by Eugene—and the lure of materialism—as personified by his father—that partly dictated the theme of *Beyond the Horizon*.

O'Neill, in his writing, wasted nothing of what he liked to refer to as his "life-experience." In his early one-act sea plays, he dwelled on his exploits as an alienated youth who shipped out as a sailor. And for *Beyond the Horizon*, the first of his full-length plays to win him a Broadway production, he mined an unhappy love triangle in which he'd recently been entangled.

The rivalry between Andrew and Robert Mayo over Ruth Atkins was based on O'Neill's tempestuous love for Louise Bryant, an aspiring writer who happened to be the lover of John Reed. A heralded if controversial journalist, Reed had befriended O'Neill in his early Greenwich Village days, when O'Neill was struggling to be recognized. Reed invited O'Neill to join the newly formed Provincetown Players on Cape Cod, and was among the first and most enthusiastic supporters of his talent as a playwright—as was Louise Bryant.

Louise, a free spirit and a symbol of the bohemian lifestyle of the World War I era, wanted both Reed and O'Neill. And for a time she allowed O'Neill to believe he would be her final choice. In fairness to O'Neill, he did initially wrestle with the temptation to betray his good friend, Reed—just as young Robert Mayo, in *Beyond the Horizon*, struggles not to hurt his brother.

But, after a brief love affair, Louise left O'Neill, who was only just beginning to emerge as a promising playwright. She chose instead to follow the thriving Reed to Russia, where they both covered the Revolution, and where Reed famously gathered the material for his classic *Ten Days That Shook the World*. (Reed died of typhus in Russia at the age of thirty-three and was buried in the Kremlin wall.)

In *Beyond the Horizon*, it was not much of a stretch for O'Neill to turn the two rivals for the girl into brothers, rather than mere friends. O'Neill and his brother,

Jamie, were themselves rivals—not for a girl, but for the affections of their mother (and to a lesser degree the approval of their father). Jamie, indeed, was growing particularly envious of his younger brother at the time O'Neill was writing *Beyond the Horizon*. Alcoholic for years, Jamie finally had been forced to abandon a mediocre career as an actor. Fully aware that he was a failure, he could not control his jealousy over his brother's burgeoning success.

If Louise Bryant was the inspiration for Ruth Atkins in *Beyond the Horizon*, the later scenes in which she and Robert quarrel bitterly seem more to reflect O'Neill's relationship with Agnes Boulton, the woman he married on the rebound from Louise.

Agnes, who supported herself as a writer of pulp-magazine fiction, was a pretty, vivacious brunette, whose resemblance to Louise was what first attracted O'Neill. Initially awed by O'Neill, she strove to accommodate his sometimes imperious—and often childish—demands. While he could work for long stretches with extraordinary concentration, he could plunge into wild drinking binges, during which he was prone to jealous rages. The neediness for mothering that he displayed not only with Agnes but with all the women to whom he was attached stemmed, it would seem, from the fact of his mother's withdrawal into morphine addiction while he was growing up. (Ella O'Neill had, by now, made a remarkable recovery from her addiction; both she and James warmly welcomed Agnes as a daughter-in-law.)

O'Neill and Agnes had vowed to live an idealistic—and childless—life of mutual creativity and total devotion to each other's needs, with the utopian (if naive) pledge that each was free to leave the marriage at any time.

Agnes did her best. During the early years of the marriage, she attempted—with O'Neill's professed encouragement—to achieve a more elevated literary career for herself. But at the same time, O'Neill expected her single-minded attention in helping him cope with the demands made on him in the wake of his new celebrity. The Broadway run of *Beyond the Horizon* was hailed by critics as the first authentically American tragedy and brought him the first of his four Pulitzer Prizes.

Agnes tried to accommodate his need for seclusion and quiet for his writing, and patiently helped him recover from his drinking binges. And she stood by him stoically as his father died a prolonged and painful death from cancer.

Always, O'Neill was fiercely at work. During the same year that he was involved in the Broadway production of *Beyond the Horizon*, he was also writing both *Anna Christie* and *The Emperor Jones*, along with several other plays. As his notebooks and work diaries attest, ideas for plays swirled in his mind by the dozens; he often worked on two or three plays at the same time and was constantly jotting notes for future work. And by the time of his success with *Beyond the Horizon*, O'Neill and Agnes—despite their vows—had produced a son, Shane, born in October 1919.

As he did in *Beyond the Horizon*, O'Neill once again drew on his "life-experience" for *The Emperor Jones*. The effect of the tropical forest, he explained, "was honestly come by. It was the result of my own experience while prospecting for gold in Spanish Honduras."

He failed to note that his gold-prospecting expedition (three years before he began writing plays) had been arranged by his father. James O'Neill had managed to get Eugene out of the country to disentangle him from an ill-considered commitment. Eugene, at twenty-one—jobless and drifting—had gotten a young woman his own age, Kathleen Jenkins, pregnant and out of obligation had married her. James O'Neill, perhaps believing an annulment could be arranged, was cannily trying to put as much distance as possible between Eugene and the Jenkins family.

Eugene found the Honduran jungle pure hell and was almost joyful when, after months of fruitless searching for gold, he was stricken with malaria and was, as he put it, "invalided back to New York" (where, not long after, he and Kathleen were divorced).

As for the character of Brutus Jones, O'Neill drew on his friendship with a black bartender named Adam Scott, a fixture in the New London, Connecticut, of O'Neill's youth. Scott was an elder of the Baptist Church and was happy at times to explain the seeming contradiction of his two occupations: "I'm a very religious man, but after Sunday, I lay my Jesus on the shelf."

Scott's bravado, his religious conviction and his superstition became the traits of Brutus Jones. O'Neill even reproduced some of Scott's figures of speech in the play, as in these lines: "Doesn't you know dey's got to deal wid a man was member in good standin' o' de Baptist Church? . . . [But] it don't git me nothin' to do missionary work for de Baptist Church. I'se after de coin an' I lays my Jesus on de shelf for de time bein'."

O'Neill often tried to explain his ability to work on several projects at once—as in the case of *The Emperor Jones* and *Anna Christie.*

"I never try to force an idea," he told an interviewer for *American Magazine* in 1922. "I think about it, off and on. If nothing seems to come of it, I put it away and forget it. But apparently my subconscious mind keeps working on it; for, all of a sudden, someday, it comes back to my mind as a pretty well-formed scheme."

One such literary preoccupation was the social plight of the prostitute. O'Neill had sympathetically depicted prostitutes in his early attempts at poetry and in a one-act play called *The Web.* Much later, he was to revisit them with compassionate humor as the self-styled "tarts" in *The Iceman Cometh.*

But *Anna Christie* was his first full-fledged study of a fallen woman redeemed by love. In some ways she foreshadowed Josie Hogan, the formidable earth mother of *A Moon for the Misbegotten*, who, out of self-loathing, pretends to be promiscuous; apart from Mary Tyrone of *Long Day's Journey Into Night*, Josie is O'Neill's most powerfully conceived female protagonist.

The actual model for Anna was a woman named Marie. She was the companion of an early mentor of O'Neill, Terry Carlin, who—after a successful career as an engineer—had dropped out of society. It was Carlin who introduced O'Neill to the anarchist movement, which later became a significant element of *The Iceman Cometh.* And the first act setting of *Anna Christie*, a saloon called Johnny-the-Priest's, is based on a Fulton Street rooming house called Jimmy-the-Priest's, frequented by O'Neill early in his career, and also used as a partial setting for the saloon in *The Iceman Cometh.*

Carlin's Marie, like O'Neill's Anna, had tried being a "nurse girl" at one time, before taking to the streets. The speech O'Neill wrote for Anna about finally feeling clean and happy on her father's barge was modeled on a letter from Marie to Carlin in which she declared herself to be washed clean and reborn.

The play, however, gave O'Neill trouble from its inception and he ultimately came to believe he had never brought it off. He had originally written a play based mainly on the character of Anna's father, Chris Christopherson, which was a flop when it tried out in Atlantic City in March 1920, a month after *Beyond the Horizon* opened on Broadway. In its rewritten version, it became the sort of play O'Neill—with his focus on tragedy—had not previously attempted: It was, at least on the surface, a romantic play with a touching love story and an almost happy ending.

O'Neill seemed to imply that Anna could truly be redeemed by her love for the sailor Mat Burke. But yet he had not wanted to leave audiences with the impression that she and Mat would live happily ever after, even though Anna herself believed she had achieved her happy ending.

"The sea outside—life—waits," O'Neill wrote on February 5, 1921, to the critic George Jean Nathan, to whom he had sent a script of the play. "The happy ending," he added defensively, "is merely the comma at the end of a gaudy introductory clause, with the body of the sentence still unwritten."

When it opened on Broadway in November 1921, *Anna Christie* received unanimously good reviews (and brought O'Neill a second Pulitzer). But O'Neill was so angry with the critics for interpreting the ending as happy that he gave the play's press agent, Oliver Saylor, a statement to distribute to the press:

"I hereby set down 'Anna Christie' as the very worst failure I have experienced," he wrote, "and the most ironical joke ever played on me—for probably its success depends on the audience believing just what I did not want them to. . . . A kiss in the last act, a word about marriage, and the audience grows blind and deaf to what follows."

How many playwrights have ever complained publicly about a *favorable* review?

Well before *Anna Christie* opened, O'Neill was already at work on *The Hairy Ape*. Now thirty-three, O'Neill was a major theater presence—unyielding in his insistence on the tragic view, and clearly in pursuit of new challenges. As his career flourished, Agnes Boulton's withered. The cracks in the marriage were beginning to show.

"I have . . . started 'The Hairy Ape' with a mad rush," O'Neill wrote to a friend in December 1921. He and Agnes were living in Provincetown, then still a quiet seaside retreat for artists. "Think I have got the swing of what I want to catch. . . . It is one of those plays where the word 'inspiration' has some point—that is, you either have the rhythm or you haven't and if you have you can ride it, and if not, you're dead."

The play's protagonist, Yank, was inspired by O'Neill's anomalous friendship with a ship's stoker, a Liverpool Irishman named Driscoll—in O'Neill's words "a giant of a man and absurdly strong." O'Neill, in his early twenties and—to his great delight—recently certified as an able-bodied seaman, had sailed with Driscoll on the passenger steamship SS *New York*. Alienated as he was from his family's milieu, the youthful O'Neill had a remarkable affinity for sailors, gangsters, circus performers, prizefighters, cops and bartenders; they all felt protective toward him.

It was in 1911, after O'Neill, at twenty-three, had almost reached the bottom of his own self-destructive, drink-sodden behavior, that he learned Driscoll had committed suicide by jumping overboard during a voyage in the fogbanks off Newfoundland.

O'Neill brooded about the why of Driscoll's suicide, for he had believed that Driscoll, of all people, "wasn't the type who just gave up," and he concluded that Driscoll's sense of belonging had been shaken. In *The Hairy Ape*, he supplied a dramatic reason for Yank's disintegration by theorizing that his faith in the importance of his superhuman endurance in the stokehold is shattered.

The Hairy Ape was scheduled to open at the Provincetown Theater in Greenwich Village on March 9,

1922, and was in rehearsal when, on February 16, O'Neill received a telegram from his brother, Jamie, from California, informing him that their mother had been stricken with a brain tumor. The two had traveled to California to attend to some real estate holdings of James O'Neill's. Ella died on February 28.

In New York, O'Neill was busy attending rehearsals not only for *The Hairy Ape*, but for another off-Broadway production of a play called *The First Man* (poorly conceived and a flop, as it turned out). Emotionally fragile as he was, he spent a ghastly week. Communications from his brother about arrangements to bring their mother's body east were erratic and O'Neill realized that Jamie—who had sworn off alcohol after their father's death—had started drinking again. The tension of attending final rehearsals of two plays and anticipating the arrival of his mother's remains accompanied by his drunken brother was almost too much for him.

As it happened, the train carrying Jamie and his mother's body was scheduled to arrive on the very night of the opening of *The Hairy Ape*. O'Neill couldn't bring himself to meet the train and guiltily delegated that duty to a friend. He soon learned the story of his brother's debauched journey: On her deathbed, Ella had been confronted once again with Jamie's intractable drunkenness. In his despair, for the entire train journey home, Jamie had locked himself in a compartment with a prostitute while his mother's body lay in the baggage car. O'Neill turned his back on his brother permanently. (Two decades later, he told the tale in *A Moon for the Misbegotten*, his final work—yet another example of "life-experience" he wove into his plays. The play was O'Neill's belated effort to absolve not only Jamie but himself, for his initial lack of compassion.)

It was through *The Hairy Ape* that O'Neill met his third wife, Carlotta Monterey. More famous for her beauty than for her talent, Carlotta replaced the actress who created the role of the haughty Mildred Douglas when the production moved uptown for a successful Broadway run. But it was not until four years later—in 1926—that O'Neill and Carlotta began a love affair. He left Agnes and eloped to Europe with Carlotta (and that is the beginning of a whole other story).